SUSTAINABLE PEACE OF THE SOUTH CHINA SEA

The 20th Anniversary of Signing the Declaration
on the Conduct of Parties in the South China Sea

Series on Asian Regional Cooperation Studies

Print ISSN: 2717-5456
Online ISSN: 2717-5464

Chief Editor: GAO Fei *(China Foreign Affairs University, China)*
Deputy Chief Editor: GUO Yanjun *(China Foreign Affairs University, China)*

Track II Diplomacy usually refers to an unofficial process with a government background. It plays an important role in promoting regional cooperation in Asia. The main tasks of Track II Diplomacy are to analyze problems, make policy recommendations, and provide intellectual support for official cooperation. Participants are mainly experts and scholars engaged in policy research as well as the government officials participating in their private capacities. The Institute of Asian Studies (IAS) at China Foreign Affairs University is China's focal point for three most influential Track II mechanisms of this region, namely the Network of East Asian Think-tanks (NEAT), the Network of ASEAN-China Think-tanks (NACT) and the Network of Trilateral Cooperation Think-tanks (NTCT). IAS is proud to launch Series on Asian Regional Cooperation Studies jointly with the World Scientific Publishing, the most reputable English academic publisher in Asia. The purpose of this series is not only to motivate more scholars to get involved in Track II Diplomacy of Asia, but also to increase the recognition of the three networks by reaching out to a wide audience. Based on the platforms of NEAT, NACT and NTCT, this series will invite outstanding scholars to conduct in-depth research on significant and challenging issues in Asian regional cooperation, through conference proceedings, scholarly monographs, textbooks and translations with high academic standards and strong policy relevance.

Published

Vol. 11: *Sustainable Peace of the South China Sea:*
The 20th Anniversary of Signing the Declaration on the Conduct of
Parties in the South China Sea
edited by GUO Yanjun and Pou Sothirak

Vol. 10: *Preventive Diplomacy in Non-Traditional Security Issues:*
ASEAN-China Public Health and Environmental Cooperation
edited by YANG Yue and QIAO Youlin

Vol. 9: *Digital Economy and the Sustainable Development of ASEAN and China*
edited by YANG Yue

Vol. 8: *Sustaining Peace in ASEAN and the Asia-Pacific:*
Preventive Diplomacy Measures
edited by GUO Yanjun and I Gusti Agung Wesaka Puja

Vol. 7: *Preventive Diplomacy, Peacebuilding and Security in the Asia-Pacific*
Evolving Norms, Agenda and Practices
edited by GUO Yanjun and MIAO Ji

The complete list of the published volumes in the series can also be found at
http://www.worldscientific.com/series/sarcs

Series on Asian Regional Cooperation Studies—Vol. 11

SUSTAINABLE PEACE OF THE SOUTH CHINA SEA
The 20th Anniversary of Signing the Declaration on the Conduct of Parties in the South China Sea

Edited by

GUO Yanjun
China Foreign Affairs University, China

POU Sothirak
Cambodian Center for Regional Studies, Cambodia

World Scientific

NEW JERSEY · LONDON · SINGAPORE · BEIJING · SHANGHAI · HONG KONG · TAIPEI · CHENNAI

Published by

World Scientific Publishing Co. Pte. Ltd.
5 Toh Tuck Link, Singapore 596224
USA office: 27 Warren Street, Suite 401-402, Hackensack, NJ 07601
UK office: 57 Shelton Street, Covent Garden, London WC2H 9HE

Library of Congress Control Number: 2024029731

British Library Cataloguing-in-Publication Data
A catalogue record for this book is available from the British Library.

Series on Asian Regional Cooperation Studies — Vol. 11
SUSTAINABLE PEACE OF THE SOUTH CHINA SEA
The 20th Anniversary of Signing the Declaration on the Conduct of Parties in the South China Sea

Copyright © 2025 by World Scientific Publishing Co. Pte. Ltd.

All rights reserved. This book, or parts thereof, may not be reproduced in any form or by any means, electronic or mechanical, including photocopying, recording or any information storage and retrieval system now known or to be invented, without written permission from the publisher.

For photocopying of material in this volume, please pay a copying fee through the Copyright Clearance Center, Inc., 222 Rosewood Drive, Danvers, MA 01923, USA. In this case permission to photocopy is not required from the publisher.

ISBN 978-981-12-9602-4 (hardcover)
ISBN 978-981-12-9603-1 (ebook for institutions)
ISBN 978-981-12-9604-8 (ebook for individuals)

For any available supplementary material, please visit
https://www.worldscientific.com/worldscibooks/10.1142/13925#t=suppl

Desk Editors: Nambirajan Karuppiah/Lum Pui Yee

Typeset by Stallion Press
Email: enquiries@stallionpress.com

Acknowledgments

This book is the major outcome of cooperation between China Foreign Affairs University (CFAU) and the Cambodian Institute for Cooperation and Peace (CICP), supported by "the Fundamental Research Funds for the Central Universities" from CFAU. Fourteen chapters are incorporated in this book and written by distinguished researchers, think tankers, and political scientists from Cambodia, China, Indonesia, Lao PDR, Malaysia, Myanmar, Singapore, Thailand, and Vietnam. These chapters provide discussions from the perspective of both Chinese as well as ASEAN scholars on respective and joint DOC- and COC-related experiences, practices, and ways together for a sustainable peace of the South China Sea, in memory of the 20th anniversary of signing the Declaration on the Conduct of Parties in the South China Sea, as the book project initiated in the year of 2022.

The long-awaited book would not have been possible without the wisdom and research efforts of all the contributing authors. Thanks also to colleagues of CICP and CFAU, notably Wu Lin, Li Fujian, Li Zhengyang, and Zhang Yingjin who have provided enormous support and contributed resourceful ideas to the project. Three Ph.D. candidates from CFAU, Li Hang, Wang Shiyu, and Jiang Xue, deserve recognition and to be honorably mentioned for their hard work and dedication. The co-editors are also deeply indebted to the editors from the World Scientific Publishing Co. in editing and supporting this book.

This collection of works will attract academics, think tankers, practitioners, and Ph.D. candidates interested in implementation of the DOC, negotiations on the COC, and ASEAN–China relations.

© 2025 World Scientific Publishing Company
https://doi.org/10.1142/9789811296031_fmatter

Disclaimer

The views expressed in the writings that appear in the volume are strictly those of the individual authors and do not necessarily reflect the views of the editors, the China Foreign Affairs University, the Cambodian Institute for Cooperation and Peace, the authors' affiliations, or any governmental organizations of the People's Republic of China and member states of ASEAN. The chapters in this publication were written between the second and the fourth quarter of 2022 (Q2–Q4 2022). Many views may have reflected situations at the time, and thus some facts, figures, and/or views may have had further developments by the time this publication is released.

Contents

Acknowledgments		v
Disclaimer		vii
Chapter 1	Twenty Years of the Declaration on the Conduct of Parties in the South China Sea: China–ASEAN Relations *Zhu Feng and Liu Zhe*	1
Chapter 2	The DOC and China–ASEAN Maritime Cooperation *Zhao Qinghai*	29
Chapter 3	Substantive Issues Surrounding the COC Consultation: Forging a Legal Path Forward for the Negotiators *Kong Lingjie*	49
Chapter 4	Historical Interaction of China–ASEAN Economic Cooperation and Security Governance: From the Perspective of DOC *Zhang Jie*	71
Chapter 5	Institutional Effectiveness and Mechanisms of the Implementation of the DOC *Wu Lin and Zhu Wenhan*	95

Chapter 6	Roads toward Sustainable Peace through the Declaration on the Conduct of Parties in the South China Sea *Pou Sothirak*	125
Chapter 7	Provisional Arrangements under UNCLOS: A Comparative Analysis for the South China Sea Code of Conduct *Aristyo Rizka Darmawan*	147
Chapter 8	The Underlying Economics of Conflict and Peace in the South China Sea *Mana Southichack*	161
Chapter 9	Together for Sustainable Peace of the South China Sea *Bounphieng Pheuaphetlangsy, Sounanda Bolivong, and Haknilan Inthalath*	177
Chapter 10	The DOC and Dispute Management in the South China Sea: Maintaining Dialogue, Maximizing Convergences *Kuik Cheng-Chwee*	193
Chapter 11	A Stronger DOC toward the Successful Completion of a Reliable COC: The ADMM in the Context of the South China Sea Issue *U. Zeyar Oo*	209
Chapter 12	ASEAN, China, and the South China Sea *Ong Keng Yong and Nazia Hussain*	231
Chapter 13	The DOC at 20: A Thai Perspective *Kavi Chongkittavorn*	245
Chapter 14	ASEAN's 20 Years of Continued Efforts to Engage China on the South China Sea: Lessons from the DOC and the Way Forward *Nguyen Hung Son*	253

Chapter 1

Twenty Years of the Declaration on the Conduct of Parties in the South China Sea: China–ASEAN Relations

Zhu Feng and Liu Zhe

*China Center for Collaborative Studies of the South China Sea,
Nanjing University, Jiangsu Province, China
zhufeng@nju.edu.cn*

Abstract

The emergence of the South China Sea dispute has deep historical origins and objective geopolitical factors. The intervention and interference of extraterritorial powers in the South China Sea issue have also added to the complexity of the dispute, making the South China Sea issue develop into a political dispute with the nature of a power struggle. Therefore, the principle of consensus is crucial to maintaining peace and stability in the South China Sea. The signing of the Declaration on the Conduct of Parties in the South China Sea (DOC), which has guaranteed the overall stability and control of the situation in the South China Sea for two decades, is a fundamental proposition and institutional design for China and ASEAN countries to respect each other's interests and aspirations, establishing the fundamental tone and logical starting point for maintaining long-term peace and stability in the South China Sea, as well as a valuable practice of multilateralism in Southeast Asia. China's "Dual-Track Approach" design for a reasonable solution to the South China Sea dispute has prevented the relationship between China and ASEAN from being shaken by the South China Sea dispute while maintaining the existing cooperation mechanism between China and ASEAN and returning the solution to the elements of the South China Sea dispute itself, avoiding the situation in the South China Sea from getting out of control. Based on the implementation of the DOC, the advancement of the "Code of Conduct in the South China Sea" (COC) will promote the reconfiguration of the existing regional security order, make a more significant contribution to peace and development in the South China Sea region, and promote China–ASEAN relations to new heights.

Keywords: Declaration on the Conduct of Parties in the South China Sea, DOC, ASEAN, South China Sea Dispute, COC

In November 2002, government representatives of China and ASEAN countries solemnly signed the Declaration on the Conduct of Parties in the South China Sea (DOC) in Phnom Penh, Cambodia. The DOC is the first political document signed by China and ASEAN countries on the South China Sea issue, as well as the first international multilateral document on regional dispute management signed by China. Over the past two decades, China and ASEAN countries have jointly guaranteed overall stability in the South China Sea. Both sides have successfully implemented the purposes and principles of the DOC, jointly upheld the direction of the times of peace and friendship, actively managed differences and enhanced mutual trust through official consultation mechanisms and a dual-track approach, also effectively carried out a series of consultations and undertaken cooperative activities including marine environmental protection, marine scientific research, the safety of navigation and communication at sea, search and rescue operation as advocated by the DOC. It can be said that the DOC is a useful attempt based on rules and order in the

South China Sea, which not only ensures freedom and safety of navigation in the South China Sea but also creates favorable external conditions for the rapid economic development of China and ASEAN countries over the past two decades. Based on the DOC, China and ASEAN countries are continuing to advance COC negotiations and China is willing to work with ASEAN countries to uphold the principle of seeking common ground while reserving differences and mutual benefit and jointly promoting the development of the situation in the South China Sea in a positive direction.

I. The Complexity of the South China Sea Dispute and the Necessity of Regularized Control

The South China Sea is the largest marginal sea in Asia, located between the Pacific Ocean and the Indian Ocean, with many neighboring countries, including continental countries (China), Peninsular marginal countries (Vietnam), and island and archipelagic countries (Malaysia, Indonesia, Philippines, etc.). Owing to the diversity of geographical environment, and production and lifestyle, countries around the South China Sea show diversity in cultures, nationalities, and religions. According to the clear concept of modern territorial sovereignty, the countries around the South China Sea have established different forms of political systems with different subjects of state power, such as people's representative system, monarchy, republican system, and parliamentary system put forward different demands for the rights and interests in the South China sea. As Nicholas Taring has said, "the diversity of geography, culture, and ethnicity makes it a difficult task for anyone to present any holistic view of Southeast Asian history."[1]

From the historical perspective, most countries around the South China Sea were included in the political suzerain-vassal system and economic tributary system with China as the core. After the colonial

---

[1] Nicholas Taring, eds., *The Cambridge History of Southeast Asia (Chinese Version)*, translated by He Shengda, Kunming: Yunnan People's Publishing House, 2005, p. 471.

process of the "Pacific Silk Road" started by Western countries, the surrounding areas of the South China Sea gradually changed progressively from the suzerain-vassal system to the Westphalia system. In 1884, Vietnam signed the Treaty of Hue with France and officially became a colony. After that, in 1899, Paul Doumer, the French governor of Indochina, proposed to build lighthouses in the Xisha and Nansha Islands to exert jurisdiction rights over the sea passage,[2] which aimed at maintaining its political advantage in the surrounding areas of the South China Sea. In the early 20th century, the Qing government sent naval forces to inspect and name the islands and reefs of the Xisha Islands. During World War II, France partly occupied the islands and reefs of the Nansha Islands and Xisha Islands twice. Later, Japan gained sea and air control over the South China Sea by war to consolidate its expansion in Southeast Asia, and then completed its actual control over Xisha Islands and Nansha Islands, which were newly named "New South Islands" by Japan. With the end of World War II, the Chinese government formally regained its sovereignty over the South China Sea including the Nansha islands and Xisha islands from Japan, based on the Cairo Declaration and the Potsdam Proclamation. And in accordance with historical facts, the Chinese government published the Location Map of the South China Sea Islands in 1947, which specified the geographical coordinates of the intermittent line in the South China Sea. At the same time, France, the Saigon regime of South Vietnam and the Kuomintang regime which retreated to Taiwan also claimed sovereignty over the islands and reefs of the Nansha and Xisha Islands. During this period, the countries around the South China Sea did not publicly claim sovereignty over the South China Sea, nor did the so-called "South China Sea dispute" exist.

From the late 1960s to 1990s, with the convening of the United Nations Conferences on the Law of the Sea, concepts such as exclusive economic zones and 200 nautical-mile maritime rights aroused attention among the international community. The confrontation

---

[2]Stein Tønnesson, "The South China Sea in the Age of European Decline," *Modern Asian Studies* 40 (2006): 3.

between the United States and the Soviet Union in the Cold War also made the strategic status of the South China Sea rise sharply.[3] Nicolas Spykman, a famous American geopolitical scientist, once compared the South China Sea to the Mediterranean Sea in Asia.[4] From the strategic perspective, the possession of the South China Sea means controlling important maritime passages from the Strait of Malacca to Japan and from East Asia to West Asia, Africa, and Europe, which will directly affect the strategic defense situation of the Indo-China region. In addition, with the outbreak of the fourth Middle East War and the world oil crisis in the 1970s, the importance of marine oil and gas resources has been rising, and the great discovery of oil in the South China Sea has also stimulated the attention of neighboring countries to marine resources. From that time, the Philippines, Vietnam, Malaysia, Brunei, and other countries gradually began to claim sovereignty over the Nansha Islands, and illegally occupied the South China Sea islands and reefs by military means and carried out unilateral fishing as well as exploring and drilling for oil and gas.

In 1992, with the end of the bipolar pattern, the former Soviet Union's military strength in Asia continued to weaken while the U.S. military withdrew from the Subic Naval Base in the Philippines, resulting in an unprecedented power vacuum in the South China Sea.

---

[3] During the Cold War, the United States regarded the South China Sea as the "First Island Chain" of its "Island Chain Strategy" in the Asia-Pacific region, thus creating an "unsinkable aircraft carrier" against the Soviet Union. In the 1970s, the Philippines and the Saigon regime of South Vietnam both requested the United States for security protection of their claims on sovereignty in the South China Sea. However, the United States did not agree to those requests because Sino-U.S. relations were at a critical stage of normalization at that time, while the South China Sea had also become an important "middle zone" for the United States and the Soviet Union to contend for hegemony: the United States has a naval base in Subic Bay in the South China Sea, while the Soviet Union has obtained the right to use Cam Ranh Bay and Da Nang in Vietnam. Refer to Bradley Lynn Coleman, eds., *Foreign Relations of the United States*, 1969–1976, Volume B-12, Documents on East and Southeast Asia, 1973–1976, United States Government Printing Office Washington, 2010, pp. 1–5.

[4] Nicolas Spykman, *The Geography of the Peace (Chinese Version)*, translated by Yu Haijie, Shanghai: Shanghai People's Publishing House, 2016, p. 55.

At this time, as a regional organization, ASEAN, which has started the process of security integration, has also begun to pay attention to the South China Sea issue.[5] In July 1992, at the ASEAN Foreign Ministers' Meeting held in Manila, Philippines, ASEAN issued the ASEAN Declaration on the South China Sea, which proposed that the South China Sea dispute should be resolved by peaceful means, encouraged all parties to act with restraint, and took the principles established in the Treaty of Amity and Cooperation in Southeast Asia as the basis for formulating international COC,[6] which symbolized that ASEAN began to focus on the South China Sea dispute in the capacity of a regional security community. In the following period, Vietnam, the Philippines, and other countries took more unilateral actions in the South China Sea. In 1992, Vietnam and Malaysia reached an agreement on the joint exploitation of oil and gas in the South China Sea. In 1995, foreign ministers of the Philippines and Indonesia expressed "welcome to participate in the joint development of the Nansha Islands to promote the settlement of disputes,"[7] which made the South China Sea dispute develop toward a more complex multilateral direction around resource development.

---

[5] In 1971, ASEAN Ministerial Conference adopted the Declaration of Zone of Peace, Freedom and Neutrality (ZOPFAN), declaring "to exert initially necessary efforts to secure the recognition of, and respect for, Southeast Asia as a Zone of Peace, Freedom and Neutrality, free from any form or manner of interference by outside Powers," and "make concerted efforts to broaden the areas of cooperation which would contribute to their strength, solidarity and closer relationship" and "consistent with the spirit and principles of the Charter of the United Nations," such as "without resorting to the threat or use of force" and "resolve their international disputes by peaceful means." Refer to ZOPFAN, ASEAN Concord, and the Treaty of Amity and Cooperation ASEAN 50, November 2017, pp. 17–48.

[6] The ASEAN Secretariat, "ASEAN Declaration on the South China Sea," July 22, 1992, https://cil.nus.edu.sg/wp-content/uploads/2017/07/1992-ASEAN-Declaration-on-the-South-China-Sea.pdf (Accessed December 26, 2022).

[7] Bhakti, Ikrar Nusa, "11. Bilateral Relations between Indonesia and the Philippines: Stable and Fully Cooperative," *International Relations in Southeast Asia: Between Bilateralism and Multilateralism*, edited by N. Ganesan and Ramses Amer, Singapore: ISEAS Publishing, 2010, pp. 287–312.

In 1995, China had an accidental friction with the Philippines over the Mischief Reef of the Nansha Islands, and the ASEAN Foreign Ministers' Meeting of the same year issued the Statement on the Recent Situation in the South China Sea, expressing concern about the situation in the South China Sea. In 1996, the ASEAN Foreign Ministers' Meeting in Jakarta proposed the necessity to formulate the COC. With the successful process of ASEAN integration, ASEAN's South China Sea policy has been gradually recognized and supported by most member countries. Since China–ASEAN relations have been upgraded to a "Full Dialogue Partner" status, China has also realized that the South China Sea issue has become a regional issue with ASEAN as its core. Therefore, since 1996, China and ASEAN have started negotiations on the COC and signed the DOC in Phnom Penh, Cambodia, in November 2002, which reached four basic principles: freedom of navigation, self-restraint, confidence-building, and maritime cooperation.[8]

With ASEAN's involvement, the South China Sea issue has changed from an issue of historical colonialism, differences in the behavior of national subjects, and unilateral development of marine resources to a regional security issue composed of multilateral powers, and therefore the South China sea has been characterized by "Regional Security Complex."[9] From the perspective of regionalism, the countries around the South China Sea have become interdependent in terms of security with ASEAN, which can help ASEAN more significantly intervene in disputes as a community. Meanwhile, the South China Sea issue has gradually evolved from the conflict of territorial sovereignty and maritime jurisdiction over the islands and reefs in the South China Sea to an international hot spot, with its characteristics transformed from an ASEAN issue to an international issue. On March 8, 2009, there was a confrontation between USNS

---

[8]The ASEAN Secretariat, "Declaration on the Conduct of Parties in the South China Sea," October 17, 2012, https://asean.org/declaration-on-the-conduct-of-parties-in-the-south-china-sea/ (Accessed December 20, 2022).
[9]Barry Buzan and Ole Wæver, *Regions and Powers: The Structure of International Security*, Cambridge: Cambridge University Press, 2003, p. 138.

Impeccable and Chinese vessels in the South China Sea. In the next year, Hillary Clinton, the Secretary of State of the United States, publicly stated that the United States has a national interest in the South China Sea,[10] which illustrates that the U.S. policy on the South China Sea issue has changed from neutrality or limited intervention to active intervention.[11] Jiang Yu, the spokesperson of the Chinese Foreign Ministry in 2010, said at a regular press conference that China resolutely opposes the intervention from countries unrelated to the South China Sea issue and opposes the internationalization, multilateralization, and expansion of the South China Sea issue, which will not solve the problem, but make it more complicated.[12]

Subsequently, the United States, Japan, India, Australia, France, the United Kingdom, and other countries have expanded their military presence or utilized other ways to project influence in the South China Sea. Under internationalization progress, the maritime disputes between the claimant countries have gradually intensified. The most representative one was the ruling released by the Permanent Court of Arbitration in The Hague in 2016 on the case unilaterally initiated by the Philippines regarding China's claims and activities in the South China Sea. On the premises of insufficient admissibility of evidence, determination of facts, and unclear definition of applicable international laws and the performance of its duties, the Permanent Court of Arbitration in The Hague completely ignored the historical and jurisprudential basis of China's sovereignty over islands and reefs in the South China Sea and its maritime rights and interests. It also

---

[10]U.S. Department of State, "Remarks by Secretary of State Hillary Rodham Clinton, Hanoi, Vietnam," July 23, 2010, https://2009--2017.state.gov/secretary/20092013clinton/rm/2010/07/145095.htm (Accessed December 24, 2022).

[11]Wu Shicun, *The Origin and Development of the South China Sea Dispute: International Study of the History of the South China Sea Dispute*, Beijing: Chung Hwa Book Company, 2022, p. 23.

[12]*Regular Press Conference of Ministry of Foreign Affairs of China*, Information Office of the State Council of the People's Republic of China, September 21, 2010, http://www.scio.gov.cn/xwfbh/gbwxwfbh/fbh/Document/769019/769019.htm (Accessed December 21, 2022).

created a negative national image of China trying against the entire international community, while foreign forces came on stage, intending to complexify the South China Sea issue, such as Japan and Australia, publicly stating that it was necessary for the parties concerned to accept the "ruling."[13] However, other ASEAN countries showed different attitudes towards the outcome of the South China Sea arbitration case. Hun Sen, Cambodian Prime Minister, claimed that the "arbitration" was clearly politically motivated and that Cambodia would not support the ruling.[14] Myanmar also stated with Cambodia, saying that it would not support any judgment of the arbitration court.[15] At that time Thongloun Sisoulith, Prime Minister of Laos, also made it clear that Laos supports China's principles and positions on the arbitration case[16] when he met with the Premier of China, Li Keqiang. In addition, Malaysia and Brunei, both members of "five countries and six parties," did not clearly express their position on the ruling.[17] Because of the consensus decision-making approach, ASEAN could not make a collective statement, as it only in

---

[13] *Arbitration between the Republic of the Philippines and the People's Republic of China Regarding the South China Sea (Final Award by the Arbitral Tribunal) (Statement by Foreign Minister Fumio Kishida)*, Ministry of Foreign Affairs of Japan, July 12, 2016, https://www.mofa.go.jp/mofaj/press/danwa/page4_002172.html, https://www.dfat.gov.au/news/news/Pages/australia-supports-peaceful-dispute-resolution-in-the-south-china-sea (Accessed December 11, 2022).

[14] *China Daily*, "Cambodia not to support arbitration court's decision over South China Sea: PM," June 28, 2016, https://www.chinadaily.com.cn/world/2016-06/28/content_25889328.htm (Accessed December 28, 2022).

[15] *Khmer Times*, "Cambodia and Myanmar in joint stand on South China Sea dispute," July 5, 2016, https://www.khmertimeskh.com/25448/cambodia-and-myanmar-in-joint-stand-on-south-china-sea-dispute/ (Accessed December 15, 2022).

[16] The State Council of the People's Republic of China, "Lao PM voices support for China's stance on South China Sea arbitration," July 15, 2016, http://english.www.gov.cn/premier/photos/2016/07/15/content_281475394069446.htm (Accessed December 15, 2022).

[17] Yang Guanghai, *The Response and Policy Trend of ASEAN Countries and Organizations to the South China Sea Arbitration Case*, Peace and Development, 2016(05), pp. 119–132.

a minimum sense expressed "serious concern" about the situation in the South China Sea in the ASEAN Joint Communique and hoped that all parties would fully and effectively implement the DOC and then reach the COC as soon as possible.[18]

As a political farce, the "South China Sea Arbitration Case" has not only failed to resolve disputes reasonably and effectively but also created new ones, making the situation in the South China Sea increasingly complex. Firstly, the ruling of the South China Sea Arbitration has been labeled as "international rule of law" by some countries, which prominently try to expand jurisdiction in the name of discretion and to implement "Judicial Law-making" in the name of treaty interpretation. The negative impact on the efforts of regional countries to resolve disputes through peaceful negotiations and maritime cooperation promoted by China and ASEAN countries under the framework of the DOC and the consultation on the COC should not be underestimated.[19] The lack of relevant international law also makes it more difficult to effectively resolve disputes in the South China Sea from the legal dimension in the future. Secondly, it has increased the unilateral actions of some claimant countries in the South China Sea, such as expanding the construction of islands and reefs, strengthening the management of the sea area, and developing oil, gas, and fishery resources. In 2017, Indonesia renamed the exclusive economic zone in the northern part of the Natuna Islands as "North Natuna Sea" and stressed that Indonesia would not recognize China's declaration of sovereignty within "the nine-dash line" in the South China Sea submitted to the United Nations in 2009. In addition, Vietnam, Malaysia, and other countries have also strengthened their unilateral activities in exploring and drilling for oil and gas at sea area, while there has been a confrontation between China and

---

[18]The ASEAN Secretariat, "Joint Communique of the 49th ASEAN Foreign Ministers' Meeting," July 24, 2016, https://asean.org/wp-content/uploads/2016/07/Joint-Communique-of-the-49th-AMM-ADOPTED.pdf (Accessed December 24, 2022).
[19]Ding Duo, *Analysis on the Negative Influence and Spillover Effect of the South China Sea Arbitration and Comment on The South China Sea Arbitration Awards: A Critical Study*, Asia-Pacific Security and Maritime Affairs, 2018(05), pp. 60–73.

Vietnam at Wanan Tan, causing tension at sea. Thirdly, the United States and other foreign powers have increased their military involvement in the South China Sea under the disguise of "rule." For example, the United States has been playing up China's action as the so-called "Gray Zone" activities, which aim at increasing its military presence in the South China Sea, using the "Freedom of Navigation Program" as an excuse to carry out intelligence gathering, close-in reconnaissance and other military activities in the South China Sea, in addition, to expand military exercises, enhance law enforcement training and equipment grants to the coast guard forces of the claimant countries in the south China sea, and strive to build up rule-making dominance in the region. Fourthly, the United States and other countries outside the region have combined the South China Sea issue with a comprehensive strategy of suppressing China to maintain the "hegemonic maintenance" of the Western countries led by the United States in the Asia-Pacific region.[20] In July 2020, Pompeo, U.S. Secretary of State, issued a statement in Washington on China's sovereignty over islands and reefs in the South China Sea and its maritime claims,[21] in which he publicly criticized China's position and openly denied China's claims of maritime rights in the South China Sea, which marked that the U.S. government's policy on the South Chinese Sea had changed from "selective intervention" to "comprehensive intervention." It not only subverts the international practice of disputes over international sovereignty and maritime rights and interests that non-parties should not illegally interfere but also

---

[20]Qin Yaqing observes that the United States, as a hegemonic power, would like to maintain a power distance between itself and other countries, set at a constant that is considered safe, which is the so-called hegemonic maintenance. Refer to Qin Yaqing, *Hegemonic System and International Conflicts: American Support in International Armed Conflicts (1945–1988)*, Shanghai: Shanghai People's Publishing House, 1999, p. 136.
[21] *U.S. Department of State*, "U.S. Position on Maritime Claims in the South China Sea," July 13, 2020, https://2017-2021.state.gov/u-s-position-on-maritime-claims-in-the-south-china-sea/index.html#:~:text=In%20the%20South%20China%20Sea%2C%20we%20seek%20to%20preserve%20peace,or%20force%20to%20settle%20disputes (Accessed December 19, 2022).

profoundly reflects the intention of the United States and some countries outside the region to become the decision-makers of the South China Sea rules. Fifthly, the South China Sea dispute has developed into different "camps" and the central position of ASEAN has been squeezed. As a sustained consensus pursued by ASEAN countries, its centrality relies on the strong and sustained leadership of ASEAN as a regional community, and ASEAN should play its due role as a regional organization in resolving disputes, crisis management, and pragmatic reduction of tensions. However, Japan, Australia, the United Kingdom, and other countries continue to intervene in the South China Sea affairs utilizing diplomacy and military and expand their military presence in the South China Sea, through various bilateral and multilateral mechanisms led by the United States. Such unilateralism makes ASEAN's central position at risk of being marginalized and squeezes the communication channels between ASEAN and China as well as other member countries. Sixthly, the expansion and globalization of the South China Sea's nature as a maritime security complex. The United States, Japan, and other countries have placed the South China Sea in an important position of their "Indo-Pacific Strategy," and the advocacy of the South China Sea security has been upgraded to a new thought for Western countries to effectively improve the flexibility and diversity of their security strategies, thus extending the connotation of the "China Threat Theory." Mahan once emphasized the key role of geographical environment in strategy that the strategic value of any location depends on its traffic conditions, military force, and resources,[22] while the three factors mentioned above have been expanded into new "issue identities" to varying degrees according to the South China Sea dispute, thus affecting the preferences and interests of different countries, and leading to an absence of conceptual identity among different claimant countries, which is undoubtedly not conducive to a

---

[22] Alfred Thayer Mahan, *Naval Strategy Compared and Contrasted with the Principles and Practice of Military Operations on Land*, New York: Little Brown and Company Press, 1911, p. 306.

reasonable settlement of the South China Sea dispute within a rational framework.

As aforementioned, the universal complex characteristics of the South China Sea dispute lie in the different perceptions of the existing regional order among different countries, and the contradiction of perceptions usually lies in the accusation that parties concerned in disputes "undermine the rule-based international order," while parties fail to reach consensus on the rule-based international order itself. This phenomenon exists not only between China and different claimant countries but also between others. One of the most notable interest conflicts is the overlapping of the "exclusive economic zones" claimed by the countries around the South China Sea, and the Malaysian Coast Guard has confronted Vietnamese fishermen at sea over illegal fishing incidents.[23] In addition, there are also disputes between several claimant countries over the sovereignty of specific sea areas, such as the dispute between Malaysia and Indonesia over the Ambalat Sea and the Sulawesi Sea, and the dispute between the Philippines and Malaysia over the sovereignty of Sabah. Regional maritime disputes represent different national interest orientations, so the most prominent manifestation is the different interpretation of rules and the strengthening of relevant discourse rights, which makes the South China Sea issue not only limited to the issue of law and rules but also a political dispute with the nature of power struggle.

As the basis of international order, only the balance of interests can make regional relations move towards a benign and normal track. Therefore, at the level of disputes in the South China Sea, forming consensual principles is very important, because only in a way that parties, under a stable and orderly framework, restrain their behavior according to the corresponding principles, and form a predictable interaction mode, can the South China Sea dispute be truly broke and solved. Therefore, in dealing with disputes, we should take into

---

[23] *South China Morning Post*, "South China Sea clash raises Vietnam–Malaysia tensions after fisherman shot dead," https://www.scmp.com/week-asia/politics/article/3097863/south-china-sea-clash-raises-vietnam-malaysia-tensions-after (Accessed December 18, 2022).

account the basic security concerns of all stakeholders and strive to reach a consensus and understanding acceptable to all parties, and this rule-based consensus also needs to meet the conventional interests of China and countries around the South China Sea, considering the relations between China and the claimant countries, the internal relations among ASEAN countries and the relations between China and foreign powers. In addition, we should respect the actual power pattern and maintain a proper balance of power to sustain peace and stability in the South China Sea, ensure freedom and safety of navigation, and constantly develop economic mutual benefits with a win–win relationship.

II. The Role and Value of the Declaration on the Conduct of Parties in the South China Sea

The DOC is a milestone document in China–ASEAN Dialogue Relations that embodies the maximum common understanding formed by China and ASEAN in the process of resolving the South China Sea dispute and seeking consensus, which also reflects the basic proposition and system design of China and ASEAN countries to respect interests and demands of all parties. In terms of content, the DOC clearly defines the basic norms governing state-to-state relations following the principles of the Charter of the United Nations, the 1982 UN Convention on the Law of the Sea, the Treaty of Amity and Cooperation in Southeast Asia, the Five Principles of Peaceful Coexistence, and other universally recognized principles of international law (Article 1),[24] which lays the foundation for settling disputes fairly and reasonably and under the principles recognized by the international community. At the same time, the DOC clarifies the basic principles of resolving the South China Sea dispute, that is, the universally recognized principles of international law that the parties concerned undertake to abide by, including the 1982 United Nations

---

[24] *The ASEAN Secretariat*, "Declaration on the Conduct of Parties in the South China Sea," October 17, 2012, https://asean.org/declaration-on-the-conduct-of-parties-in-the-south-china-sea/ (Accessed December 12, 2022).

Convention on the Law of the Sea, as stated in Article 4, to resolve their territorial and jurisdictional disputes by peaceful means, without resorting to the threat or use of force,[25] through friendly consultations and negotiations by sovereign states directly concerned. In addition, the DOC establishes self-restraint and crisis management provisions to avoid aggravating regional tensions. Article 5 of the DOC commits the parties to exercise self-restraint in the conduct of activities that would complicate or escalate disputes and affect peace and stability including, among others, refraining from action of inhabiting the presently uninhabited islands, reefs, shoals, cays, and other features and to handle their differences in a constructive manner,[26] which has pointed out the specific direction for avoiding the expansion of disputes and clarifying crisis management in the South China Sea.

Although the DOC is the basic provision of the COC consultation, it has played a positive role as a milestone in the current process of resolving the South China Sea dispute. From the perspective of maintaining long-term stability, the DOC sets the basic tone and logical starting point for the COC consultation, establishes a set of guiding framework and principled thinking for controlling disputes and development of maritime security in the South China Sea, and provides a clear guiding ideology for resolving conflicts between territorial sovereignty and maritime jurisdiction claims. After the signing of the DOC, although the South China Sea dispute remains complex, the maritime situation is generally stable and controllable, and there have been no extreme maritime incidents such as the illegal armed occupation of islands and reefs and local wars, which means that the DOC has provided a "safety valve" for the situation in the South China Sea approved by all parties. Furthermore, the principle of "safeguarding the freedom of navigation in and overflight above the South China Sea" put forward in the DOC has also been implemented by countries around the South China Sea, which not only safeguards the basic civil functions of the South China Sea based on

---

[25] *Ibid.*
[26] *Ibid.*

peace but also promotes the economic and development interests of the coastal countries. The "freedom of navigation and overflight" in the DOC based on international law also effectively defines military crossing and civil acts at sea, which plays a positive role in avoiding conflicts, especially the uncontrollable risk of a military conflict at sea.

Moreover, China and ASEAN countries have also gradually set up a relatively stable maritime crisis management and security dialogue mechanism under the basis of "holding dialogues and exchange of views as appropriate between their defense and military officials and exchanging, on a voluntary basis, relevant information"[27] in Article 5 and "the Parties concerned stand ready to continue their consultations and dialogues concerning relevant issues, through modalities to be agreed by them, including regular consultations on the observance of this Declaration, for the purpose of promoting good neighbourliness and transparency, establishing harmony, mutual understanding and cooperation, and facilitating a peaceful resolution of disputes among them"[28] in Article 7. The mechanism benefits the future development of institutionalism in the South China Sea. In December 2004, China and ASEAN countries held the first Senior Officials' Meeting on the implementation of the follow-up actions of the DOC in Kuala Lumpur and decided to establish a Joint Working Group Meeting on the implementation of the DOC on the basis of the Senior Officials' Meeting. Heretofore, 19 Senior Officials' Meetings (SOMs) and 37 Joint Working Group (JWG) meetings have been held in total. Even during the difficult times of the epidemic, the consultation has been carried forward by video conference, which is of great significance to the firm and effective implementation of the DOC and the acceleration of the COC consultation and which has also played an irreplaceable role in properly handling maritime emergencies. In addition, China and ASEAN have launched an informal meeting mechanism of defense ministers since February 2011, which has become the main channel for discussing security issues in the

---

[27] *Ibid.*
[28] *Ibid.*

South China Sea, creating conditions for enhancing political mutual trust and security relations between China and ASEAN.

The DOC has also played an important role in promoting maritime cooperation between China and ASEAN countries, as stated in Article 6 "marine environmental protection, marine scientific research, the safety of navigation and communication at sea, search and rescue operation, and combating transnational crime, including but not limited to trafficking in illicit drugs, piracy and armed robbery at sea, and illegal traffic in arms."[29] China and ASEAN countries have carried out practical maritime cooperation in the five areas of cooperation advocated by the DOC such as marine environmental protection and scientific research. In March 2005, China, the Philippines, and Vietnam signed the Joint Marine Seismic Undertaking, which agreed that the oil companies of the three countries would undertake data gathering and processing of two-dimensional or three-dimensional seismic data over 3 years in a 143,000km^2 area of the South China Sea and assess the oil resources in the agreement area by interpreting a certain number of existing two-dimensional seismic lines.[30] JMSU has made valuable progress in preliminary cooperation mechanisms for the joint exploration and development of oil in the South China Sea by carrying out marine scientific research in a multilateral manner. In addition, China has signed respectively with Indonesia, Malaysia, Brunei, and other countries the Memorandum of Understanding on Cooperation in the Marine Field, the Agreement on Cooperation in Marine Science and Technology, and the Memorandum of Understanding between China and Brunei on Marine Environmental Protection and Oil and Gas Field Development as all documents mentioned above lay a foundation for rational use of resources by cooperation and help develop marine science in the countries around the South China Sea. China and ASEAN countries have also carried out a series

---

[29] *Ibid.*
[30] *China and the Philippines Reached Consensus on Resolving Relevant Disputes in the South China Sea,* The State Council Information Office of the People's Republic of China, July 13, 2016, http://www.scio.gov.cn/ztk/dtzt/34102/34818/34827/Document/1483634/1483634.htm (Accessed December 12, 2022).

of cooperation on the basis of implementing Article 6 of the DOC in the field of non-traditional security. In 2014, China and ASEAN jointly adopted the Statement on Strengthening Cooperation and Coordination in Maritime and Aeronautical Search and Rescue. In October of the same year, China and ASEAN decided to establish a "hotline platform among search and rescue agencies" and a "hotline among foreign ministries on maritime emergencies," a table-top exercise on search and rescue, and a China–ASEAN Remote Sensing Satellite Data Sharing and Service Platform and so on.[31] On April 27, 2016, China and ASEAN countries held the 11th Senior Officials' Meeting on the Implementation of the DOC in Singapore and adopted a work plan for the implementation of the DOC from 2016 to 2017, and expressed common will to establish three technical cooperation committees on navigation safety and search and rescue, marine scientific research and environmental protection, and combating transnational crimes at sea as soon as possible.[32] In 2018, a seriously ill Vietnamese fisherman suffering from a sudden illness at sea needed emergency treatment. A Chinese Coast Guard 46101, which received a distress signal from Vietnamese fishermen at sea, quickly dispatched its medical personnel to provide first aid and coordinated the naval military doctors stationed on Chenhang Island to rush to the scene. After multi-party rescue efforts, the fishermen were out of danger and Vietnamese Coast Guard Commander Ruan Guangdan sent a special letter to sincerely thank the Chinese Coast Guard and relevant functional departments for their humanitarian aid.[33] On December 2, 2021, the Belize-registered bulk carrier "Narimoto Maru," which was

---

[31] The ASEAN Secretariat, "Chairman's Statement of 17th ASEAN-China Summit," December 29, 2014, https://asean.org/wp-content/uploads/images/Chairmans_statement_of_17th_ASEAN-China_Summit.pdf (Accessed December 12, 2022).
[32] *The 11th Senior Officials' Meeting on the Implementation of the Declaration on the Conduct of Parties in the South China Sea was Held in Singapore,* Ministry of Foreign Affairs of China, April 29, 2016, https://www.fmprc.gov.cn/web/wjb_673085/zzjg_673183/bjhysws_674671/xgxw_674673/201604/t20160429_7671464.shtml (Accessed December 24, 2022).
[33] *China Successfully Rescued a Vietnamese Fisherman Who Was Suddenly Seriously Ill in Xisha Sea Area,* Central People's Government of the People's Republic of China,

bound for Taipei from Lumut, Malaysia, was in distress 450 nautical miles south of Sanya. The China Maritime Search and Rescue Center responded quickly and cooperated with the Vietnamese Maritime Search and Rescue Agency to participate in the rescue. All 18 crew members were rescued and taken to Vietnam for resettlement.[34] In addition, China has signed memorandums of cooperation with the maritime police and maritime rescue agencies of Indonesia, Malaysia, the Philippines, and other countries, which has created favorable conditions for bilateral and multilateral maritime law enforcement exchanges and non-traditional security cooperation, standardizing the handling mode of emergencies in the disputed area of the South China Sea and effective communication among maritime law enforcement agencies.

All the time, some claimant countries and countries outside the region have advocated that only the "third-party mechanism" is the priority to solve the South China Sea issue. The practice of the DOC over the past 20 years has proved that China and ASEAN countries are fully capable of solving maritime disputes independently. As a regularized model with East Asian characteristics, the DOC is an effective way to gather and maintain consensus on the South China Sea dispute, taking into account the basic security and economic interests of all parties, abandoning the zero-sum thinking of "either this or that," and defining the norms and bottom lines of maritime behavior that should be abided by all countries around the South Chinese Sea. The DOC points out the direction for peace and stability in the South China Sea and the construction of regional maritime rules, while the practice of the DOC is of great significance to the practice of multilateralism in Southeast Asia in the context of the particularity and complexity of the South China Sea issue.

January 24, 2018, http://www.gov.cn/xinwen/2018-01/24/content_5260134.htm (Accessed December 24, 2022).

[34]*China and Vietnam Successfully Rescued 18 Crew Members of a Belizean Bulk Carrier in Distress in South China Sea*, Website of Chinanews, December 2, 2021, https://www.chinanews.com.cn/sh/2021/12-02/9621031.shtml (Accessed December 2, 2022).

III. China's Design for a Reasonable Solution to the South China Sea Dispute: "Dual-Track Approach"

As one of the main parties to the South China Sea dispute, China has spared no effort to promote the establishment of maritime rules in the South China Sea since the adoption of the DOC. While implementing the spirit of the DOC, China has farsightedly put forward a "dual-track approach" to resolve the South Chinese Sea issue, which suggests that the relevant disputes are to be resolved through friendly consultations and negotiations between the states directly concerned, without outside intervention and "third-party mechanism." On the other hand, peace and stability in the South China Sea are jointly maintained by China and ASEAN countries, and China recognizes that ASEAN countries, as important members in building the centrality of ASEAN, can play an important role in peace and stability in the South China Sea. China advocates the joint efforts of all parties while fulfilling the obligations of the DOC, which reflects China's institutional innovation for the peaceful settlement of disputes by combining the principles of international cooperation with the principles of peaceful settlement of disputes.

The design of the "dual-track approach" is also a response to the complexity of the South China Sea issue as the South China Sea dispute covers many elements, including the territorial sea, exclusive economic zone, delimitation of the continental shelf, construction of islands and reefs, maritime law enforcement, resource development, freedom of navigation, and so on. For some time, the South China Sea dispute has expanded to political, social and other fields, resulting in public sentiment and even many new controversial issues. Therefore, an innovative mode of international dispute settlement needs to go beyond the scope of traditional legal forms and integrate with political and social dimensions.[35] The "dual-track approach" takes into account the particularity of the historical relations between China and

---

[35] Jacob Bercovitch and Richard Jackson, "Conflict resolution in the twenty-first century: Principles, methods and approaches," *International Studies Review* 42 (2009): 881.

the countries around the South China Sea, as well as the universality of the development of friendly relations between China and ASEAN. The way of direct negotiation and consultation with the countries concerned is conducive to dealing with problems sincerely and efficiently through the "point-to-point" approach, and truly understanding the interests and demands of the target countries. Meanwhile, it also clarifies the respective rights and obligations of the parties and non-parties to the South China Sea dispute, which can effectively avoid the situation that non-parties to the dispute are involved in complex territorial sovereignty disputes and are forced to take sides, which can also control differences, avoid the expansion of the problem, and more effectively restrict some parties' attempt to coerce ASEAN through the South China Sea dispute and thus affect the overall relationship between China and ASEAN.[36] From the perspective of international practice, the vast majority of land and maritime boundary delimitation has been settled through direct consultation and negotiation, such as the agreement reached between Malaysia and Singapore on the territorial sea boundary through bilateral negotiations as well as the Agreement between China and Vietnam on the Delimitation of the Territorial Seas, Exclusive Economic Zones and Continental Shelves of the two Countries in Beibu Gulf/Bac Bo Gulf.

Looking back on the complex development of the South China Sea dispute, the proposal of the "dual-track approach" also marks that China has shifted from completely refusing to discuss the South China Sea issue on any multilateral occasion to recognize that the issue shall be discussed under a certain multilateral framework, which is an adjustment made by China's side considering the new situation and is characterized by a policy shift from a "vague strategy" to a "clear strategy," focusing on pragmatism and balance. At the same time, the "dual-track approach" also reflects the increasingly important role of ASEAN as a regional community in the positive development of the South China Sea dispute. With the acceleration of the process of ASEAN integration, the mutual distrust caused by the

---

[36]Wu Shicun, "Dual-track approach" is the key to achieving win–win cooperation in the South China Sea," *World Affairs* 9 (2015), p. 35.

history of Southeast Asian countries has been gradually broken, and more and more ASEAN member countries have realized the spillover effects of ASEAN integration on security and development issues. With the signing of the DOC, ASEAN has distinguished the overall regional security order from the issue of national sovereignty on the premise of guaranteeing the independent rights and interests of the claimant countries, which not only ensures the limited goal of the COC (that is, to control rather than resolve conflicts) but also creates conditions for China to support the "dual-track channel" to deal with the South China Sea issue.

China has always supported ASEAN's organizational capacity building and institutional building. In 2012, the State Oceanic Administration of China issued the Framework Plan (2011–2015) for international cooperation in the South China Sea and adjacent seas and launched more than 70 marine science and technology cooperation projects. In 2013, on the occasion of the "golden decade" of the China–ASEAN strategic partnership, General Secretary Xi Jinping put forward the strategic concept of building the "2nd Century Maritime Silk Road" during his visit and started from the existing regional cooperation mechanism to build a strategic platform to reproduce the prosperity of the Maritime Silk Road together. In the same year, Chinese Premier Li Keqiang delivered a speech at the East Asia Summit in Brunei, proposing the construction of a "multilateral security cooperation mechanism in East Asia," in which the construction of China–ASEAN relations was listed as an important goal. So far, China and ASEAN have accumulated various security cooperation mechanisms beyond mere economic cooperation, such as the leadership meeting mechanism, the ministerial meeting mechanism, the working dialogue mechanism, the ASEAN Regional Forum (ARF) mechanism, and so on to constantly expand consensus.

From the perspective of the problem origin and settlement channels of the South China Sea dispute, the South China Sea issue is a problem in East Asia, a problem of seeking common ground while reserving differences, resolving contradictions, and enhancing the process of cooperation among countries around the South China sea, and a problem of whether China–ASEAN relations can achieve interconnection beyond the economic and social common market which is a major step to further upgrade the institutional cooperation in establishing effective cooperative relations, managing and solving their own problems in the political, security, and strategic fields.[37] However, due to the narrow geopolitical concept of the United States and other foreign powers and the strategic attempt to suppress China in an all-around way, the South China Sea issue has become increasingly complex and turbulent from a simple issue of territorial sovereignty and the distribution of maritime elements. It presents that Western countries have stirred up the situation again following the historical colonialism in the South China Sea, which has gradually become a stormy place under the interference of big powers in East Asian affairs. On December 31, 2022, the Southern Theater of China released a video of a U.S. military plane deliberately changing its flight altitude and dangerously approaching a China's aircraft over the South China Sea on December 21, disregarding repeated warnings by China, which seriously violated the Code of Conduct for the Safety of Air and Sea Encounters between China and the United States, as well as relevant international laws and practices. The situation in the South China Sea is always at risk of accidental fire. However, it is ridiculous that before the Chinese side released the video of the encounter, the U.S. side deliberately misled public opinion, reversed black and white, and made a counter-charge, accusing the Chinese military aircraft of "dangerous proximity" in an attempt to confuse the international audience. Historical experience tells us that more and more Western and foreign countries involved in the South China Sea issue will only make the South China Sea fall into the "sea of suffering," not only cannot it solve the problem but will breed more new problems and disputes. As far as ASEAN is concerned, although it pursues the strategy of "great power balance," ASEAN also realizes that once the South China Sea issue becomes the stage of a great power game, it will make the existing situation develop out of control, and even make

---

[37]Zhu Feng, "Dual-track approach" is the best way to deal with the South China Sea dispute," *China News Weekly* 685 (2014).

ASEAN lose the choice of "normative power." At the ASEAN Summit in 2019, Malaysian Prime Minister Mahathir said that U.S. warships should not be allowed to enter the South China Sea on the premise of guaranteeing freedom of navigation and overflight, otherwise, it would lead to tension in the South China Sea.[38]

Under the theme of peaceful development and win–win cooperation between China and ASEAN countries, the "dual-track approach" is the only choice to settle the South China Sea dispute, which can not only avoid the turbulence of the existing all-round cooperation between China and ASEAN due to the South China Sea dispute but also return to the elements of the South Chinese Sea dispute itself on the basis of maintaining the existing cooperation mechanism between China and ASEAN. Leaving the right to resolve the issue to the countries concerned is a respect for sovereign states and basic facts, as well as a respect for history. Meanwhile, under the framework of regionalism, China also believes in ASEAN's normative ability to manage and govern the South China Sea dispute. The development process of China–ASEAN relations in the new century shows that the cooperation between China and ASEAN can not only inject strength into the mitigation and regulation of the South China Sea dispute but also create more realistic and feasible solutions for restoring peace in the South China Sea and promoting the common economic development of surrounding countries.

IV. From DOC to COC: The New Height of China–ASEAN Relations

The adoption of the DOC and the "dual-track approach" to deal with the South China Sea dispute reflects the growing willingness and ability of sovereign states and regional communities to shape the order and also means that the discourse power of regional affairs in the South China Sea has gradually shifted to claimant countries and ASEAN. On the issue of maintaining and promoting security and

---

[38] *Malaysiakini*, "No warships in ASEAN waters, Dr M tells US," https://www.malaysiakini.com/news/452039 (Accessed November 15, 2022).

stability in the South China Sea, China and ASEAN have highly consistent interest demands, and the relevant norms of conduct have also established a basic consensus. However, the complexity of the South China Sea issue and the new situation and problems in geopolitics call for China and ASEAN countries to formulate new rules on the basis of implementing the DOC, namely the "Code of Conduct in the South China Sea" (COC). The consultation of the "COC" is the common mission of China and ASEAN to safeguard the security of the South Chinese Sea, which benefits the relevant stakeholders in the South China sea dispute.

Although the DOC has played an important role in maintaining the overall peace and stability of the South China Sea in the past two decades, it is not a binding international legal document in nature, but a political commitment between China and ASEAN countries. At the same time, the DOC is a phased document, which aims to leave some policy space for the agreement of "COC." From the content point of view, the provisions of the DOC also have some limitations, such as insubstantial content and vague definitions, such as whether the maritime rights in the South China Sea are exclusive or inclusive and shared, which need to be clearly explained further, and maritime cooperation and development also need more operational solutions. As an upgraded version of the DOC, the COC focuses on "substance, effectiveness and operability."[39]

Long before the signing of the DOC, China and ASEAN had already put the establishment of the COC on the agenda. After the Mischief Reef incident in 1995, China and the Philippines reached eight codes of conduct to resolve the South China Sea issue. In July 1999, the Sixth ASEAN Regional Forum welcomed the consultation between China and ASEAN within the framework of the ASEAN Regional Forum in its statement and announced that ASEAN was formulating a "COC," and China also agreed to negotiate a code of

---

[39]Refer to *Premier Li Keqiang's Speech at the 23rd China–ASEAN Summit (Full Text)*, Ministry of Foreign Affairs of China, November 13, 2020, http://switzerlandemb.fmprc.gov.cn/web/gjhdq_676201/gjhdqzz_681964/lhg_682518/zyjh_682528/202011/t20201113_9386044.shtml (Accessed December 17, 2022).

conduct in 1999. The last part of the DOC issued in 2002 also stated that "the future adoption of the COC would further promote peace and stability in the region,"[40] which shows the close relationship between the DOC and the COC. To some extent, the DOC is a phased outcome of the consultation process of the "COC."

So far, China has presented a great open attitude in the negotiations on the "COC" and has released full goodwill and sincerity. At present, the consultation of the "COC" has entered the second round of the review stage, which means that the formulation of the "COC" has entered the "deep water area" of text consultation, and will involve more sensitive topics, such as the applicable sea area of the COC, the supervision mechanism of the COC, and the relationship between the COC and other laws. The current COC framework document has embodied the governance mechanism of coastal countries, such as strengthening security cooperation between China and ASEAN, preventing and managing maritime security, etc. During the COC consultation, China and ASEAN have also reached "byproducts" such as the Joint Statement between China and ASEAN Countries on the Application of the Code for Unplanned Encounters at Sea in the South China Sea. The "COC" for airspace management in the South China Sea is also in the process of negotiation and formulation. Therefore, it is reasonable to believe that on the basis of existing mechanisms and norms, the "COC" will form more binding regional rules that meet the needs of all parties and conform to international law.

In the development process of China–ASEAN relations, the COC consultation is of great significance. Once the formulation of the COC is completed, it will probably become the most important maritime security cooperation mechanism in East Asia and produce a strong reconstruction effect on the existing regional order, which, under the framework of solving the South China Sea issue, can regulate the relations among the countries around the South China Sea and also determine the rules and ways of interaction between states.

---

[40]*The ASEAN Secretariat*, "Declaration on the Conduct of Parties in the South China Sea," October 17, 2012, https://asean.org/declaration-on-the-conduct-of-parties-in-the-south-china-sea/ (Accessed December 20, 2022).

Therefore, a fair, reasonable, and creative regional order can not only realize the common vision of all countries but also promote the distribution of public goods in the region and achieve a certain degree of power balance, thus contributing to regional peace and development. More importantly, in the context of the internationalization of the South China Sea dispute, the consensus of the "COC" on relevant issues and the stable expectation of cooperation and security between China and ASEAN countries will greatly reduce the space for the United States and other foreign powers to deeply intervene in the South China Sea dispute and implement the strategy of maritime hegemonism. Based on the construction of institutionalism cooperation and relationship networks, the COC will also enhance the practical cooperation of maritime civil and non-traditional security on the existing basis, and will greatly enhance the resilience of China–ASEAN relations.

In November 2022, in the joint statement on the 20th Anniversary of the DOC, China and ASEAN countries reaffirmed that the DOC is a milestone document in China–ASEAN Dialogue Relations, appreciated the progress made in the negotiation on the "COC," and reaffirmed that the future adoption of the "COC" further promote regional peace and stability.[41] The process from the DOC to the COC has also provided new impetus for deepening the China–ASEAN comprehensive strategic partnership, and made greater contributions to the Asian region's independent participation in global governance and effective management of international crises.

V. Conclusion

Whether the future of the South China Sea is win–win cooperation or a zero-sum game depends on the independent choice of China and ASEAN countries. During the 20 years after the signing of the DOC, China–ASEAN relations have achieved leapfrog development, which

---

[41] *The ASEAN Secretariat*, "Joint Statement on The 20th Anniversary of the Declaration on the Conduct of Parties in the South China Sea," November 12, 2022, https://asean.org/joint-statement-on-the-20th-anniversary-of-the-declaration-on-the-conduct-of-parties-in-the-south-china-sea/ (Accessed December 23, 2022).

demonstrates the importance of China and ASEAN's practice of multilateralism, adherence to the diplomatic concept of "amity, sincerity, mutual benefit and inclusiveness" and rules for regional governance. However, at the same time, we also need to be soberly aware that the good vision from the DOC to the COC does not mean that the South China Sea region has completely shaken off the influence of Western powers during this new Cold War, on the contrary, countries outside the region will not give up any "window of opportunity" to intervene in the South China Sea issue and the domain of regional issues is also constantly updated while the strategic competition of great powers has entered an era of comprehensive factor confrontation. Therefore, to cope with the possible turbulence in the South China Sea in the future, China and ASEAN should maintain strategic strength, work together to deal with the new problem, support and uphold the dialogue and cooperation based on multilateralism, and construct China–ASEAN relations into a strategic force to shape and lead the new trend of the Asian regional pattern.

Furthermore, we also need to realize that the South China Sea issue is not the whole of China–ASEAN relations. The security and stability of the situation in the South China Sea is only a partial reflection of regional governance in the South China Sea, and the cooperation between China and ASEAN countries in building a community with a shared future is bound to be comprehensive. In November 2020, the 23rd China–ASEAN Summit issued the Plan of Action to Implement the China–ASEAN Strategic Partnership for Peace and Prosperity (2021–2025). The "Plan" includes a Ten-Point plan for future China–ASEAN cooperation, covering cooperation issues in various fields and multi-level cooperation mechanisms, which reflects the good prospects for the future development of China–ASEAN relations and the determination for sustained cooperation. During the recovery period of the world economy in the post-epidemic era, China and ASEAN also urgently need to implement economic and trade cooperation, consolidate the construction of the Regional Comprehensive Economic Partnership Agreement, add impetus to regional economic cooperation, and tie a more tenacious and solid bond between China and ASEAN.

Chapter 2

The DOC and China–ASEAN Maritime Cooperation

Zhao Qinghai

Center of Maritime Security and Cooperation, China Institute of International Studies, Beijing, China
zhaoqinghai@ciis.org.cn

Abstract

Since the signing of the Declaration on the Conduct of Parties in the South China Sea, China and ASEAN members have made useful explorations on the joint development of marine oil and gas resources, cooperation in less sensitive fields, and maritime confidence and security-building measures. In some fields, substantive progress has been secured, which is credited to all parties' adherence to the spirit of cooperation of international law, consensus on cooperation, guidance of the implementation of the DOC, adoption of a step-by-step approach in a sequential manner starting with easier ones, and China's active provision of public goods for cooperation. However, current cooperation in the South China Sea has been facing barriers caused by long-existing maritime disputes, major-power competition, and domestic politics of countries in the region. Under this circumstance, China and ASEAN states should build a sense of a community with a shared future, manage and control differences properly, make a balanced effort in the DOC implementation and COC consultations, strive to foster a synergy between the 21st Century Maritime Silk Road and the ASEAN Outlook on the Indo-Pacific, focus on blue economy development, and cooperate in regional maritime governance. In doing so, the two sides can jointly push forward cooperation in the South China Sea to a higher level and safeguard peace and stability in the region.

Keywords: DOC, COC, Maritime Cooperation, China–ASEAN Relations

The People's Republic of China (PRC) and 10 member states of the Association of South-East Asian Nations (ASEAN) signed the Declaration on the Conduct of Parties in the South China Sea (DOC) in November 2002 in Phnom Penh, Cambodia. Over the past two decades since then, China and ASEAN countries have made remarkable progress by upholding the purposes and principles of the DOC and implementing arrangements for practical maritime cooperation laid out therein. Therefore, a comprehensive review of past achievements and a sum-up of previous experience will be of great practical significance to further advancing peace and stability in the South China Sea (SCS) and deepening maritime cooperation between China and ASEAN member states.

I. Progress in China–ASEAN Maritime Cooperation since the Signing of the DOC

The DOC reflects the political willingness of China and ASEAN member states to defend stability in the South China Sea, advance mutual trust, and elevate cooperation. Philippine scholar Rommel C. Banlaoi points out, "The DOC was a milestone in China–ASEAN relations as it highlighted the need to cooperate rather than compete in the South China Sea so China and ASEAN can enjoy peace, prosperity and security with each other."[1] The DOC has clear

---

[1] Rommel C. Banlaoi, "China–ASEAN Relations At 30: Pursuing Maritime Cooperation In South China Sea," November 6, 2021, https://www.eurasiareview.com/

requirements for conducting maritime cooperation, as Article 6 states that "Pending a comprehensive and durable settlement of the disputes, the Parties concerned may explore or undertake cooperative activities. These may include the following: a. marine environmental protection; b. marine scientific research; c. safety of navigation and communication at sea; d. search and rescue operation; and e. combating transnational crime, including but not limited to trafficking in illicit drugs, piracy and armed robbery at sea, and illegal traffic in arms."[2] This serves as a guidance framework for the two sides to promote practical maritime cooperation. Over the course of the past two decades, China and ASEAN, guided by the spirit of cooperation of the DOC, have explored and innovated ways to conduct maritime cooperation, which has already made substantive progress.

(i) *Active Explorations on Joint Development of Maritime Oil and Gas Resources*

In March 2005, national oil companies of China, the Philippines, and Vietnam signed a Tripartite Agreement for Joint Marine Seismic Undertaking in the Agreement Area in the South China Sea, under which the three parties designed seismic work programs and conducted a joint survey of possible oil deposits in this area. In October, China and Vietnam launched joint exploration and exploitation of transboundary oil and gas resources in the Beibu Bay (Gulf of Tonkin). Oil companies from the two countries signed an Agreement on Oil and Gas Cooperation in the Beibu Gulf. Moreover, the two sides agreed to initiate delimitation negotiations on sea areas outside the mouth of Beibu Bay and promote consultations on joint development of oil and gas in the South China Sea. As of December 2021, China and Vietnam have successfully held 12 rounds of consultation of the working group for consultation on maritime joint development.

06112021-china-asean-relations-at-30-pursuing-maritime-cooperation-in-south-china-sea-analysis/.
[2]"Declaration on the Conduct of Parties in the South China Sea," May 14, 2012, https://asean.org/declaration-on-the-conduct-of-parties-in-the-south-china-sea-2/.

China National Offshore Oil Corporation and Brunei National Petroleum Company Sendirian Berhad signed the Memorandum of Understanding on Commercial Cooperation in the Oil and Gas Sector in November 2011, and signed an Cooperation Agreement in Beijing on April 2, 2013. Three days later during Sultan Haji Hassanal Bolkiah's visit to China, the governments of China and Brunei issued a Joint Statement, agreeing to support relevant enterprises of the two countries to carry out joint exploration and exploitation of maritime oil and gas resources under the principle of mutual respect, equality, and mutual benefit. Progress in joint development has also been achieved between China and the Philippines. During President Rodrigo Roa Duterte's visit to China in October 2016, China and the Philippines signed a Joint Statement and 13 agreements on cooperation. A November 2018 visit to the Philippines by Chinese President Xi Jinping witnessed the signing of the Memorandum of Understanding in Cooperation on Oil and Gas Development between the Government of People's Republic of China and the Government of the Republic of the Philippines. When President Duterte visited China in August next year, both sides confirmed the official establishment of the Oil and Gas Development Inter-Governmental Joint Steering Committee in accordance with the Memorandum of Understanding, and the Terms of Reference on Inter-Governmental Joint Steering Committee and Inter-Entrepreneurial Working Group on Oil and Gas Development between China and the Philippines.

Cooperation on oil and gas development between China and other countries in the South China Sea has yet to reap fruits, but it has created a favorable atmosphere for China to discuss with related countries the idea of "pursuing joint development while shelving disputes" and offered useful experience.

(ii) *Remarkable Results in Maritime Cooperation in Less Sensitive Fields*

China has signed inter-governmental and inter-departmental agreements on maritime cooperation with Indonesia, Malaysia, Thailand, and Cambodia. Joint Committee Meetings with these countries have been convened on a regular basis. A number of cooperation programs have been confirmed and carried out and indeed yielded fruitful results. China respectively established joint ocean observation stations with Malaysia and Cambodia. China also worked with Indonesia to build China–Indonesia Centre for Ocean and Climate and China–Indonesia Padang Joint Ocean Observation Station. As for Thailand, China–Thai Joint Laboratory on Climate and Marine Ecosystem was established and joint investigations have already been put in place. As for Vietnam, the China–Vietnam Agreement on Fishery Cooperation in the Beibu Gulf took effect on June 30, 2004. The following-up implementation has contributed to protecting fishery resources in the Bay, establishing a stable relationship for fishing activities, and further advancing bilateral relations between the two nations. In 2012, the two sides built an expert group for low-sensitive maritime cooperation. As of June 2022, a total of 15 rounds of negotiations within the group have been held. Over the past years, the two countries have set up joint projects including the Cooperation on Marine Environment Management in the Beibu Gulf and fishery release activity for restocking in the Bay. Besides, a broad consensus has been reached on signing agreements on maritime search and rescue operations, maritime cooperation, fishery emergency hotline and sustainable fishery development in the Beibu Bay.

(iii) **Breakthroughs in Traditional and Non-traditional Security Cooperation**

As of late November 2021, navies of China and Vietnam have carried out 31 joint patrols in the Beibu Bay since their first operation in 2006. Joint military drills have been also held between China and Malaysia, which have evolved into three-way China–Malaysia–Thailand joint military exercises over time. In October 2018 and April 2019, China–ASEAN military exercises were successfully held in the north of the South China Sea and nearby sea areas of Qingdao, lifting China–ASEAN cooperation on maritime security to a higher level. At the ASEAN–China Senior Officials' Meeting on the Implementation of the DOC in the South China Sea (SOM-DOC) in

April 2016, all parties reaffirmed commitment to the implementation of "early harvest measures," including the adoption of the "MFA-to-MFA hotline for maritime emergencies" and "China–ASEAN Member States maritime emergency rescue hotline." In October 2017, China and other ASEAN littoral countries held a joint field exercise for maritime search and rescue in sea areas of Zhanjiang.

(iv) *Initial Success of Establishing Maritime Cooperation Mechanisms and Rules*

A total of five meetings have been held since the establishment of the China–Philippines Bilateral Consultation Mechanism in the South China Sea in May 2017. A Joint Coast Guard Committee on Maritime Cooperation was also founded between the China Coast Guard and the Philippine Coast Guard. In September 2019, China and Malaysia agreed on building a bilateral consultation mechanism on maritime issues. China and Vietnam also established a mechanism for regular meetings between the heads of delegations of governmental border negotiation. By far, China has established with all ASEAN claimants except for Brunei dialogue and consultation mechanisms on disputes in the South China Sea.[3] These consultation mechanisms have provided a platform for understanding each other's SCS policies, managing differences, preventing and controlling maritime accidents, and upgrading maritime cooperation. China and ASEAN states have cooperated to hold the China–Southeast Asian Countries Marine Cooperation Forum five times. At the 19th China–ASEAN Summit in September 2016, leaders of all parties deliberated and approved the Joint Statement on the Application of the Code for Unplanned Encounters at Sea (CUES) and agreed on its adoption and application in the South China Sea. The CUES

---

[3]Wu Shicun and Chen Xiangmiao, "Chen Xiangmiao: Review and prospect of China–ASEAN cooperation in the South China Sea: Based on rules construction" (中国 — 东盟南海合作回顾与展望：基于规则构建的考量), *Asia-Pacific Security and Maritime Affairs* 6 (2019): 42.

serves as clear guidance to promote safe practices and standard procedures when there are unplanned encounters between naval vessels and aircraft of the two sides.

Consultations on the Code of Conduct for the South China Sea (COC) have made major progress. After the resumption of consultations in 2013, a draft Framework COC and a Single Draft Negotiating Text (SDNT) were announced respectively in 2016 and 2017. Involving parties finished the first reading of SDNT and reached a new consensus on the second reading. The COC can help manage maritime crises and accumulate mutual trust. More importantly, it will serve as a regulation on maritime practices and measures of related countries and as an institutional arrangement for "what can and cannot do" and "what should and should not do," further laying a foundation for the future order of practical maritime cooperation featuring openness and rule in the South China Sea.

II. Successful Experience of China–ASEAN Maritime Cooperation

Sustained progress in China–ASEAN maritime cooperation is attributable to the continuous deepening of bilateral political and economic relationships. Besides, a critical driving force for maritime cooperation is that related countries have been resolute in forging consensus on cooperation and adopting pragmatic and feasible approaches on the basis of observing basic principles of international law.

(i) *Upholding the Spirit of Cooperation of International Law and Treaties*

The DOC states clearly that "The Parties reaffirm their commitment to the purposes and principles of the Charter of the United Nations, the 1982 UN Convention on the Law of the Sea (UNCLOS), the Treaty of Amity and Cooperation in Southeast Asia (TAC), the Five Principles of Peaceful Coexistence, and other universally recognized principles of international law which shall serve as the basic norms governing state-to-state relations."⁴ One thing that should be given special focus is Article 123 of the UNCLOS that stipulates, "States bordering an enclosed or semi-enclosed sea should cooperate with each other in the exercise of their rights and in the performance of their duties under this Convention. To this end they shall endeavour, directly or through an appropriate regional organization: (a) to coordinate the management, conservation, exploration and exploitation of the living resources of the sea; (b) to coordinate the implementation of their rights and duties with respect to the protection and preservation of the marine environment; (c) to coordinate their scientific research policies and undertake where appropriate joint programmes of scientific research in the area."⁵ Article Four of Chapter Three of the TAC also stipulates, "The High Contracting Parties shall promote active cooperation in the economic, social, technical, scientific and administrative fields as well as in matters of common ideals and aspirations of international peace and stability in the region and all other matters of common interest." Article Eight notes, "The High Contracting Parties shall strive to achieve the closest cooperation on the widest scale and shall seek to provide assistance to one another in the form of training and research facilities in the social, cultural, technical, scientific and administrative fields." Both the UNCLOS and the TAC hold that China and ASEAN member states have an obligation to push forward maritime cooperation. "Along with the DOC, the TAC has become the effective cornerstone of China–ASEAN maritime cooperation in the South China Sea."⁶ In 2003, China acceded to the TAC, laying an important political foundation for maritime cooperation between China and ASEAN countries.

---

⁴"Declaration on the Conduct of Parties in the South China Sea," May 14, 2012, https://asean.org/declaration-on-the-conduct-of-parties-in-the-south-china-sea-2/.
⁵"United Nations Convention on the Law of the Sea" (联合国海洋法公约), *The Ocean Publisher*, 2013, pp. 87.
⁶Rommel C. Banlaoi, "China–ASEAN Relations at 30: Pursuing Maritime Cooperation In South China Sea," November 6, 2021, https://www.eurasiareview.com/06112021-china-asean-relations-at-30-pursuing-maritime-cooperation-in-south-china-sea-analysis/.

(ii) *Driving Maritime Cooperation through Consensus*

Since the 1990s, platforms such as Workshop on Managing Potential Conflicts in the South China Sea, ASEAN Regional Forum, ASEAN Maritime Forum, and Expanded ASEAN Maritime Forum have worked on discussing plans for the settlement of regional maritime disputes, protection of maritime security, and pragmatic technique cooperation. After a long period of promotion and publicizing, countries in this region have reached a relatively high consensus on protecting the sea environment, preventing the depletion of fishery reserves, defending the safety of navigation and communication at sea, launching maritime confidence-building measures, conducting search and rescue operations, and combating transnational crimes. For example, enhancing maritime cooperation has been encompassed in the ASEAN Plus Three Cooperation Work Plan (2013–2017). In 2015, the ASEAN Summit issued the Statement on Enhancing Regional Maritime Cooperation. In the statement on marine sustainability adopted by the East Asia Summit in 2020, all parties reaffirmed their commitment to enhance regional maritime cooperation in dealing with marine plastic rubbish, strengthen sustainable marine economic development, protect and preserve the marine and coastal environment, including biodiversity, ecosystem, and resources, as well as in protecting people who depend on oceans from harmful activities and other threats such as land-based and sea-based pollution. Relevant consensus produces a social environment conducive to maritime cooperation between China and ASEAN member states.

(iii) *Making the Implementation of the DOC as a Booster of China–ASEAN Maritime Cooperation*

In order to better implement the DOC, China and ASEAN countries co-established the mechanism of meetings of senior officials and joint working groups. As of June 2021, the Meeting of Senior Officials on the implementation of the DOC in the South China Sea has been chaired 19 times. As of May 2022, ASEAN and China have hosted 36 meetings of the Joint Working Group of the DOC in the South China

Sea (JWG). All these meetings have played an important role in boosting China–ASEAN maritime cooperation. In 2011, China and ASEAN passed the Guidelines for the Implementation of the DOC, paving the way for driving the implementation of the DOC and maritime cooperation. To this end, a number of maritime cooperation programs have been carried out. For example, China and ASEAN member states adopted the Declaration for a Decade of Coastal and Marine Environmental Protection in the South China Sea (2017–2027) proposed by the Philippines. Since the 16th SOM-DOC in October 2018, China and ASEAN member states have updated the DOC implementation plan for 2016–2021 and confirmed a batch of new projects for practical maritime cooperation.

(iv) *Following a Step-by-Step Approach in a Sequential Manner Starting with Easier Ones*

The South China Sea dispute has a long history with complicated differences. In view of the different policy priorities of different countries, it is a must to take into full account the sensitivity of cooperation fields, strike a balance between various interests, and address the concerns of all parties so as to elevate maritime cooperation in the South China Sea. At the workshop on commemoration of the 20th anniversary of the DOC in the South China Sea, Chinese State Councilor and Foreign Minister Wang Yi pointed out, "The DOC captures the essence of the East Asian culture, such as seeking consensus and accommodating the comfort level of all parties. It also reflects the maximum common understanding of regional countries on the South China Sea issue. In implementing the DOC, we always follow the Asian tradition of respecting each other and honoring our words."[7] For years, in accordance with five cooperation areas confirmed in the DOC, China and ASEAN member states have got priorities straight after an overall consideration of the degree of mutual

---

[7] Wang Yi, "Carrying Forward the DOC Spirit and Forging Consensus to Jointly Build a Sea of Peace, Friendship and Cooperation," July 25, 2022, https://www.fmprc.gov.cn/mfa_eng/zxxx_662805/202207/t20220725_10727703.html.

trust, the differences in interests and aspirations, the sensitivity of cooperation fields, and the demand of countries in the SCS. The two sides have worked out lists for implementing the DOC cooperation tasks following a step-by-step approach in a sequential manner starting with easier ones, and have deepened maritime cooperation in the South China Sea following a "consensus-oriented and result-oriented" way.

(v) *Playing China's Active Role as a Provider of Public Goods for Maritime Cooperation*

Regional maritime cooperation is a common course of all countries, but it usually requires certain countries to act as a spearhead or provide intellectual and financial support. At the General Debate of the 75th Session of the UN General Assembly, Chinese President Xi Jinping said, "In particular, major countries should act like major countries. They should provide more global public goods, take up their due responsibilities and live up to people's expectations."[8] In advancing cooperation in the South China Sea, China has consistently shouldered its due responsibilities as a major country. In 2011, the Chinese government established the China–ASEAN Maritime Cooperation Fund, providing necessary financial support for practicing maritime practical cooperation.[9] In 2012, the China–Indonesia Maritime Cooperation Fund was started. From 2013, China has spearheaded the establishment and operation of the East Asia Marine Cooperation Platform and China–ASEAN Maritime Cooperation Center. In 2018, the South China Sea Tsunami Advisory Center hosted and supported by China was put into trial operation, providing a public service of advisories on potential tsunamis in the region.

---

[8]"Statement by H.E. Xi Jinping at the General Debate of the 75th Session of the United Nations General Assembly (full text)"(习近平在第七十五届联合国大会一般性辩论上的讲话), *Xinhuanet*, September 22, 2020.
[9]Wen Jiabao stated that China will set up a 3 billion yuan fund to promote maritime cooperation between China and ASEAN (温家宝：中方将设30亿元基金促中国东盟海上合作), *China News*, November 18, 2011.

China also launched its Framework Plan (2011–2015) and Framework Plan (2016–2020) for international cooperation in the South China Sea and adjacent seas, receiving positive responses from neighboring countries in the region.

III. Challenges Facing China–ASEAN Maritime Cooperation

Despite all the fruitful results achieved in the past, China and ASEAN countries have been facing various disruptions to their maritime cooperation. The past two decades after the signing of the DOC have witnessed a China–ASEAN maritime cooperation that features more negotiations but fewer implementations, more bilateral work but less multilateral ones, more cooperation in less sensitive fields but less in key areas such as joint development and maritime search and rescue, and stable consultation mechanisms but a lack of specific cooperation ones.[10] The growing competition between major countries results in a more complicated situation in the SCS and more barriers facing China–ASEAN maritime cooperation.

(i) *Constraints Caused by Maritime Disputes*

China and ASEAN Countries are hard to find accommodations in maritime disputes as they concern state's sovereignty and dignity, national feelings, and resources and space needed for national development. Disputes on islands and reefs have resulted in conflicts between China and ASEAN countries from time to time against fishery resources and oil and gas reserves, which stoke mutual suspicion and eroded mutual trust. Considering the development gap and unresolved major differences, ASEAN claimants remain suspicious and worried about China-led initiatives on cooperation in many fields,

---

[10]Wu Shicun and Chen Xiangmiao, "Chen Xiangmiao: Review and prospect of China–ASEAN cooperation in the South China Sea: Based on rules construction" (中国 — 东盟南海合作回顾与展望：基于规则构建的考量), *Asia-Pacific Security and Maritime Affairs* 6 (2019): 42.

fearing that China will leverage those initiatives to establish regional dominance and impose its SCS policies and claims on them. Although ASEAN claimants realize the importance of marine environmental protection including fishery release activity for restocking, and for the safety of sea lanes, they hold a negative attitude toward China's proposal for establishing three technical committees on marine research and environmental protection, navigation safety, search, and rescue, and combating transnational crimes. Relevant proposals were made as early as 2008. Yet it was in May 2017 that the 14th SOM-DOC deliberated and approved a "Non-paper on the steps towards the establishment of the technical committees." No concrete follow-up has been made because of a lack of willingness of ASEAN member states. In recent years, China has proposed to establish a Blue Partnership with ASEAN, while the latter only wants to build a Blue Economic Partnership. Nevertheless, relevant cooperation agreements have seen a general lack of progress.

(ii) *Disruptions Posed by Major Powers' Strategic Competition*

Maritime cooperation has become an important leverage for major powers to interfere in regional affairs with a view to settling major problems facing maritime governance and seeking dominance or voice in regional affairs. Apart from a variety of bilateral maritime cooperation, major countries put forward with ASEAN and other regional organizations maritime cooperation initiatives, including the Indo-Pacific Oceans Initiative proposed by India, Japan's Free and Open Indo-Pacific Strategy, and a series of maritime cooperation measures reached at the ASEAN–U.S. Special Summit. As the U.S. launches strategic competition against China in a comprehensive manner, sea-related issues have been used by the U.S. to contain China's development. It leverages maritime disputes between China and neighboring countries to lobby those countries for greater maritime pressure on China. Cooperation in the SCS has been more of a political and security issue used for geopolitical competition. Fearing that China may play down its role in the region and even exclude it from regional affairs, the U.S. depicts China as a revisionist country that is breaking the rule-based order and imposing coercion on regional states, which not only vilifies China but also undermines regional maritime cooperation and disrupts consultations on the COC. Mechanisms including bilateral alliances, ASEAN–U.S. Summit, Quadrilateral Security Dialogue, and Five Eyes Alliance have been made a tool to build a cooperation network targeting and excluding China in terms of safety at sea and maritime diplomacy. The U.S. promised a new investment of $60 million in strengthening cooperation between the U.S. Coast Guard and ASEAN countries,[11] during the ASEAN–U.S. Special Summit in mid-May 2022. During the Quad Leaders' Tokyo Summit in late May 2022, the U.S., Australia, India, and Japan announced the Indo-Pacific Partnership for Maritime Domain Awareness, promising to build a maritime picture that integrates the Pacific Islands, Southeast Asia, and the Indian Ocean region to transform the ability of partners to fully monitor the waters on their shores.[12] The U.S. has been seeking to drive a wedge between China and ASEAN countries by provoking conflicts in the South China Sea. The temptation and lobbying of the U.S. have successfully roped some Southeast Asian nations into countering China through security cooperation with major powers outside the region. Their suspicion of China's cooperation initiatives has greatly contained regional maritime cooperation.

(iii) *Barriers to Cooperation Laid by Domestic Politics of Disputant Parties*

A higher priority of the ocean in national strategy has attracted people's great concerns about the belonging of related islands and reefs, maritime delimitation, and the development of marine resources. Against the backdrop, tough positions on related disputes have

---

[11] *The White House*, "ASEAN–U.S. Special Summit 2022, Joint Vision Statement," May 13, 2022, https://www.whitehouse.gov/briefing-room/statements-releases/2022/05/13/asean-u-s-special-summit-2022-joint-vision-statement/.

[12] *The White House*, "Fact Sheet: Quad Leaders' Tokyo Summit 2022," May 23, 2022, https://www.whitehouse.gov/briefing-room/statements-releases/2022/05/23/fact-sheet-quad-leaders-tokyo-summit-2022/.

somehow evolved into something about "political correctness" in some claimant countries. Domestic public acceptance has been at the top of the list for governments when conducting maritime cooperation. In particular, they have to take all the things into consideration and think twice before making proper decisions when cooperation involves disputed waters. Multilateral maritime cooperation in particular providing regional public goods and services has faced a cold shoulder because some claimants lack political willingness for common cooperation in order to pursue unilateral claims over sea waters and maximize interests in resource development. Instead, those countries have acted unilaterally to consolidate and expand vested interests, which has resulted in undermining the atmosphere for maritime cooperation. For example, in disputed waters, some ASEAN claimant countries have taken unilateral actions to explore and exploit oil and gas, take over unoccupied islands and reefs, and conduct fishery activities within the "nine-dash line." Those practices would tend to cause escalated conflicts between related countries, fuel maritime tensions, lower political mutual trust, and provide fewer opportunities for practical cooperation. Take China–Philippines cooperation as an example. When President Gloria Macapagal Arroyo was in office, the Philippines' joint exploration deal with China and Vietnam failed to withstand the wide protests of domestic opponents. When it came to President Duterte, China–Philippines maritime cooperation once showed good momentum. However, as Duterte is scheduled to step down from the President's post, oil and gas discussions with China in the South China Sea were announced to be completely terminated in June 2022 out of concerns for domestic politics. Such uncertainty and inconsistency in policy throughout administrations will only drive credit deficits high for future cooperation.

IV. Thoughts on Deepening China–ASEAN Maritime Cooperation under the DOC

The majority of countries in the South China Sea highly rely on the ocean to grow economy. Therefore, maritime cooperation concerns the development and security of all parties in this region. At the

Special Summit to Commemorate the 30th Anniversary of China–ASEAN Dialogue Relations, President Xi Jinping stressed, "Joint efforts are needed to safeguard stability in the South China Sea and make it a sea of peace, friendship and cooperation," and "We may also energize the China–ASEAN Countries Joint Research and Development Center of Marine Science and Technology, build the Partnership on Blue Economy, and promote marine sustainable development."[13] President Xi's speech chartered a way for deeper China–ASEAN maritime cooperation. To sustain China–ASEAN cooperation in the South China Sea, the following principles and directions should be given priority.

(i) *Building a Strong Sense of a Maritime Community with a Shared Future, under Which Differences are Managed and Controlled Properly*

On the occasion of the 70th founding anniversary of the Chinese People's Liberation Army Navy in 2019, President Xi initiated a proposal for building a maritime community with a shared future. He said, "The blue planet humans inhabit is not divided into islands by the oceans, but is connected by the oceans to form a community with a shared future, where people of all countries share weal and woe." The philosophy calls for joint efforts to seek win–win cooperation on maritime security, address common threats and challenges at sea, and safeguard maritime peace, tranquility, development, and prosperity. It conforms to the defining trend of the times and serves the long-term interest of all parties. Therefore, it should be upheld as a guideline for addressing maritime affairs by littoral countries in the SCS and other countries in the world. China and ASEAN member states should manage and control differences properly with a "dual-track" approach in the spirit of a maritime community with a shared future.

---

[13] Xi Jinping, "For a Shared Future and Our Common Home, Speech by H.E. Xi Jinping, President of the People's Republic of China, at the Special Summit to Commemorate the 30th Anniversary of China–ASEAN Dialogue Relations" (命运与共　共建家园　——　在中国　——　东盟建立对话关系30周年纪念峰会上的讲话), *Guangming Daily*, November 23, 2021.

Pending the settlement of disputes, the two sides should stick to prevent marine accidents with maritime security and confidence-building measures, manage differences under the framework of regional rules, and construct a new framework of regional rules through positive consultations.

(ii) *Proceeding Consultations on the COC with the Implementation of the DOC*

The full and faithful implementation is a joint commitment made by China and 10 ASEAN countries. There is no paradox between advancing consultations on the COC and the implementation of the DOC because the former is a main objective as well as a part of the latter. Both the designed are to "provide stronger institutional safeguards for managing differences and advancing cooperation."[14] Looking forward, China and ASEAN member states should make steady progress in consultations on the COC under the framework of full and effective implementation of the DOC. Balanced efforts should also be paid to set up working mechanisms for implementing the DOC under the framework of the COC. Practical maritime cooperation, as an important component of the COC in the future, should get further expansion and more safeguards with regard to both mechanisms and measures.[15]

(iii) *Seeking Greater Synergy between the 21st Century Maritime Silk Road (MSR) and the ASEAN Outlook on the Indo-Pacific (AOIP) to Form a Long-Term Mechanism for Maritime Cooperation*

In the initiative proposed by China to build the MSR, the South China Sea is a main starting point and ASEAN countries are the main

---

[14] Wang Yi, "Carrying Forward the DOC Spirit and Forging Consensus To Jointly Build a Sea of Peace, Friendship and Cooperation," July 25, 2022, https://www.fmprc.gov.cn/mfa_eng/zxxx_662805/202207/t20220725_10727703.html.
[15] Wu Shicun, *The South China Sea Dispute: Origin and Development* (南沙争端的由来与发展), *Zhonghua Book Company*, 2022, pp. 302–303.

partners. The AOIP published in June 2019 outlines its positions and claims on maritime cooperation as follows: (1) settling disputes in a peaceful way, promoting maritime safety and security, and freedom of navigation and overflight, and addressing transnational crimes, including trafficking in persons or of illicit drugs, sea piracy, robbery and armed robbery against ships at sea; (2) advancing cooperation for sustainable management of marine resources, promoting maritime connectivity, protecting livelihood of coastal communities and supporting small-scale fishing communities, developing blue economy, and promoting maritime commerce; (3) conducting cooperation to address marine pollution, sea-level rise, marine debris, preservation and protection of the marine environment and biodiversity, and promoting green shipping; (4) carrying technical cooperation in marine science collaboration, research and development, sharing experience and best practices, capacity-building, managing marine hazards and marine debris, and raising awareness on marine and ocean-related issues.[16] At the ASEAN Secretariat in July 2022, Wang Yi said that China, "would like to increase synergy and cooperation with ASEAN on the implementation of the Outlook to produce cooperation outcomes at an early date."[17] ASEAN's claims on maritime cooperation are in line with China's positions, which lends a greater practical possibility to fostering synergy between the MSR and AOIP. The two sides can conduct discussions on establishing consultation mechanisms for cooperation and providing financial support in order to form long-term relations featuring stable and sustainable cooperation.

---

[16]"ASEAN Outlook on the Indo-Pacific," June 23, 2019, https://asean.org/asean2020/wp-content/uploads/2021/01/ASEAN-Outlook-on-the-Indo-Pacific_FINAL_22062019.pdf.

[17]Wang Yi, "Peace, development, autonomy, inclusiveness and firm practice of open regionalism" (和平、发展、自主、包容 坚定践行开放的区域主义), *International Studies* 4 (2022): 6.

(iv) *Making the Pie of Interests Bigger and Taking Blue Economy Cooperation as a Major Course*

In recent years, China has been a driving force in establishing a Blue Economy Partnership with ASEAN. Adopted at the 38th ASEAN Summit in October 2021, ASEAN Leader's Declaration on the Blue Economy agrees to explore cooperation on the blue economy in areas as follows: marine environmental protection; Illegal, Unreported and Unregulated (IUU) fishing; marine and coastal ecosystems protection; sustainable aquaculture and fishing practices; sustainable production and consumption; biotechnology; marine industrial development; marine pollution; marine litter and plastic pollution; food security; trade; coastal tourism and heritage conservation; maritime transport; security and safety of navigation; data, statistics, and data analytics; as well as capacity-building, digitization and innovation. China can conduct serious research on ASEAN member states' main aspirations and then leverage its own industrial and technical strength to advance the establishment of China–ASEAN Blue Economy Partnership. To this end, China can conduct work in two fields in the short term. One is marine aquaculture, which has a low threshold for finance and skills but is of great help for improving fishermen's livelihood and relieving stress of the depletion of marine fishery resources. China can leverage its strength in finance, technical research and development, and market to provide debt assistance, technical services, and a consumer market to ASEAN countries. The other is economic cooperation in the bay areas. China and littoral ASEAN countries can join hands to build the Pan South China Sea economic cooperation zone by engaging in cooperation with regard to port infrastructure connectivity, and industries and industrial estates near the port area.

(v) *Jointly Pushing Ahead with Agenda on Regional Ocean Governance*

The South China Sea is a common home for China and other littoral countries in this region. Therefore, problems of this region require concerted efforts of all littoral countries. In line with Goal 14 of the UN's 2030 Agenda for Sustainable Development, China and ASEAN member countries can conduct joint research on marine ecology and environment to assess ecological challenges facing the SCS. In response to most urgent problems of regional ecology including the degradation of coral reefs and reduction in fishery resources, China and other littoral countries in the SCS can establish a consultation committee consisting of their departments of ocean and environmental protection, mobilize experts and scholars in related fields to set up joint experts' technical working groups, launch a restoration fund for coral reefs and a special fund for fishing resources investigation and conservation, with a focus on practical maritime cooperation in terms of restoring coral reefs, protecting endangered marine species and conducting technical research and development in marine aquaculture.

Improving governance for marine plastic litter. Consensus has been reached on dealing with marine debris, in particular plastic litter, at the East Asia Summit, ASEAN Plus Three Summit, and ASEAN Leaders' Summit. In early March 2022, the fifth session of the United Nations Environment Assembly adopted the End Plastic Pollution, a legally binding treaty, which establishes an Intergovernmental Negotiating Committee to complete a treaty that allows for governance across the full life cycle of plastic products including production, design, recycling, and disposal. Therefore, conducting governance cooperation on marine plastic litter conforms to regional aspirations and the defining trend of the world. Under the circumstances, China and ASEAN can cooperate with each other to exchange experience and data with regard to monitoring and tracking marine plastic litter, managing plastic debris, and building waste-free cities.

Chapter 3

Substantive Issues Surrounding the COC Consultation: Forging a Legal Path Forward for the Negotiators*

Kong Lingjie

*China Institute of Boundary and Ocean Studies,
Wuhan University, China
konglingjie@whu.edu.cn*

Abstract

The DOC, signed by China and the ASEAN member states in 2002, sets out the objective of adopting a code of conduct in the South China Sea. The parties arrived at the Framework of the COC in 2017, and endorsed the Single Draft Negotiating Text in 2018, and completed the first reading of the text in 2019. The second reading is in progress. In the next phase of the consultation, apart from the procedural matters, the parties need to deal with several substantive

---

*Grant information: This chapter benefited from a key research project of the National Social Science Foundation of China.

issues of foundational importance for further elaborations and adoption of the text, which include, among others, the legal nature of the COC, its geographical scope of application, relationship with DOC, implementation mechanism, and relationship with other countries. Adopting a more substantive and effective COC at an early date serves the fundamental interest of the countries and peoples in the region as well as the international community.

Keywords: South China Sea, Security, Declaration on the Conduct of Parties, Code of Conduct

I. Progress of the COC Consultation

The notion of managing the South China Sea issue by a code of conduct for the claimant States can be traced back to the early 1990s. The ASEAN Declaration on the South China Sea, announced by the foreign ministers of six ASEAN member states in July 1992, commands all parties concerned to establish a code of international conduct over the South China Sea on the basis of the principles of the 1976 Treaty of Amity and Cooperation in Southeast Asia.[1] On the basis of the draft text prepared by the Philippines and Vietnam, ASEAN member states adopted the ASEAN Regional Code of Conduct in the South China Sea in November 1999.[2] The negotiation between China and ASEAN countries commenced in March 2000 in Hua Hin, Thailand. By then, China had also prepared its own version of the document. The intensive negotiations among the parties in the subsequent 20 months did not end up with a code of conduct but instead a Declaration on the Conduct of Parties.[3] The representatives of ASEAN member states and China signed the Declaration on the Conduct of Parties in the South China Sea (DOC) in Phnom Penh,

---

[1] The ASEAN Declaration on the South China Sea, adopted in Manila, the Philippine on 22 July 1992, para. 4.

[2] ASEAN Regional Code of Conduct in the South China Sea, adopted in November 1999.

[3] Carlyle A. Thayer, "ASEAN, China and the Code of Conduct in the South China Sea," *SAIS Review of International Affairs* 33 (2013): 76.

Cambodia on November 4, 2002.[4] The DOC is seen by the parties as a milestone instrument of historical significance in ASEAN–China relations, and also the starting of a new chapter for the 11 countries to collectively maintain peace, stability, security, and order in the South China Sea region.

Pursuant to paragraph 10 of the DOC, the parties acknowledged that the adoption of a code of conduct (COC) would further promote peace and stability in the region. To this end, the parties agreed to work, on the basis of consensus, toward the eventual attainment of this objective.[5] This paragraph states the need for a COC, the parties' commitment to attain this objective, and the consensus approach for adopting the COC. However, it does not indicate when the parties should begin the consultation, how the text should be formulated, elaborated, and adopted, and when the COC should be concluded. Nor does this paragraph and other provisions of the DOC say anything about the nature of the COC, its relationship with the DOC, and the major parts and substantive provisions of the COC. In other words, the parties only agreed in 2002 to work toward the eventual adoption of a COC on the basis of consensus in their implementation of the DOC. Issues surrounding the COC consultation, both procedural and substantive, are left to the COC negotiators.

Adoption of the COC is regarded by the parties as an integral part of the work for a full and effective implementation of the DOC. In this connection, the parties adopted the Guidelines for the Implementation of the DOC in July 2011 (Guidelines).[6] Under paragraph 6 of the Guidelines, the parties reaffirmed the conviction that full and effective implementation of the DOC should lead to the

---

[4]Declaration on the Conduct of Parties in the South China Sea, signed in Phnom Penh, Cambodia on November 4, 2002.
[5]Paragraph 10 of the DOC reads: "The Parties concerned reaffirm that the adoption of a code of conduct in the South China Sea would further promote peace and stability in the region and agree to work, on the basis of consensus, towards the eventual attainment of this objective."
[6]Guidelines for the Implementation of the Declaration on the Conduct of Parties in the South China Sea, adopted in Bali, Indonesia on July 20, 2011.

eventual realization of a COC.[7] In the year 2012, the Philippines, ASEAN, and Indonesia released their draft text, proposed elements, and zero draft for the COC.[8] On August 5, 2013, Chinese Foreign Minister Wang Yi announced that the parties had agreed to commence the COC consultation. At the 6th ASEAN–China Senior Officials' Meeting on the Implementation of the DOC (SOM-DOC) and the 9th ASEAN–China Joint Working Group on the Implementation of the DOC (JWG-DOC) held in September 2013, the parties kicked off the consultation.

After an in-depth exchange of views on certain key procedural matters of the COC consultation, the parties endorsed the Framework of the Code of Conduct in the South China Sea (Framework) in August 2017.[9] The Framework served as the basis for further negotiation of the COC, particularly the formulation of a draft negotiating text. The Framework indicates that the COC is composed of three major parts, namely the preambular provisions, general provisions, and final clauses.[10]

Part one is to set out the basis of the COC, its relationship with the DOC, and the significance of the conclusion of the COC, and aspirations of the parties.

Part two constitutes the main body of substantive provisions of the COC. It is divided into three sections, i.e., the objectives of the COC, the principles of the COC, and the basic undertakings of the parties. The basic undertakings section contains provisions governing

---

[7] Paragraph 6 of the Guidelines reads: "The decision to implement concrete measures or activities of the DOC should be based on consensus among parties concerned, and lead to the eventual realization of a Code of Conduct."

[8] Carlyle A. Thayer, "ASEAN'S Code of Conduct in the South China Sea: A litmus test for community-building?" *The Asia-Pacific Journal* 10 (August 2012); Mark J. Valencia, "Navigating differences: What the 'Zero Draft' Code of Conduct for the South China Sea says (and doesn't say)," *Global Asia* 8(1) (March 2013).

[9] Framework of the Code of Conduct in the South China Sea, adopted in Manila, the Philippines on August 6, 2017.

[10] Ian Storey, "Assessing the ASEAN–China framework for the Code of Conduct for the South China Sea," *Perspective of Yusof Ishak Institute* 62 (2017), https://www.iseas.edu.sg/images/pdf/ISEAS_Perspective_2017_62.pdf.

the conduct of parties with regard to the duty to cooperate, promotion of practical maritime cooperation, self-restraint and promotion of trust and confidence, prevention of incidents, management of incidents, and other undertakings.

Part three contains provisions on the mechanism for implementation and review of the COC, non-parties to the COC, and its entry into force.

Adoption of the Framework accelerated the formulation of a draft negotiating text. In August 2018, China and the ASEAN member states endorsed a Single Draft Code of Conduct in the South China Sea Negotiating Text (SDNT).[11] The SDNT is said to be A4-sized 19 pages long.[12] A small part of its text is from the Framework, and a large part is inputs from all parties. The JWG-DOC is tasked by the parties to read the SDNT under the leadership of the SOM-DOC.

The principal work of the first reading is to streamline the text, especially the provisions proposed by the parties separately, to reduce duplications and redundancies embodied in various parts, sections, and provisions of the document, and to consolidate the text where necessary, possible, and feasible. This sounds essentially a language editing work. It can be exceptionally laborious when the number of provisions is large, and the workload for streamlining the text is heavy. In July 2019, the parties announced that the first reading of the SDNT had been completed ahead of schedule.[13] According to Ian Storey, during the first reading, the parties had removed overlapping text, and inserted comments from the parties.[14]

---

[11] Single Draft Code of Conduct in the South China Sea Negotiating Text, adopted in Singapore on August 3, 2018.
[12] https://thediplomat.com/2018/08/a-closer-look-at-the-asean-china-single-draft-south-china-sea-code-of-conduct.
[13] https://www.chinadailyasia.com/articles/150/234/212/1564567550878.html?newsId=90597.
[14] Ian Storey, "As ASEAN and China discuss a Code of Conduct for the South China Sea, America looks on skeptically," *ISEAS Commentary of the Yusof Ishak Institute*, October 24, 2019, https://www.iseas.edu.sg/media/commentaries/as-asean-and-china-discuss-a-code-of-conduct-for-the-south-china-sea-america-looks-on-sceptically-by-ian-storey.

After a brief review and reflection meeting, the parties decided to proceed straight to the second reading of the SDNT. For the purpose of further consolidating the text, the JWG-DOC can employ the following tools: (a) use different colors for the texts to indicate their sources, (b) use brackets and other symbols to distinguish the agreed and non-agreed parts of the text, (c) append dissenting and separate opinions and declarations of the parties to the text; and (d) label certain provisions proposed by the parties as alternative options. As a matter of fact, the consolidation of the SDNT is a process for the parties to gradually narrow their differences, forge consensus and reach agreement on the underlying substantive issues surrounding the provisions.

The second reading of the SDNT was disrupted by COVID-19. The JWG-DOC was not able to meet physically until May 2022.[15] On October 1–3, 2022, at the 37th JWG-DOC, the parties resumed the second reading.[16]

Reading of the SDNT, transforming the text with inputs from the 11 parties into a single, coherent and unified document in particular, can be an extremely tough job. This important work appears to be more challenging for the JWG-DOC when the positions and views of the parties on a wide range of procedural matters and substantive issues of foundational importance for the COC consultation are varied, divided, and opposing to each other. These substantive issues include, among others, (a) the legal nature of the COC, (b) the geographical scope of application of the COC, (c) the relationship between the COC and DOC, (d) the implementation mechanism of the COC, and (e) the relationship between the COC and other countries.

In respect of the major steps, approaches, methods, and other procedural matters for the COC consultation, the parties have not

---

[15]https://asean2022.mfaic.gov.kh/posts/2022-05-27-News-The-36th-Meeting-of-the-ASEAN-China-Joint-Working-Group-on-the-Implementation-of-the-Declaration-on--09-52-00.

[16]https://asean2022.mfaic.gov.kh/posts/2022-10-07-News-The-37th-Meeting-of-the-ASEAN-China-Joint-Working-Group-on-the-Implementation-of-the-Declaration-of--11-41-08.

released any information. It remains unclear whether there will be a third reading of the SDNT. Nor is it clear what concrete steps the parties are to take for further elaborations of the text. Will the parties establish a handful of sub-drafting committees tasked to rewrite relevant parts of the SDNT? Are the parties to resort to informal diplomacy? What is clear is that the parties agree to adopt at an early date a more substantive and effective COC on the basis of consensus. In other words, before they have a draft COC agreeable and acceptable for each of the eleven countries, they can hardly complete the consultation and adopt the COC.

Before the outbreak of COVID-19 and after the SDNT was adopted, Chinese Premier Li Keqiang and Foreign Minister Wang Yi expressed the hope on several occasions that the parties endeavor to complete the consultation and adopt the COC within three years.[17] However, the parties do not have an agreed timetable for the COC consultation or a deadline for its conclusion. All parties have reaffirmed on numerous occasions their commitment to accelerate the COC consultation process and their will to adopt a more substantive and effective COC at an early date.

II. Substantive Issues Surrounding the COC Consultation

(i) *Common Ground of the Parties on the COC Consultation*

Before we turn to the key issues surrounding the COC consultation, the consensus of the parties in respect of the objectives, subject matters, and legal basis of the COC should be briefly introduced.

---

[17]Premier Li Keqiang said in his keynote speech at the 44th Singapore Lecture that China is ready to work with ASEAN countries to "strive to conclude consultations on a code of conduct (COC) in the South China Sea in three years' time." https://chinaplus.cri.cn/chinaplus/news/politics/11/20181115/210030.html. At the ASEAN–China Ministerial Meeting on July 31, 2019, State Councilor and Foreign Minister Wang Yi stated that completion of the first reading was a major progress in the consultation, and "an important step toward the goal of concluding the consultations within three years." http://www.chinadaily.com.cn/a/201908/01/WS5d42214fa310d83056402178.html.

The parties to the COC consultation can be categorized into the following groups: (a) the parties to the COC and other countries, (b) the parties directly concerned with the territorial and maritime disputes in the South China Sea and other States, (c) the coastal States of the South China Sea and other States.

First, China and the ASEAN member states are the signatories to the DOC. They are the parties to the COC consultation. They will be the parties to the COC. ASEAN is not a party to the consultation or a party to the document. It is also unlikely that the parties are to adopt a COC, which is open to other countries.

Second, the COC consultation is premised on the so-called "dual-track approach" for managing the South China Sea issue. This approach, proposed by Brunei and advocated by China, requires the territorial and maritime disputes to be settled peacefully through direct talks by the parties directly concerned, and stability in the South China Sea is to be maintained by China and ASEAN countries.[18] The COC is not an instrument to settle the outstanding territorial and maritime disputes. Rather, it is an instrument containing a set of norms to regulate and guide the conduct of the parties, to avoid conflicts arising from the enduring disputes. Where differences arise, the parties should manage the conflicts by the norms, institutions, and mechanisms established under the COC, to avoid aggregation, extension, and complication of the disputes. The parties are also encouraged to build mutual trust through confidence-building measures and practical maritime cooperation so that all parties can collectively maintain order, security, and stability in the region.

Third, not all parties to the COC are coastal states within the meaning of the 1982 United Nations Convention on the Law of the Sea (UNCLOS). The DOC is not an instrument concluded by the coastal States in the South China Sea solely for the purpose of

---

[18]Wang Yi, "Handle the South China Sea Issue through the 'dual-track' Approach," August 9, 2014, https://www.fmprc.gov.cn/mfa_eng/gjhdq_665435/2675_6654 37/2747_663498/2749_663502/201408/t20140810_518825.html.

operationalizing regional cooperation under the regime of Article 123 of the UNCLOS for semi-enclosed seas.[19]

Fourth, in terms of the subject matter, the COC can be characterized a maritime security instrument, which is adopted by China and ASEAN member states on the basis of international law, including the UNCLOS. The UNCLOS comes into play only because the conduct regulated by COC takes place on the sea and under the legal regimes of the seas established by the UNCLOS. On top of that, the COC should also be drafted on the basis of general international law, especially those having a bearing on conflict management, mutual trust, confidence building, and maritime cooperation. Provisions of the COC may be more specific, substantive and detailed than the existing rules on the conduct of the parties in the South China Sea.

Pending the conclusion of the COC and without a publicly accessible SDNT, it is unwise to speculate at this stage how the parties are to resolve the key issues surrounding the COC consultation. However, it is both timely and necessary to examine these issues from an international legal perspective when the second reading of the SDNT is approaching an end. It should be noted that these issues are principally political in nature. Only the parties are in a position to negotiate, compromise, and find agreeable solutions to them. As a public international lawyer, my intention is to assist the JWG-DOC to find agreeable solutions on the basis of a better understanding of the legal aspects of relevant questions.

(ii) *Legal Nature of the COC*

A preliminary issue for the negotiators to tackle is the legal nature of the COC. To be more specific, should the COC be: (a) a treaty, (b) a non-legally binding political instrument, or (c) an instrument of a mixed nature, partly legally binding and partly non-legally binding?

---

[19]Pursuant to Article 123 of the UNCLOS, Costal States bordering a semi-enclosed sea shall endeavor, directly or through an appropriate regional organization, to implement cooperation and coordination in a variety of fields.

Certain parties have expressed the view that the COC should be a legally binding treaty. First, the drafting history of the DOC implies that the COC shall be a treaty. Before and during the DOC negotiation, certain countries had proposed and insisted on a legally binding instrument. Eventually, China and ASEAN countries only agreed to conclude the DOC, a political instrument.

Second, in light of this historical context, under paragraph 10 of the DOC, the parties *reaffirm* that they agree to work toward the adoption of a COC. Should the parties agree in paragraph 10 of the DOC, a political instrument, to adopt another political instrument, they would not have chosen to employ the term "reaffirm." They have already adopted numerous declarations, guidelines, and other documents of a political nature in their subsequent implementation of the DOC. The parties' true intention as reflected in paragraph 10 of the DOC must be the adoption of a legally binding COC.

Third, the DOC has not been fully and effectively implemented in the past two decades mainly because it does not prescribe concrete legal obligations targeting specific conducts of the parties, and it does not contain a robust monitoring, compliance, and implementation mechanism. The parties have agreed to adopt a more effective COC. A legally binding can ensure the effectiveness of the COC.

As to the nature of the COC, China and other parties have not yet openly expressed their positions and views. They may argue that the COC does not necessarily need to be a legally binding instrument. First, the text of the DOC, paragraph 10 in particular, does not give any indication about the legal nature of the COC. Second, an instrument is not legally binding does not mean it is not effective. Third, compliance with a legally binding treaty and a political instrument both depends on the goodwill and political commitment of the parties. Fourth, a non-legally binding COC can better accommodate the divergent views of the parties on the core substantive issues.

In any event, only the parties are in a position to make a decision on this issue. Hopefully, they are able to reach an overall consensus or agreement on this point at an early phase of the consultation. From the perspective of elaborations of the draft text, it is not a good idea for the parties to put aside this issue and save it to the last phase of negotiation. This will create enormous difficulties for the JWG-DOC to further consolidate the text after the completion of the second reading. Once the parties had made a choice at a late stage of the negotiation, the JWG-DOC would have to substantially modify a large number of provisions and the terms employed thereof.

Pursuant to the rule of general international law on characterizing the legal nature of an international instrument, the distinction between a legally binding instrument and a non-legally binding instrument relies primarily on the fact whether the instrument in question has created new legal obligations for the parties or not.[20] An instrument that merely states the political commitment of the parties shall not be regarded as a treaty. Nor can an instrument be taken as a legally binding treaty if it merely repeats the obligations conferred upon the parties by the existing treaties and reaffirms the parties' commitment to fulfill these obligations.

If all parties agree to conclude a legally binding COC, they basically should draft it like a treaty. In this connection, the form or designation of the instrument is not decisive of its status as a treaty. They can draft the text in the format of treaties and with the major parts of treaties. The parties can reaffirm their commitment to universally recognized principles of international law as enshrined in the Charter of the United Nations and the Treaty of Amity and Cooperation in Southeast Asia (TAC), including the principles of sovereignty and territorial integrity, non-interference in domestic affairs of other States, prohibition of threat of use/use of force, peaceful settlement of disputes, non-aggregation of disputes, general duty of cooperation to ensure peace, security and stability in the South China Sea, etc.

---

[20] *Vienna Convention on the Law of Treaties*, Article 2(1)(a); *Aegean Sea Continental Shelf* (Greece v. Turkey), *Judgment, ICJ Reports 1978*, p. 3 at p. 39, para. 96; *Maritime Delimitation and Territorial Questions* (Qatar v. Bahrain), *Jurisdiction and Admissibility, Judgment, ICJ Reports 1994*, p. 112 at pp. 120–22, paras. 23–29; Land and Maritime Boundary (Cameroon v. Nigeria; Equatorial Guinea intervening), *Judgment, ICJ Reports 2002*, p. 303 at pp. 427, 429, paras. 258, 262–263.

The parties can reaffirm the commitment to fulfill their obligations under UNCLOS, the 1972 International Regulations for Preventing Collisions at Sea (COLREGs), the 1974 International Convention for the Safety of Life at Sea (SOLAS), and the 1979 International Convention on Maritime Search and Rescue (SAR), particularly the obligations to use the South China Sea exclusively for peaceful purposes, to respect sovereignty, sovereign rights and jurisdiction of the coastal States in their territorial sea, exclusive economic zone and continental shelf, the undertakings pending maritime delimitation for reaching provisional arrangements and not to jeopardize or hamper the final solutions, to protect and preserve marine environment, to respect the rights of other States in the South China Sea, etc.

When it comes to confidence building, practical maritime cooperation, and conflict management in the South China Sea, the parties do not undertake many specific obligations from the existing treaties, apart from the principles of general international law. Thus the COC needs to prescribe new and concrete legal obligations for the parties. By the same token, when it comes to self-restraint, prevention of conflicts, and management of conflicts, the COC needs to contain provisions enumerating the activities that the parties shall and should not do, and also the procedures the parties shall and should follow when a conflict arises. They may choose to employ different terms, e.g., shall, should, undertake and shall endeavor, to qualify the binding nature of the obligations for the parties. They may also use different terms to distinguish absolute obligations and due diligence obligations. Nevertheless, the COC can hardly be regarded as a legally binding treaty if it does not contain any provisions setting out new legal obligations for the parties apart from the obligations they have already undertaken under other sources of international law.

That being said, the question is how international lawyers can help when the negotiators cannot reach an agreement on this point. A quick answer is to leave this matter deliberately ambiguous. They may seek guidance from the DOC, which does not explicitly prescribe its own nature. You may further question what will happen when the nature of the COC is called into question. Characterization of the nature of the COC should rely primarily on an interpretation of the text of the COC provisions, taking into account its drafting history, the subsequent State practices, and other relevant circumstances. At the negotiating table, the parties may have to find neutral terms and phrases that do not indicate the legal nature of the COC. The draft text and statements of the negotiators may be taken as *travaux preparatoire* of the COC. The negotiators may tend to be more cautious and careful with their words. In any event, when they choose to be deliberately ambiguous on this point, the nature of the COC will be left in the hands of future interpreters, and misinterpretation is a risk that the drafters should try to avoid.

Lastly, for all parties, adopting a legally binding COC means that reaching an agreement on a variety of issues and the relevant provisions of the COC will be more difficult and even impossible. No party should expect to restrain the conduct of other parties at no cost for itself. Reciprocity and mutuality lie at the heart of compromise.

(iii) *Geographical Scope of the COC*

The second issue is the geographical scope of application of the COC. More specifically speaking, the question is should the COC explicitly define its own territorial scope of application or that of its substantive provisions. This does not sound to be a serious question at all. The COC is a code of conduct for peace, security, and cooperation in the South China Sea, and in this sense, it governs all activities of the parties in the South China Sea. However, this can be a very controversial issue for the negotiators. In fact, when they lay their eyes on each other at the negotiating table, they will realize right away that the claimant States even have given different names to the disputed islands and features and the seas.

During the DOC negotiation, the territorial scope of the application was also an issue on which divided views were expressed. As mentioned earlier, the ASEAN Regional Code of Conduct applies to disputed areas of the Spratlys and the Paracels in the South China Sea. It does not further clarify the nature, scope, and limit of the disputed areas. Apparently, on the part of China, including the Paracels in the scope of application of the DOC was unacceptable. The term "South China Sea" is used in the preamble, paragraphs 3 and 10 of the DOC. The DOC does not define this term. The preamble mentions the need to promote a peaceful, friendly, and harmonious environment in the South China Sea and the enhancement of peace, stability, growth, and prosperity in the region. Paragraph 3 reaffirms the parties' respect for and commitment to the freedom of navigation in and overflight above the South China Sea. Paragraph 10 states the parties' commitment to adopt a code of conduct in the South China Sea. The term "South China Sea" as employed in the DOC largely refers to the region.

The substantive provisions do not have a defined territorial scope of application either. For instance, paragraph 5 does not enumerate the uninhabited islands, reefs, shoals, cays, and other features or the sea areas of their locations. Paragraph 6 encourages the parties concerned to explore or undertake cooperative activities, the modalities, scope, and locations of which should be agreed upon by the parties concerned prior to their actual implementation.

As to the territorial scope of application of the COC, the positions and views of the parties concerned appear to be even more divided. Since the adoption of the DOC, especially in the past decade, on the part of the Philippines, Vietnam, Malaysia, Indonesia, and China, their positions and claims on the subject matters, legal nature, scope, and means of settlement of the territorial and maritime disputes in the South China Sea have been specified and clarified. Particularly, in the award delivered in 2016, the South China Sea Arbitration Tribunal found that China is not entitled to draw strait baselines or archipelagic baselines for the Spratly Islands; none of the high-tide features of the Spratly Islands is capable of generating an exclusive economic zone or continental shelf; certain low-tide elevations and submerged features form part of the continental shelf of the Philippines; and China's claims to historic rights, or other sovereign rights or jurisdiction, with respect to maritime areas of the South China Sea are contrary to the UNCLOS and without legal effect to the extent that they exceed the geographic and substantive limits of China's entitlements under the Convention.[21] On the part of China, it claims sovereignty, sovereign rights, jurisdiction, and historic rights in the South China Sea.[22]

Now, the question is what the negotiators can do about it when they cannot reach agreement on this point. The consultation can get stuck in a deadlock when a certain party or parties insists on defining the geographical scope, which is opposed by other parties. Should they follow the steps of the DOC, and choose not to define its territorial scope? What will be the effect, consequences, and implications if the COC does not explicitly define its geographical scope of application? In this regard, the parties should bear in mind that the continuous existence of the South China Sea disputes is the underlying *raison d'tre* for them to adopt the COC, despite the change and adjustments of the positions, claims, and arguments of the parties concerned in respect of the disputes. Since the COC and DOC largely govern the same subject matter, the parties can follow the approach of the DOC, and accordingly choose not to define "South China Sea." The provisions concerning self-restraint, confidence building, and conflict management can choose not to specify the islands and maritime features and sea areas in which the dispute, incident, and conflict occur. The provisions concerning pragmatic maritime cooperation can leave the parties concerned to decide the locations of specific programs.

The COC drafters should not lose sight of the view that ambiguities in the claims of the parties concerned in the South China Sea are obstacles to reaching provisional arrangements and operationalizing practical maritime cooperation because the parties are not clear about the nature and boundaries of their respective rights, jurisdiction, duties, and obligations in the seas. In this connection, they may consider incorporating the without-prejudice clause into the COC. These provisions can state explicitly that the provisions contained in the COC shall be interpreted as a renunciation by any party of previously

---

[21] *The South China Sea Arbitration* (The Philippines v. China), Award, July 12, 2016.
[22] Statement of the Ministry of Foreign Affairs of the People's Republic of China on Settling Disputes between China and the Philippines in the South China Sea Through Bilateral Negotiation, July 12, 2016.

asserted rights, claims, title to sovereignty, sovereign rights, and jurisdiction in the South China Sea. The act of any party relating to the implementation of the COC shall be regarded as a recognition of the positions and claims of the parties in respect of the territorial, sovereignty, sovereign rights, and jurisdiction disputes.

(iv) *The Relationship between the DOC and the COC*

The third issue is the relationship between the DOC and the COC. The answer to this question appears to be straightforward and clear. The DOC is widely seen by the parties as a milestone document, which states their collective commitment to enhance mutual trust and confidence, and cooperation in the South China Sea, and full and effective implementation of the DOC thereby contributes to the maintenance of peace and stability in the region. Adoption of the COC constitutes an important and integral part of the full and effective implementation of the DOC. Thus the spirit and principles of the DOC should be incorporated into the COC. When the COC is adopted, several questions arise naturally. Should the DOC be replaced by the COC? Is there still a need for the parties to continue their work on the full and effective implementation of the DOC? Shouldn't they move to the next phase and a new chapter of their relationship with regard to maintaining peace and security in the South China Sea, and focus on the full and effective implementation of the COC instead of the less comprehensive and substantive DOC?

In the case that the DOC and COC are both legally binding treaties, they are largely in a relationship between successive treaties relating to the same subject matter. The rules of general International Law as reflected in Article 30 of the 1969 Vienna Convention on the Law of Treaties (VCLT) shall apply to resolve any incompatibilities and conflicts between the DOC and COC. Where the spirit and principles of the DOC are fully incorporated into and are well reflected in the provisions of the COC, especially when the COC is a legally binding instrument, the DOC, as a political instrument, will be replaced by the COC. Provisions of the COC prevail over those of the DOC. In this scenario, the DOC continues to exist as a historical instrument.

The DOC may serve as a context for the interpretation of certain provisions of the COC.

The parties have agreed to adopt a more substantive and effective COC. The word "substantive" implies that the COC will be more comprehensive in terms of subject matters, more specific in terms of conduct of parties, and more concrete in terms of obligations and commitment for the parties. The word "effective" indicates that the COC will very likely establish an inclusive, robust, and efficient implementation mechanism. Attention can be laid more on how the negotiators can make the COC more substantive and effective. The Framework of the COC contains an item on the connections between the DOC and the COC. The negotiators must have been aware of the close inter-connection and interactions between the two instruments. The COC can include a provision highlighting the historical significance of the DOC, articulating the close ties between the two instruments, and reaffirming the parties' commitment to the spirit and principles of the DOC in accordance with the provisions of the COC. The drafters of the COC should also try to make the two documents and their implementation mechanisms compatible, complementary, and consecutive to each other.

(v) *Implementation Mechanism of the COC*

Implementation is crucial for the success of any international instruments irrespective of their legal nature. The DOC has been criticized for not establishing an effective implementation mechanism. With respect to practical maritime cooperation, the DOC only encourages the parties to explore the modalities for cooperation on a voluntary basis. In the past two decades, the parties have established the SOM-DOC, JWG-DOC, and MFA-to-MFA hotline among the foreign ministries for immediate and effective exchange of views and coordination with regard to emergencies occurring at sea. The parties have agreed to adopt a more effective COC, and the implementation mechanism is an essential part of the text of the COC. The question is how they can make the COC more effective in terms of compliance, reporting, review, and monitoring of the instrument. In this respect, some observers even recommend the parties to create a commission or council by reference to the Arctic Council.

The negotiators must think very carefully about what to do with the existing mechanisms, platforms and channels. In this regard, it is unwise to reinvent the wheel. It took the parties decades of joint efforts to build them. They should better build upon what they have, and make necessary adjustments and improvements, in order to ensure they can function more efficiently and effectively under the framework of the COC. The JWG-DOC and SOM-DOC can be renamed respectively as JWG-COC and SOM-COC. They can be designated as the principal organs for reporting and monitoring the implementation of the COC. The COC can include provisions on matters concerning their functions, powers, decision-making and so forth. The COC can encourage the parties to adopt rules of procedure for the JWG-COC and SOM-COC to ensure their functional efficiency.

The parties can consider establishing separate implementation mechanisms for practical maritime cooperation in various areas, mutual trust and confidence-building measures, and conflict and incident avoidance, and management and settlement. The COC can also encourage the parties to seek assistance and technical support from experts and eminent persons. If the negotiators cannot reach agreement on the details of these mechanisms, they can leave them open. The golden rule is what works better prevails over what looks or sounds better.

(vi) *Relationship between the COC and Other Countries*

Countries outside of the South China Sea region watch closely the progress of the COC consultation. They claim to be stakeholders in the South China Sea issue. The United States and its allies even expressed their views on certain substantive issues concerning the COC. For instance, before the parties commenced the COC consultation, they called upon them to adopt a legally binding instrument and to establish a rules-based order for the South China Sea. When China and ASEAN countries finished the first reading of the SDNT, they alleged that the

PRC used the COC to legitimize their unlawful maritime claims, to evade its obligations under international law and the COC would be harmful to the region.[23] China and the ASEAN countries, on the other hand, state repeatedly that peace, security, and stability are of foundational interest to themselves and the international community. They ask the United States and its allies to respect their efforts and achievements in the COC consultation.

Pursuant to the general rule regarding third States of a treaty, as reflected in Article 34 of the VCLT, a treaty does not create either obligations or rights for a third State without its consent. Where the parties choose to conclude a legally binding COC, this general rule applies to the issue concerning third States. The COC, not open for accession to States other than China and the ASEAN member states, does not create obligations for the third States. Where the parties are to conclude a non-legally binding COC, the third State issue will not arise. Irrespective of the nature of the COC, the parties can encourage the third States to respect the principles contained in the COC. Further, the coastal States of the South China Sea shall respect the rights and freedoms enjoyed by third States under UNCLOS, especially the freedoms of navigation and overflight in the South China Sea. Equally important, the third States shall respect the rights, duties, and jurisdiction of the coastal States, and comply with the laws and regulations adopted by the coastal States in accordance with the provisions of UNCLOS.

III. Prospects of the COC Consultation

Lastly, I should say a few words on the outlook of the COC consultation. It is notable that the views of observers are widely divided on this point. Some of them even frequently change their views. They

---

[23]Ian Storey, "As ASEAN and China Discuss a Code of Conduct for the South China Sea, America Looks on Skeptically," *ISEAS Commentary of the Yusof Ishak Institute*, October 24, 2019, https://www.iseas.edu.sg/media/commentaries/as-asean-and-china-discuss-a-code-of-conduct-for-the-south-china-sea-america-looks-on-sceptically-by-ian-storey.

called upon the parties to accelerate the consultation on one occasion, alleging that a legally binding COC was crucial for establishing rules-based order for the South China Sea. They later asserted that the COC would be useless because it cannot restrict or restrain the increasingly provocative acts and excessive claims of the PRC in the South China Sea. I am an international lawyer. I am not in a position to predict when the COC can be concluded. I am not even able to tell whether it can be adopted eventually. Above all, the principle of consensus governs the whole consultation process. When a party chooses on its own or under the influence of other States not to participate in the consultation, the consultation will come to an impasse. As long as there is a single party refusing to accept the draft text, the eleven countries will not be able to adopt the COC. This is the power of the consensus principle.

As we all know, this is not the first time for China and ASEAN member States to sit together with the goal of formulating a set of norms to guide and regulate the conduct of parties in the South China Sea. However, this is indeed the first time for China and the ASEAN countries to sit at the table, adopt a Framework for the COC, formulate a Single Draft Negotiating Text, read the text, streamline the text, reduce the redundancies, consolidate the text, and work toward a single uniform and unified text agreeable for all parties. They began the process basically with nothing at hand. They seem to be very clear about where they are at the moment, where to go in the next phase, and what they aspire to achieve at the end. They have made good progress so far. This is the magic power of the consensus approach.

I would like to remind the negotiators that nothing worth having comes easily. When the second reading is completed, the parties are likely to enter a more challenging phase for elaborations of the text. Each party has to make their own hard decisions and choices. All parties can only reach a consensus by careful choice of terms, words, and phrases. Delicate balances must be properly stricken. Some may be of the view that the consensus approach will prolong the consultation. It may be a good time to bring the ASEAN tradition of informal diplomacy into play. Decisions that are not suitable to be made at the

JWG-DOC level should be referred immediately to SOM-DOC for guidance. Political resolve may be critical for the parties to arrive at a mutually agreeable COC text.

Confucius, the great Chinese philosopher, said, "君子和而不同,小人同而不和." This famous sentence, included in the *Analects of Confucius*, encourages the COC negotiators to enlarge their real consensus, narrow their real differences, and reach real agreement that reflects their true mind, will, intent, and aspirations. After the COC is concluded, it will be a pity if there are still some negotiators who allege that they said something they did not mean to say at the negotiating table, this is not what they meant when they said this at the negotiating table, and even worse, they do not take what said at the negotiating table seriously.

Chapter 4

Historical Interaction of China–ASEAN Economic Cooperation and Security Governance: From the Perspective of DOC

Zhang Jie

*National Institute of International Strategy,
Chinese Academy of Social Sciences, Beijing, China
zhang_jie@cass.org.cn*

Abstract

The South China Sea issue is an important security issue in China–ASEAN relations. Promoting the signing and implementation of the Declaration on the Conduct of Parties in the South China Sea (DOC) and the consultation of the Code of Conduct for the South China Sea (COC) are important ways for China and ASEAN to maintain stability in the South China Sea. The signing of the DOC has enhanced the strategic mutual trust between China and ASEAN and pushed the bilateral cooperation onto the "fast track." In turn, the comprehensive and high-quality regional cooperation has provided the "ballast" for the implementation of the DOC. At present, in the face of the challenges posed by the deep involvement of the U.S. and its allies in the South China Sea, it is important to review and summarize the experience of China and ASEAN in dealing with the South China Sea issue and promoting regional cooperation. On this basis, all parties can consider the Global Development Initiative and the Global Security Initiative as guides to continue to focus on regional economic cooperation and achieve sustainable security in the region through sustainable development.

Keywords: China–ASEAN Relations, DOC, Regional Cooperation, Security Governance

I. Introduction

The South China Sea issue is about the long-standing dispute over territorial sovereignty and maritime rights and interests between China and some Southeast Asian countries. Since the establishment of dialogue relations in the 1990s, China and ASEAN countries subsequently initiated political consultations on the South China Sea issue and reached the Declaration on the Conduct of Parties in the South China Sea (DOC) in 2002. The DOC was the first political statement on the South China Sea issue signed by China and ASEAN, which contained a political consensus on the peaceful resolution of conflicts and a major agenda for cooperation in the South China Sea. Since the signing of the Declaration, there have been no large-scale military conflicts in the South China Sea. At the end of 2022, to commemorate the 20th anniversary of the signing of the DOC, China and ASEAN issued a joint statement, which said the DOC has made an important contribution to maintaining stability in the South China Sea.[1]

---

[1] "Joint Statement on the 20th Anniversary of the Declaration on the Conduct of Parties in the South China Sea," website of Ministry of Foreign Affairs of the People's Republic of China, November 14, 2022, https://www.fmprc.gov.cn/eng/zxxx_662805/202301/t20230105_11001064.html.shtml (Accessed January 25, 2023).

It is determined by the strategic position and spillover effects of the South China Sea issue that the existence of the DOC has a broader value and significance, which is highlighted by the deepening of China–ASEAN strategic mutual trust and comprehensive development. At the same time as the DOC was signed, China and ASEAN also concluded the Framework Agreement on Comprehensive Economic Cooperation between China and ASEAN and the Joint Declaration of ASEAN and China on Cooperation in the Field of Non-traditional Security Issues. Since then, China acceded to the Treaty of Amity and Cooperation in Southeast Asia (TAC) in 2003 and became the first strategic partner of ASEAN. In 2013, China proposed the initiative of building a China–ASEAN community with a shared future. In 2021, China and ASEAN announced the establishment of a comprehensive strategic partnership. After years of joint efforts, China–ASEAN relations have become one of the most vibrant, enriching, and mutually beneficial relations among ASEAN's dialogue partnerships, and have become a model of regional cooperation in East Asia, making significant contributions to peace, stability, development, and prosperity in the Asia-Pacific region.[2] Based on such perseverance, in the third decade of the 21st century, though the strategic competition between China and the U.S. is intensifying, the general trend that both China and ASEAN adhere to maintaining stability and economic cooperation in the South China Sea has not fundamentally changed.

Taking the South China Sea issue as a case, it is of great academic value and practical significance to study the historical process that China and ASEAN properly dealt with disputes, maintained regional stability, and achieved mutual benefit and win–win cooperation. This chapter reviewed in stages the development of DOC and the main

---

[2] "Joint Statement of the ASEAN–China Special Summit to Commemorate the 30th Anniversary of ASEAN–China Dialogue Relations: Comprehensive Strategic Partnership for Peace, Security, Prosperity and Sustainable Development," website of the State Council of the People's Republic of China, November 22, 2021, http://english.www.gov.cn/news/topnews/202111/22/content_WS619b825ec6d0df57f98e54bc.html.

achievements of China–ASEAN regional cooperation in the same period. Then, it analyzed the internal impetus and successful experience of carrying out these two processes, the DOC and regional cooperation, simultaneously. The chapter roughly divides the development of DOC into three stages, basically one stage every 10 years, while China–ASEAN regional cooperation is also synchronized and upgraded every 10 years, which shows the two processes have obvious synchronization. The comparative study by dividing different stages shows that the consensus on development is the most fundamental driving force of China–ASEAN relations. The two sides have thus formed a consensus to put aside the disputes and focus on regional cooperation. In turn, the realization of mutual benefit and win–win cooperation has further strengthened the sense of community between China and ASEAN, enabling all parties to be self-restraint and maintain the basic stability in the South China Sea. At present, "promoting security through development, ensuring development through security," as the practical experience, has been deepened by China into the Global Development Initiative (GDI) and Global Security Initiative (GSI). In the next stage, China and ASEAN should consider these two initiatives as guides to seek regional peace and prosperity together.

II. The First Phase (1992–2002): The Signing of the DOC and the Beginning of Regional Cooperation

Founded in August 1967, ASEAN had little interaction with China for more than 10 years after its establishment due to the influence of the Cold War. It was only after the end of the Cold War that China and ASEAN began to engage with each other as China gradually restored and established diplomatic relations with Southeast Asian countries. This was a mutual choice because in the early 1990s China accelerated the pace of reform and opening up and chose Southeast Asia as a breakthrough direction. During the same period, with the resolution of regional affairs such as the Cambodia issue, ASEAN also began to turn to regional economic cooperation, accelerating the construction of dialogue relations with major external countries alongside building an intra-regional free trade area.

In July 1991, then Chinese Foreign Minister Qian Qichen attended the 24th ASEAN Foreign Ministers' Meeting for the first time and proposed that "China is willing to further strengthen cooperation with ASEAN and establish dialogue with ASEAN in the political, economic, scientific and technological and security field." "China respects and supports ASEAN's proposal to establish a peaceful, free, neutral and nuclear-free zone in Southeast Asia, and supports ASEAN's efforts to strengthen regional economic cooperation, safeguard its resources and economic rights and interests, and establish a new international economic order."[3] ASEAN responded positively, and then the China–ASEAN dialogue was officially launched, in July 1992, and China and ASEAN established a consultative partnership.

Due to historical reasons and long-term estrangement, China and ASEAN countries lack political and security mutual trust, thus the South China Sea issue has become the most important security issue between the two sides. In 1992, China and ASEAN countries began consultations to formulate a political statement on the South China Sea issue. According to the recollection of the then Chinese diplomat in charge of Asian affairs, the common desire of all parties at that time was to respect each other, treat each other as equals, and focus on cooperation. Therefore, when they all got together, they talked about the South China Sea issue, and all parties agreed that it was their responsibility to find manageable ways to deal with the conflicts arising from the South China Sea issue.[4] After extensive working-level consultations, by December 1997, China and the ASEAN countries met at the summit level and formed a joint statement in which they explicitly committed to resolve their differences or disputes through

---

[3]"Qian Qichen met with 6 ASEAN foreign ministers, reiterated China willing to strengthen cooperation and establish dialogue relations with ASEAN," ("钱其琛会见东盟6国外长时重申中国愿同东盟加强合作建立对话关系") *People's Daily*, July 21, 1991, 6th edition.

[4]Conference presentation by Chinese delegates, "China–ASEAN DOC 20th Anniversary Symposium," June 2022, Beijing, China.

peaceful means without resorting to force or the threat of force. The two sides agreed to resolve the South China Sea dispute through friendly consultations and negotiations in accordance with recognized international law, including the 1982 UN Convention on the Law of the Sea; and, while continuing to seek solutions, agreed to explore ways to cooperate in the regions concerned.[5]

After nearly a decade of negotiations, China and ASEAN countries signed the DOC in 2002, an important document that embodies the commitment of all parties to promote regional peace, stability, and mutual trust in accordance with international law, including the UN Convention on the Law of the Sea. It is particularly important to emphasize that the opening of political consultations on the South China Sea was a courageous attempt by China, which was more cautious about multilateral dialogue at that time and considered the multilateral mechanism to be a "siege" against China. It chose to consult with all ASEAN countries, rather than just the countries involved in the South China Sea, which in fact carries the risk of both amplifying the South China Sea issue and of ASEAN talking to China with "one voice." But China has proven to be a good seizer of this choice, turning it into a good opportunity to try to engage in multilateral dialogue. In the process, China and ASEAN have respected each other, communicated sincerely to enhance understanding and trust, and ASEAN has become more aware of China's determination to develop peacefully.

In July 1996, ASEAN upgraded China from a "consultation partner" to a "dialogue partner" and established a comprehensive dialogue partnership with China. After the financial crisis in 1997, China and ASEAN established the "Chinese–ASEAN good-neighborly partnership of mutual trust orientated toward the 21st century" for the

---

[5] "Joint Statement of the Meeting of Heads of State/Government of the Member States of ASEAN and the President of the People's Republic of China, Lumpur, Malaysia, 16 December 1997," ASEAN Main portal, June 28, 2012, https://asean.org/joint-statement-of-the-meeting-of-heads-of-state-government-of-the-member-states-of-asean-and-the-president-of-the-peoples-republic-of-china-kuala-lumpur-malaysia-16-december-1997/.

first time, and started the "10+1" as the core dialogue mechanism. They worked together with Japan and South Korea to promote East Asia cooperation. The close economic ties have enhanced mutual understanding and trust between the two sides and created conditions for the comprehensive development of East Asian cooperation, the formation of regional identity, and the building of regional rules and mechanisms. All of these created a virtuous interaction between the proper handling of the South China Sea issue in the security field and the strengthening of cooperation in the economic field. Thus, on the occasion of the signing of the DOC in 2002, China and ASEAN also signed the Framework Agreement on Comprehensive Economic Cooperation between China and ASEAN and the Joint Declaration of ASEAN and China on Cooperation in the Field of Non-traditional Security Issues. Since then, China has also acceded to the TAC in 2003, and taken the lead in establishing a strategic partnership with ASEAN. Apart from that, it was also the first to negotiate with ASEAN on the establishment of a free trade zone, explicitly support the central role of ASEAN in regional cooperation, and publicly express its willingness to sign the Protocol to the Southeast Asian Nuclear-Weapon-Free Zone Treaty (SEANWFZ Treaty). Such "primacy" has driven the regional countries to actively invest in the healthy competition of ASEAN, promoting the entire East Asian region to quickly embark on the integration path, and playing an important role in building regional strategic stability and shaping the East Asian peace system.

III. The Second Phase (2003–2012): The Stabilization of Situation in the South China Sea under the DOC and the Acceleration of Regional Cooperation

Since the signing of the DOC, China and ASEAN countries have taken it as a guide to maintain basic stability in the South China Sea and made useful attempts in maritime cooperation. In the same period, China–ASEAN cooperation entered the "golden decade," and the two sides have gradually formed the most substantive, dynamic, and leading partnership.

In accordance with the spirit of the DOC, the disputing parties have exercised relative self-restraint, thus no new occupied islands and reefs have emerged, as well as large-scale maritime frictions among countries. In addition, China and ASEAN countries have actively discussed and practiced in accordance with the spirit of the Declaration that all parties should strengthen cooperation in areas such as marine environmental protection, marine scientific research, maritime navigation and traffic safety, search and rescue, and combating transnational crimes. By mid-2011, the parties held two senior officials' meetings, set up a joint working group and held six meetings, and decided to carry out six cooperation projects on disaster prevention and mitigation, marine search and rescue, and marine scientific research in the South China Sea, of which China hosted three projects and ASEAN countries hosted others.[6] In addition, in November 2004, China and the Philippines signed an agreement on joint research on oil and gas resources in the South China Sea, after which Vietnam joined it. Then, Chinese, Filipino, and Vietnamese enterprises signed the Tripartite Agreement on Joint Marine Seismic Work in the South China Sea Consultative Area in March 2005, trying to jointly conduct offshore energy exploration.

The signing of the DOC has enhanced the strategic mutual trust between China and ASEAN countries and promoted the cooperation to enter a new stage of all-round and institutionalized construction. With "10+1" as the core mechanism, the two sides have established multi-level dialogues, including leaders, ministers, senior officials, and working groups, covering all areas of diplomacy, security, trade, investment, and transportation. At the same time, the two sides have formulated two "Action Plans for the Implementation of the China–ASEAN Joint Declaration on Strategic Partnership for Peace and

---

[6] "The Senior Officials Meeting to Implement the Declaration on the Conduct of Parties in the South China Sea reached a series of consensuses," ("落实《南海各方行为宣言》高官会达成一系列共识") website of the Embassy of the People's Republic of China in the Lao People's Democratic Republic, July 20, 2011, http://la.china-embassy.gov.cn/eng/news/201107/t20110724_1546739.htm.

Prosperity" for the period 2005–2010 and 2011–2015, and have arranged the cooperation agenda in the three pillars of political security, economy, and social culture. In the field of security, besides dealing with the South China Sea issue properly, China and ASEAN have also started cooperation in the field of non-traditional security. In November 2002, the two sides issued the Joint Declaration on Cooperation in non-traditional security, announcing that they would jointly combat terrorism, drug smuggling, human trafficking, and other kinds of transnational crimes. In terms of regional cooperation, China and ASEAN started cooperation on the establishment of a free trade area in 2002, and by January 2010, the China–ASEAN FTA entered a full implementation stage. Taking this as a pioneer, ASEAN has also started relevant negotiations with South Korea, Japan, Australia, New Zealand, India, and other countries, gradually building a network of FTAs with the framework of "10+1."

The years 2002 to 2012 were the decade when the regional cooperation between China and ASEAN entered the "fast track." The cooperation between the two sides gradually covered the whole field and made breakthroughs, thus solidifying the regional identity of mutual benefit and win–win cooperation, and laying the foundation for dealing with the challenges brought by the great power game and the reorganization of order in the Asia-Pacific region thereafter.

IV. The Third Phase (2013 to Date): The Implementation of the DOC with Consultation on the COC at the Same Time, China and ASEAN Adhere to the "Original Intention" of Cooperation

Around 2010, China's GDP surpassed Japan's and became the first in Asia and the second in the world, bringing about a fundamental change in the pattern of the Asia-Pacific region. In the face of China's rise, in order to maintain its regional dominance, the United States adjusted its long-standing "offshore balance" strategy to the "pivoting to Asia" and the "Asia-Pacific rebalancing" strategy, and even the "Indo-Pacific strategy." Accordingly, its policy toward China has changed from engagement and cooperation to competition and cooperation, and finally to comprehensive containment. In this process, the South China Sea issue has become an important "instrument" for the U.S. to implement its regional strategy. Under the banner of safeguarding freedom of navigation and overflight and establishing a rules-based regional order, the U.S. has sought the support of its allies and partner countries to create an encirclement around China. The changing regional environment has impacted the perceptions toward China and policy initiatives of ASEAN, especially the countries involved in the South China Sea. They not only share the same destiny with China economically but also have strategic doubts about China's rise, fearing that China's naval and air forces will use force to resolve the South China Sea issue as it grows stronger. At the same time, after years of rapid economic development and the cultivation of maritime awareness, the countries concerned have become more reliant on the maritime economy and have become more "firm" in their stance on the South China Sea issue. Under the influence of such factors, the situation in the South China Sea has entered a turbulent and volatile period since around 2010.

In the meantime, some events, such as the so-called South China Sea Arbitration proposed by the Philippines in 2013 and the China–Vietnam Zhongjiannan confrontation in 2014, highlighted the friction between China and some of the ASEAN countries involved in territorial sovereignty and maritime rights. The construction of islands and reefs, the development of fisheries, and oil and gas resources have led to international public opinion on sea-related issues being the regional "hot spot" constantly. In particular, the U.S. interference in the South China Sea issue has moved from behind to the front, i.e., from supporting the Philippines in bringing the so-called South China Sea Arbitration to changing its own "neutral position" on the territorial issues in the South China Sea. It has directly promoted the militarization, judicialization, internationalization, and public opinion of the South China Sea issue. By the time the "Indo-Pacific Strategy" is introduced, the U.S. competitive strategy toward China has become a key factor affecting the situation in the South China Sea.

Against the backdrop, in 2011, China and ASEAN reached an agreement on the implementation of the guiding text of the DOC. In 2013, the two sides officially launched consultations on the Code of Conduct for the South China Sea (COC), which has become an important way for China and ASEAN to jointly maintain regional stability. The DOC is an early phased diplomatic achievement reached between China and ASEAN, and the DOC undertakes the task of further developing the COC. "The parties concerned reaffirmed that the formulation of the COC would further promote stability in the region and agreed to work towards that goal on the basis of consensus among the parties."[7] However, in the 10 years after the signing of the Declaration, as the overall situation in the South China Sea remained stable, the desire and urgency of the parties to advance the consultations on the COC decreased, and therefore the number of joint working group meetings and senior officials' meetings was limited. It was not until the South China Sea issue became more volatile that the further implementation of the Declaration and the launch of the negotiation of the COC were put back on the agenda.

Despite the complexity of the situation in the South China Sea at this stage, China and ASEAN have made a series of important progress on the South China Sea by effectively addressing the crisis. First, the frequency of joint working group meetings and senior officials' meetings between China and ASEAN countries has been revitalized in order to implement the DOC and promote consultations on the COC. At the same time, bilateral maritime-related dialogue mechanisms such as China–Vietnam and China–Philippines have focused more on practical cooperation, with discussions covering both the control of frictions and the exploration of new ways of maritime cooperation. Second, the maritime crisis management mechanism has been strengthened. In September 2016, China and ASEAN countries issued the Joint Statement between China and ASEAN on the

---

[7]"Declaration on the Conduct of Parties in the South China Sea," website of Ministry of Foreign Affairs of the People's Republic of China, November 4, 2002, https://www.fmprc.gov.cn/eng./wjb_663304/zzjg_663340/gjs_665170/gjzzyhy_665174/2608_665204/2610_665208/200303/t20030304_598503.html.

Application of the Code for Unplanned Encounters at Sea (CUES) in the South China Sea and the Guidelines for the Hotline Platform of Senior Officials of Foreign Affairs of China and ASEAN in Response to Maritime Emergencies. The former aims to provide clear guidance for emergency handling and operational norms in case of accidental encounters between ships and aircraft of the navies of China and ASEAN countries in the South China Sea. The latter is to provide immediate and effective communication channels between foreign ministries of countries in case of emergency when policy intervention is needed, to control risks, discuss countermeasures and maintain stability in the South China Sea.[8] Third, various types of maritime cooperation have been promoted. In 2018, China held its first maritime military exercises with all ASEAN countries, with the intention of deepening strategic mutual trust. In addition, after the turnaround of China–Philippines relations in 2016, the two sides launched a consultation on cooperation in oil and gas development in late 2018.[9] These achievements reflect the deep foundation of cooperation between China and ASEAN and highlight the "crisis-based" cooperation model that has been developed in East Asia after a long period of practice, i.e., the more crises and difficulties arise, the more the parties can turn them into opportunities through dialogue and communication, thus forming new cooperation mechanisms and intentions.

---

[8]"The 19th China–ASEAN Summit Issues Joint Statement on the Application of the Code for Unplanned Encounters at Sea in the South China Sea," website of Ministry of Foreign Affairs of the People's Republic of China, September 8, 2016, https://www.fmprc.gov.cn/mfa_eng/gjhdq_665435/2675_665437/2727_663458/2729_663462/201609/t20160912_516895.html.

"The 19th China–ASEAN Summit Adopts Guidelines for Hotline Communications among Senior Officials of the Ministries of Foreign Affairs of China and ASEAN Member States in Response to Maritime Emergencies," website of Embassy of the People's Republic of China in the Republic of the Philippines, September 8, 2016, http://ph.china-embassy.gov.cn/eng/chinew/201609/t20160912_1162471.htm.

[9]"Memorandum of Understanding on Cooperation on Oil and Gas Development between the Government of the People's Republic of China and the Government of the Republic of the Philippines," website of Ministry of Foreign Affairs of the People's Republic of China, November 27, 2018, https://www.fmprc.gov.cn/mfa_eng/wjdt_665385/2649_665393/201811/t20181127_679548.html.

Similarly, in the field of regional cooperation, after the global financial crisis in 2008, China–ASEAN cooperation has been upgraded again, from the "Golden Decade" to the "Diamond Decade." This is mainly because both China and ASEAN have grown in their willingness and ability to shape regional cooperation in tandem, and have worked together in the same direction. On the one hand, ASEAN was committed to building its own unity and announced the establishment of the ASEAN Community in 2015 after years of efforts. On the other hand, ASEAN focused on building its own "centrality," which was formally proposed at the 12th ASEAN Summit in 2007. After the 12th ASEAN Summit in 2007, when ASEAN Centrality was formally proposed, it was solidified by kinds of ASEAN-led regional dialogue mechanisms such as the ASEAN Regional Forum (ARF), ASEAN Defense Ministers' Meeting (ADMM), and the East Asia Summit (EAS). Apart from that, it has also established many bilateral dialogue relations with more than 10 countries. In response, China, as its strategic dialogue partner, has long supported ASEAN's "centrality" and taken the initiative to strengthen the connection with regional plans such as the Master Plan on ASEAN Connectivity (MPAC) 2025 and the ASEAN Outlook on the Indo-Pacific (AOIP). In addition, during this period, China's willingness and ability to shape regional cooperation has increased significantly, and it has begun to change from being a participant and learner to a shaper and operator of regional cooperation. As China's neighborhood, Southeast Asia has naturally become China's priority in diplomacy. In October 2013, Chinese President Xi Jinping proposed in Indonesia the initiative of building the 21st Century Maritime Silk Road and a closer China–ASEAN community of destiny. In 2014, Premier Li Keqiang attended the 17th China–ASEAN Leaders' Meeting and said that China has been working with ASEAN to build a closer community with a shared future. "The China–ASEAN strategic partnership has experienced a 'golden decade' and is entering a 'diamond decade' with a higher starting point, broader connotations and deeper cooperation," said Premier Li Keqiang at the 17th China–ASEAN Leaders' Meeting in 2014. In terms of specific cooperation programs, after the "2+7" cooperation framework[10] proposed in 2013, in 2017, China proposed to upgrade the "2+7" cooperation framework into a "3+X" cooperation framework, which is based on the three pillars of political and security, economic and trade, and people-to-people exchanges, and supported by many other fields. In November 2018, the 21st China–ASEAN Leaders' Meeting adopted the "China–ASEAN Strategic Partnership Vision 2030." China became the first dialogue partner to develop a medium and long-term cooperation plan with ASEAN. The two sides emphasized the importance of connecting the MPAC 2025 with the common focus areas of China's Belt and Road Initiative (BRI), promoting complementarities between the ASEAN Community Vision 2025 and the UN 2030 Agenda on Sustainable Development, to build a model of South–South cooperation.[11] In January 2022, after a decade of joint efforts between ASEAN and China, the Regional Comprehensive Economic Partnership (RCEP) officially came into force.

The above-mentioned regional practice shows that, despite the profound changes in the regional situation and the huge disturbances in the South China Sea from outside, regional cooperation has become the "ballast" of China–ASEAN relations. Together with the basic consensus on the South China Sea formed through years of interaction between the two sides, such "ballast" eventually pushed China and ASEAN countries to jointly adhere to the "two-track" approach, relying on the implementation of the DOC and the consultation on the COC, has stabilized the overall situation in the South China Sea. Of course, with the intensification of the Sino-U.S. strategic game, especially the continued and direct involvement of the U.S. in the South China Sea, the future situation in the South China Sea

---

[10]The "2+7" cooperation framework refers to advancing cooperation in seven key areas, including politics, economy and trade, connectivity, finance, maritime affairs, security and people-to-people exchanges, on the basis of the political consensus of deepening strategic mutual trust and focusing on economic development.
[11]"ASEAN–China Strategic Partnership Vision 2030," ASEAN main portal, November 15, 2018, https://asean.org/wp-content/uploads/2018/11/ASEAN-China-Strategic-Partnership-Vision-2030.pdf.

will face more uncertainty, and in this situation, it is more relevant to continue to adhere to the spirit advocated in the DOC.

V. Major Experiences and Regional Significance of China and ASEAN in Achieving the Dual Goals of Security and Development

Since the establishment of dialogue relations, China–ASEAN cooperation has developed rapidly and made remarkable achievements, not only achieving the "leapfrog development" in relations between the two sides but also enabling the East Asian region to escape the haze of the Cold War and embark on a dynamic path of economic integration through cooperation.[12] The South China Sea issue, for example, fully confirms this conclusion, reflecting the successful practice of China and ASEAN in dealing with the two major issues of security and cooperation. These two main lines echo each other at significant points in time. Namely, the three stages of the DOC's development are also roughly the three stages of China–ASEAN regional cooperation forming a leapfrog development. In these three stages, the need to maintain regional stability and achieve development and prosperity opened the political dialogue on the South China Sea issue and eventually led to the signing of the DOC. The consultation of the DOC enhanced mutual understanding and trust among the parties. Thus after the signing of the DOC, China–ASEAN relations were guaranteed by institutional security, providing a more reliable and long-term guarantee for both sides to enhance their economic cooperation. After a decade of cooperation in the second phase, China and ASEAN interests have been deeply integrated, thus providing a "ballast" for the challenges that the DOC will face when it enters the third phase,

---

[12] Xi Jinping: "For a Shared Future and Our Common Home, Speech by H.E. Xi Jinping, President of the People's Republic of China, at the Special Summit to Commemorate the 30th Anniversary of China–ASEAN Dialogue Relations," website of Ministry of Foreign Affairs of the People's Republic of China, November 22, 2021, https://www.fmprc.gov.cn/mfa_eng/topics_665678/bj2022/yswj/202111/t20211122_10451280.html.

prompting all parties to prioritize development and adhere to a more rational and restrained approach to the South China Sea issue. China has not taken possession of new uninhabited islands and reefs because of its rising military strength, and ASEAN has always maintained the bottom line of not naming China and not talking about the South China Sea Arbitration ruling in its various statements on the South China Sea. This mutual "compromise" and understanding of each other's security concerns have jointly maintained the basic stability of the situation in the South China Sea. Generally speaking, the South China Sea issue has been disturbed by internal and external factors and the situation has fluctuated. However, China–ASEAN regional cooperation has maintained a good momentum since it entered the "fast track." The positive interaction between the two sides has finally ensured that China–ASEAN relations have completed the leapfrog development from dialogue relations, strategic partnership to comprehensive strategic partnership, achieving common development and prosperity.

Summing up the historical experience of such leapfrog development, there are at least three points.

First, both sides take development as the first principle. Since the reform and opening up, China has insisted on economic development as the center and adhered to the foreign policy of creating an amicable, secure, and prosperous neighborhood. ASEAN, on the other hand, has shifted its focus to integration and the building of a broader ASEAN-centered regional free trade network, since it achieved peace in the region in the 1990s. With development as the primary goal, both sides have formed a consensus and jointly promoted East Asian cooperation, making important contributions to making the Asia-Pacific region a center of global economic growth. The main line of development of China–ASEAN relations has always been regional cooperation. Though the South China Sea issue is the most important security issue for both sides, it is not an issue that affects the overall development of China–ASEAN relations.

Second, both sides adhere to the foreign policy of peaceful coexistence. In various political statements, including the DOC, China, and ASEAN have repeatedly reaffirmed that "the purposes and principles of the UN Charter, the 1982 UN Convention on the Law of the Sea, the TAC, the Five Principles of Peaceful Coexistence and other universally recognized principles of international law shall be the basic norms for the conduct of relations among nations."[13] China was one of the first countries to propose the Five Principles of Peaceful Coexistence, and ASEAN adopted the TAC at its first summit, which clearly states that no force or threat of force will be used in the event of disputes, and friendly consultation will be used to propose solutions. The acceptance of the TAC was set as one of the prerequisites for establishing dialogue relations with ASEAN, and China was the first country outside the Southeast Asian region to sign the TAC. In practice, China has resolved all land-based territorial disputes, except for China and India, through peaceful means since the 1990s. At the same time, ASEAN has gradually achieved peace and stability within the region since its establishment, and then successfully avoiding large-scale conflicts with major external powers and working to eliminate confrontation and war between external forces in the region. Therefore, it has always been the consensus between China and ASEAN to resolve the South China Sea disputes through dialogue and consultation in a peaceful manner.

Third, the East Asian approach is an important regional experience for China and ASEAN to jointly realize the transition from the signing of the DOC to the negotiation of the COC. The East Asian approach has been studied and expressed by scholars at home and abroad. The essence of the approach is to make decisions by consensus on the basis of sovereign equality, with the core spirit of respecting diversity, accommodating differences and progressiveness of the process, and ultimately reaching consensus. As in the case of the DOC, the initial goal was to reach COC, but in order to respect the views of all parties, they eventually adopted a flexible approach, resulting in a more lenient Declaration. According to the recollections of the then

---

[13]"Declaration on the Conduct of Parties in the South China Sea," website of Ministry of Foreign Affairs of the People's Republic of China, November 4, 2002, https://www.fmprc.gov.cn/eng./wjb_663304/zzjg_663340/gjs_665170/gjzz yhy_665174/2608_665204/2610_665208/200303/t20030304_598503.html.

diplomats, although the Declaration did not meet the wishes of any country, it was a political statement that gathered the greatest number of points of agreement and consensus among all parties. Of course, the parties did not abandon the goal of establishing the COC but agreed to a step-by-step approach that would meet the comfort zone of all parties on an equal footing.

VI. Development Prospects and China's Strategic Choice: Taking the "Dual Initiatives" as Guides to Maintain Stability in the South China Sea

With the U.S. launching a comprehensive strategic competition with China, the strategic significance of the South China Sea issue has gone far beyond territorial disputes and become an important part of the Sino-U.S. game and regional order reconstruction, and Sino-U.S. relations have become a key factor affecting the situation in the South China Sea. In the future, the changing of the situation in the South China Sea and the consultation on the COC will be inevitably influenced by this factor. China and ASEAN countries are also facing new challenges in the South China Sea, especially as the strategic anxiety and doubts about China are increasing, the speculative mentality is also growing. Some countries try to take advantage of the "window phase" before the conclusion of the COC to solidify their "sovereignty" over the occupied islands and reefs. These have increased the uncertainty and instability in the South China Sea.

In a speech delivered at the ASEAN Secretariat in July 2022, then Chinese State Councilor and Foreign Minister Wang Yi pointed out that the entire region is at a "crossroads" and there are two very different directions around the future of Asia. One is to insist on open regionalism, uphold genuine multilateralism, and prioritize development. The other is to revert to the old Cold War mentality, to make the regional economy into different "camps," and even to "NATOize" Asia-Pacific security. The choice we make today will determine where the road will lead in the future, open or closed, cooperation or confrontation, unity or division, progress or regression, and will fundamentally and long-term affect the future and destiny of the countries in the region. Similarly, on the South China Sea issue, all parties are also facing choices.[14]

Therefore, at present, dealing with the South China Sea issue also requires China and ASEAN countries to proceed from the whole situation. In recent years, China has proposed the GDI and the GSI, which provide new ideas and new paths for China and ASEAN to better deal with their relations and security matters in the future. Through the implementation of the GSI, both sides should manage their differences and provide security for sustainable development in the South China Sea. Through the implementation of the GDI, they should strengthen cooperation and innovation to provide impetus for sustainable security in the South China Sea. Ultimately, the positive interaction between sustainable development and sustainable security will provide more new opportunities and new ways to deal with the South China Sea issue.

First, implement the GDI to promote sustainable development in the South China Sea. At present, the most urgent challenge for the entire Asia-Pacific region is to avoid being coerced by the United States into abandoning the good situation of regional economic cooperation and turning to arms race and confrontation. In view of this, although it is difficult to carry out economic cooperation in the South China Sea in the short term, China and ASEAN countries can "look beyond the South China Sea." The two sides can continue to promote bilateral and multilateral economic cooperation under the framework of China and ASEAN, increase the degree of cohesion between them, and consolidate the role of economic mutual benefit as the "ballast" of stability in the South China Sea. In this regard, the GDI offers new ideas and approaches.

In 2021, President Xi Jinping proposed the GDI, calling for the building of a global development community. The Initiative proposes to focus on poverty reduction, food security, anti-epidemic and

---

[14]"Wang Yi Delivers a Policy Speech on Open Regionalism at ASEAN Secretariat," website of the Embassy of the People's Republic of China in the Kingdom of Thailand, July 12, 2022, http://th.china-embassy.gov.cn/eng/sgxw/202207/t20220713_10719199.htm.

vaccines, financing for development, climate change and green development, industrialization, digital economy, and connectivity as key areas of cooperation. Around these areas, China and ASEAN should make use of the cooperation mechanisms already established by the "10+1" and "10+3," and consider establishing more emergency mechanisms and cooperation funds related to food and energy to jointly maintain the economic development and political stability of each country.

In the longer term, China should comprehensively promote the implementation of the GDI in Southeast Asia, strengthen the connection with the economic agendas of the AOIP, adhere to the innovation drive, expand green cooperation, and seek to build new cooperation with Southeast Asia in areas such as smart cities, e-commerce, artificial intelligence applications, new energy, and environmental technology. Such new highlights will tap new dynamics to economic growth for all parties. More enterprises should be encouraged to make ASEAN their preferred destination for investment and strengthen strategic docking with ASEAN connectivity, and RCEP should be strengthened to release cooperation dividends and enhance the GDP of each country. In addition, the sub-regional cooperation mechanisms, including the Lancang–Mekong cooperation and China–East ASEAN Growth Area, should also be promoted.

At the same time, China should pay attention to promoting cooperation in science and technology innovation to stimulate new development momentum in the region, which in turn will provide new thinking and new paths for cooperation in maritime governance in the South China Sea. It should focus on studying the low-carbon economy of the ocean, and seek win–win cooperation with ASEAN countries in marine resources by using new technologies and strengthening the protection and development of the marine environment at the same time. The clean energy cooperation and offshore power generation should also be the priorities. Refer to the U.S. marine cooperation agenda with Southeast Asian countries, for example, in the use of marine resources, with the development of deep-sea exploitation technologies, develop rules, release each country's strengths, and seek joint development at different sea levels.

Second, implement the GSI to maintain peace and stability in the South China Sea. In 2022, President Xi Jinping proposed the GSI, which provides a Chinese solution to keep world peace and resolve the global security dilemma. The GSI is based on a new concept of common, integrated, cooperative, and sustainable security. Common security is different from the "zero-sum game" of the U.S. and its allies and emphasizes that while maintaining China's national security, it insists on paying attention to the reasonable security concerns of all countries. The emphasis on sustainable security reflects the Chinese characteristic of promoting security through development. The GSI also emphasizes respect for the sovereignty and territorial integrity of all countries, adherence to the purposes and principles of the UN Charter, peaceful resolution of differences and disputes between countries through dialogue and consultation, and integrated maintenance of security in traditional and non-traditional areas.

These concepts are not only a highly summarized summary of the established practices of China and ASEAN to maintain stability in the South China Sea but also still have guiding significance for expanding and deepening security cooperation in the South China Sea in the future. As Wang Yi proposed the four "continues," at the seminar held by China in July 2022 to commemorate the 20th anniversary of the signing of the DOC. The four "continues" means, to continue to guard the bottom line of peace, continue to promote dialogue and consultation, continue to deepen maritime cooperation, and continue to push forward the COC.[15]

Under the current situation of increasingly fierce competition among major powers, it is in the common interest of all countries involved in the South China Sea to insist on setting aside sovereignty disputes and maintaining the *status quo* in the South China Sea. It is

---

[15]"Wang Yi Attends and Addresses the Opening Ceremony of the Symposium Commemorating the 20th Anniversary of the Signing of the Declaration on the Conduct of Parties in the South China Sea," website of the Consulate General of the People's Republic of China in Davao, the Republic of the Philippines, July 25, 2022, http://davao.china-consulate.gov.cn/eng/zgyw_10/202207/t20220725_10727396.htm.

also the prerequisite to ensure that the regional dialogue mechanism under ASEAN's leadership can focus on the development agenda. Therefore, since 2022, although the actual activities of the countries involved in the South China Sea have not decreased, they have all tacitly kept a low profile, avoided public opinion speculation, and, in a more self-restrained manner, have guarded the bottom line of peace and controlled the continued heating up of the South China Sea issue.

In terms of security governance, the current regional and international environment makes it difficult to advance traditional security cooperation in the South China Sea. Thus all parties should focus on selective cooperation in non-traditional security areas. China can consider taking advantage of its strengths in information and high technology to provide more public goods in areas such as maritime search and rescue, as well as combating transnational crimes at sea.

China should continue to promote the consultations on the COC with ASEAN countries, seek rules and mechanisms acceptable to all parties, and try to establish a dialogue mechanism among the littoral states in the South China Sea, making it a useful addition to the ASEAN-centered regional security architecture. At present, under the regional situation where the competition between major powers is more intense, the consultation on the COC is facing multiple challenges, but maintaining the consultation process itself is an important contribution to regional stability and an important communication channel to maintain regional cooperation with ASEAN. The consultations on the COC require that all parties continue to adhere to the ASEAN way, especially China as a major power, understand the security concerns of ASEAN countries, provide predictable patterns of behavior in the form of mechanisms and institutions, and increase security trust with ASEAN countries. To this end, China should also consider releasing a Chinese proposal for regional order duly, increasing policy transparency, and easing the strategic anxiety of neighboring countries, including ASEAN countries.

Third, achieve the dialectical unity of the "dual initiatives" in the South China Sea. President Xi Jinping pointed out in the concept of overall national security that development is the master key to solve all security problems. Practice has proven that without peace, development is water without a source; without security, prosperity is wood without a root. Only by adhering to sustainable development can we achieve sustainable security. And only security with development as the key can guarantee long-term stability in the South China Sea.

After the outbreak of the Russia–Ukraine conflict, European countries' policies toward Russia have largely shaken the role of economic "ballast," and this effect has spread to the Asia-Pacific region, impacting the long-established "dualistic structure" of the region. However, unlike Russia's economic relations with Europe, China has broader and deeper economic ties with its neighbors, and its markets, investments, and industrial structure remain China's strengths in operating and shaping its neighborhood. Therefore, China should still strive to build a regional development consensus and provide a new path to break through the regional security dilemma through sustainable development.

Specifically in the South China Sea, the relevant countries have different political systems, and different national management models and are at different stages of economic development, and these differences make it difficult to implement some mutually beneficial and win–win cooperation measures in the short term. However, as the economic level of each country rises and the national governance capacity improves, it may be possible to make regional governance cooperation possible in the future. Especially with the development and utilization of new technologies, it will also provide more possibilities for countries to achieve mutual benefits in the maritime economy. Therefore, maintaining sustainable regional development will ultimately be conducive to achieving regional security and stability.

Chapter 5

Institutional Effectiveness and Mechanisms of the Implementation of the DOC*

Wu Lin[†,§] and Zhu Wenhan[‡,¶]

[†]*China Foreign Affairs University, Beijing, China*
[‡]*Southwest University of Political Science and Law, Chongqing, China*
[§]*wulin@cfau.edu.cn*
[¶]*411694844@qq.com*

Abstract

This year marks the 20th anniversary of the signing of the Declaration on the Conduct of Parties in the South China Sea (DOC). Over the past 20 years, China and ASEAN countries have established an institutional cooperation process based on a multi-level institutional framework, consultations on the Code of Conduct in the South

---

*Grant information: This chapter benefited from the Beijing Social Science Foundation Young Academic Leader Project "Research on Order Transformation and China's New Strategy of Regional Cooperation in Asia" (Grant No. 21DTR020).

China Sea (COC) and practical maritime cooperation to implement the spirit of the DOC, and have actively built a maritime order of lasting peace, win–win cooperation and rule-based governance in the South China Sea. However, there is still debate in academic and policy circles about the institutional effectiveness of the DOC and its implementation. One of the reasons for the debate cannot be ignored is the lack of an analytical framework for assessing the effectiveness of the mechanisms for implementing the DOC. This chapter attempts to put the security situation in the South China Sea, institutional strategy, and institutional cooperation tension into an evaluation framework, and by examining the historical process of the establishment and development of the implementation mechanism of the DOC, it reveals the effectiveness and limitations of institutional cooperation between China and ASEAN countries in the construction of regional order in the South China Sea, which will provide policy enlightenment for China and ASEAN countries to shape the regional order in the South China Sea in the future.

Keywords: South China Sea, Mechanisms for Implementing the DOC, Institutional Cooperation, Regional Order

I. Introduction

This year marks the 20th anniversary of the signing of the Declaration on the Conduct of Parties in the South China Sea (DOC). In 2002, representatives of the governments of China and ASEAN countries signed the DOC in Phnom Penh, Cambodia. As the first political document between China and ASEAN countries to deal with the South China Sea issue at the regional level, the DOC has confirmed the political consensus that China and ASEAN countries are committed to strengthening mutual trust and maintaining peace in the South China Sea. The DOC has laid out the basic path for the peaceful settlement of disputes in the South China Sea through consultation and negotiation and the goal of reaching the Code of Conduct in the South China Sea (COC) on the basis of consensus. The DOC has also clarified for the first time the guarantee principle of restraint by all parties before dispute resolution and established ways of seeking to build mutual trust in a spirit of cooperation and understanding, including developing and deepening practical maritime cooperation.[1] Over the past two decades, China and ASEAN countries have continuously improved and executed the mechanism for implementing the DOC, with the goal of maintaining peace and stability in the South China Sea, and have gradually established an institutional cooperation process based on an institutional framework consisting of senior officials' meeting and joint working group, consultations on the COC and practical maritime cooperation, and have actively built a maritime order of lasting peace, win–win cooperation and rule-based governance in the South China Sea.

As the most important multilateral cooperation and consultation system for dealing with the South China Sea issue, the development and implementation of the mechanism for implementing the DOC have not been smooth sailing. With the intensification of conflicts and confrontations in the international environment, the debate has focused on the core issue of whether the institutional approach based on the DOC can provide the regional order for lasting peace in the South China Sea. From their respective perspectives, academic and policy circles have failed to reach a consensus on the institutional effectiveness of the DOC and its implementation. There are many reasons for this. One of the factors that cannot be ignored is the lack of an analytical framework for assessing the effectiveness of the mechanisms for implementing the DOC completely, precisely, and comprehensively. At the critical historical point of the 20th anniversary of the signing of the DOC, facing the more complex and volatile region with intertwined risks, it is necessary to comprehensively review and sort out the origin and development of the mechanisms for implementing the DOC, to establish an evaluation framework of its effectiveness, and to reveal the effectiveness and limitations of the institutional cooperation path of the DOC in maintaining peace and shaping order in the South China Sea.

---

[1]Chinese Ministry of Foreign Affairs, "Declaration on the Conduct of Parties in the South China Sea," November 4, 2002, https://www.fmprc.gov.cn/chn/pds/ziliao/1179/t4553.htm.

This chapter is divided into four parts. The first part sorts out the existing researches on the effectiveness of the mechanisms for implementing the DOC, points out its shortcomings, and lays the foundation for the following arguments. The second part proposes an effectiveness evaluation framework of the implementation mechanism of the DOC, in which the security situation in the South China Sea, institutional strategy, and institutional cooperation tension are the core indicators of the evaluation. The third part verifies the evaluation framework based on the historical process of the mechanisms for implementing the DOC. The conclusion part discusses the policy enlightenment of this study.

II. Existing Studies on the Effectiveness of the Mechanisms for Implementing the DOC

Existing studies have discussed the effectiveness of the implementation mechanism of the DOC mainly in three aspects. The first is the role and significance of the DOC and the COC. The second is the policy interaction between China and ASEAN countries. And the third is the security situation and order in the South China Sea. Around the three aspects, the effectiveness evaluation of the implementation mechanism of the DOC by the academics can be roughly divided into two categories. One positively evaluates the institutional progress of the DOC and is cautiously optimistic that China and ASEAN countries will manage their differences and promote practical cooperation along this path. Another kind of view is relatively pessimistic, believing that there are limitations in the way to deal with the South China Sea issue, and questioning the prospect and role of the COC.

In the discussion on the role and significance of the DOC and the COC, some believe that the DOC embodies the collective wisdom and spirit of cooperation between China and ASEAN countries, and has played a leading role in promoting the stability and improvement of the situation in the South China Sea. It is a successful example of multilateralism in the settlement of regional maritime disputes, and it is also an initial attempt by countries around the South China Sea to establish rules for the regional order.² Some scholars have analyzed the basic principles of restraint, mutual respect, and political mutual trust stipulated in the DOC and their consistency with the ASEAN Way from a normative perspective, believing that the ever-strengthening consensus is a guarantee for China and ASEAN to properly respond to South China Sea security challenges.³ The academic criticism of the DOC mainly focuses on three aspects. First, the DOC lacks specific measures for follow-up actions and the establishment of organizational structures, and lacks substantive content; second, it lacks legally binding measures and penalties for violations of the DOC; third, the progress in the negotiation of the COC is quite slow, which leads to the conclusion that the mechanisms for implementing the DOC have not fully exerted its effectiveness.⁴ However, some scholars have expressed different views on the lag of the COC negotiation process. They believe that China and ASEAN countries have accelerated the COC consultations in recent years, but the intervention and interference of external forces are complicating this process. On the one hand, the United States is trying to use the COC to restrain China, and some of the claimant countries want to use the COC to confirm the territories they have occupied⁵; on the other hand, the United States has questioned the progress made by China

---

²Wu Shicun, "20 years of the Declaration on the Conduct of Parties in the South China Sea: Review and reflection," *World Knowledge* 16 (2022): 23–26.

³Alice D. Ba, "ASEAN's stakes: The South China Sea's challenge to autonomy and agency," *Asia Policy* 21 (2016): 47–53.

⁴David Groten, ed., *How Sentiment Matters in International Relations: China and the South China Sea Dispute*, Verlag Barbara Budrich, 2019, p. 86; Robert S. Ross and Øystein Tunsjø, eds. *Strategic Adjustment and the Rise of China: Power and Politics in East Asia*, Cornell University Press, 2017, p. 241; Euan Graham and Henrick Z. Tsjeng, eds, *Navigating the Indo-Pacific Arc*, RSIS Monograph No. 32, November 2014, p. 79.

⁵Hu Bo, "The pattern and trend of the competition between China and the United States in the South China Sea: A comprehensive analysis based on the three variables of power, rules and third-party factors," *Diplomatic Review* 1 (2021): 24–46; Zhang Jie, "The Asia-Pacific security situation under the background of the U.S. strategic game against China: Influencing factors, main features, and development trends," *Northern Research* 4 (2022): 68–77.

and ASEAN countries in the COC consultations. Therefore, it is not realistic to clarify the timetable and binding force of the COC at present, but insisting on an institutionalized consultation process is still an important exploration for the future establishment of a cooperative institution for states around the South China Sea.[6]

In terms of the South China Sea policy interaction between China and ASEAN countries, some scholars have noticed the development and changes in China's South China Sea policy, believing that the restoration of the implementation mechanism of the DOC at the end of 2010 and the achievement of the guidelines of the DOC in 2011 show that China is willing to take specific actions, to prevent the escalation of the situation in the South China Sea through more moderate diplomatic means.[7] Some scholars have also paid attention to ASEAN's institutional strategy, and found that ASEAN's approach to handling South China Sea disputes from the very beginning was not to "solve" disputes multilaterally but to maintain stability. Rather, it is to create a peaceful environment for the claimant states to negotiate rather than resort to armed conflict. This is not only the reason why ASEAN has been working hard to establish regional rules and norms in bilateral and multilateral ways since the 1990s, but also the key reason why ASEAN and China are committed to launching COC negotiations.[8] Some scholars focus on China–ASEAN relations and believe that the dialogue mechanism of the DOC has created positive conditions for China and ASEAN countries to carry out regional economic cooperation, peaceful coexistence, and defense cooperation. The political mutual trust and good political relations between China

---

[6]Zhu Feng and Hu Bo, ed., "The future stability of the situation in the South China Sea depends on the establishment of regional rules," *World Knowledge* 16 (2018): 18–21.

[7]Carlyle A. Thayer, "Chinese assertiveness in the South China Sea and Southeast Asian responses," *Journal of Current Southeast Asian Affairs* 30 (2011): 77–104; Rodolfo C Severino, "ASEAN and the South China Sea," *Security Challenges* 6 (2010): 37–47; M. Taylor Fravel, "China's strategy in the South China Sea," *Contemporary Southeast Asia* 33 (2011): 292–319.

[8]Kei Koga, *Managing Great Power Politics: ASEAN, Institutional Strategy, and the South China Sea*, Palgrave Macmillan, 2022, p. 248.

and ASEAN countries are conducive to solving the South China Sea issue.[9] In addition, those who question China's intention and the ASEAN way tend to view the role of the DOC implementation mechanism negatively. Some scholars, for example, argue that China is becoming increasingly "assertive" in the South China Sea and that ASEAN is lacking in formal institutions since its inception, particularly legally binding agreements and mechanisms to ensure compliance and dispute resolution, which has constrained ASEAN's ability to address regional security and economic challenges.[10]

Scholars have different judgments on the *status quo* and prospects of the security situation and order in the South China Sea, which has also led to their differences in the effectiveness of the implementation of the DOC. Many scholars have noticed the negative impact of the "Indo-Pacific Strategy" on the security situation in the South China Sea, but to what extent this factor has affected the implementation of the DOC and the policies of China and ASEAN countries is the focus of debates among scholars. For example, some scholars view 2020 as the turning point for the situation in the South China Sea. They believe that the situation in the South China Sea has shown signs of stabilization and improvement following the ruling of the South China Sea arbitration case in 2016, but the situation in 2020 is beginning to shift toward unrest, from general stability to the possibility of losing control in some areas. Therefore, it is believed that China and ASEAN countries may face difficulties in resolving the "South China Sea dilemma" through COC consultations.[11] Some scholars also believe that although there are new changes and challenges in the

---

[9]Zhang Jie and Zhu Bin, "The South China Sea factor in China–ASEAN relations," *Contemporary World* 8 (2013): 52–56; Mikael Weissmann, "The South China Sea: Still no war on the horizon," *Asian Survey* 55 (2015): 596–617.
[10]M. J. Jones and M. L. R. Smith, *ASEAN and East Asian International Relations: Regional Delusion*, Cheltenham: Edward Elgar Publishing, 2006; K. Sato, "The Rise of China's impact on ASEAN Conference Diplomacy: A study of conflict in the South China Sea," *Journal of Contemporary East Asia* 2 (2013): 95–110; N. Kipgen, "ASEAN and China in the South China Sea," *Asian Affairs* 49 (2018): 433–448.
[11]Wu Shicun, "Current situation in the South China Sea and breaking the 'South China Sea Dilemma' in China–ASEAN relations," *Journal of Ocean University of*

situation in the South China Sea, it is generally under control, because of the rising expectation of a controllable China–U.S. military competition and China's ability to control the situation.[12] They emphasized that the factors for maintaining peace and stability in the South China Sea should not be underestimated, and the implementation mechanism of the DOC will play a key role in it. However, at the same time, they cautioned against some unrealistic and high expectations, such as the COC is not an appropriate platform to resolve disputes in the South China Sea, but only the applicable norms for certain behaviors of China and ASEAN countries. The norms and rules for the entire South China Sea region are much broader.[13]

To sum up, the academic community has conducted a comprehensive discussion on the effectiveness of the implementation mechanism of the DOC from three aspects: the political document itself, China–ASEAN policy interaction, and the situation and order in the South China Sea, laying the foundation for analysis. But there are also some shortcomings. First, the development process of the mechanisms for implementing the DOC is not linear, and its effectiveness is also changing. An over-general or one-sided evaluation of its institutional effectiveness is not in line with the facts. Second, the analysis of the continuity and change in time and space of institutional cooperation between China and ASEAN countries in implementing the DOC is insufficient. On the one hand, this is because the facts of institutional cooperation are insufficiently sorted out. On the other hand, what is more important is the lack of overall and historical analysis of the implementation of the DOC and its development. Simplifying China's South China Sea policy based on the Western logic of

---

China 1 (2022): 7–11; Liu Lin, "The situation and development trend of the South China Sea outlook," *Asia-Pacific Security and Ocean Research* 2 (2021): 72–90.

[12]Hu Bo, "Short-term troubles and long-term worries coexist in the maritime situation around China," *World Knowledge* 15 (2021): 29–30.

[13]Zhu Feng and Hu Bo, ed., "The future stability of the situation in the South China Sea depends on the establishment of regional rules," *World Knowledge* 16 (2018): 18–21.

"a strong country must seek hegemony" intention, ignoring the mutual construction of regional context and regional countries. Third, there is no analytical framework for assessing the implementation mechanism of the DOC, and it is difficult to carry out detailed research on the institutional process in different periods. Based on the above three deficiencies, this chapter attempts to combine existing research and policies to propose an evaluation framework for the effectiveness of the implementation mechanism of the DOC and restore it to the historical process for verification.

III. Effectiveness Evaluation Framework of the Implementation Mechanism of the DOC

To evaluate the effectiveness of institutional cooperation in a time span of as long as two decades, three basic elements need to be considered, namely policy context, institutional strategy, and cooperation tension. First, the emergence and development of cooperative institutions depends on the policy context, and whether institutional cooperation effectively responds to and shapes the context is equally important. Second, the institutional strategy is directly related to its effectiveness, and this element is the core indicator for evaluating the implementation mechanism of the DOC. Third, there is tension in institutional cooperation, and the context of major power competition highlights this tension. It is particularly important to be able to control the tension and maintain the momentum of cooperation. Based on the three basic elements, the chapter puts the security situation in the South China Sea, institutional strategy, and institutional cooperation tension into one analytical framework, and undertakes a broad, dynamic, and comprehensive assessment of the role and limitations of the implementation mechanism of the DOC at different stages.

(i) *Security situation in the South China Sea*

As an important context variable, the security situation in the South China Sea is a prerequisite for analyzing the policies and actions of the regional states.[14] The improvement or deterioration of the situation directly affects the cognition and choice of China and ASEAN countries, which is reflected in the specific form of the implementation mechanism of the DOC. Therefore, it is obviously inaccurate to simply judge the institutional effectiveness of the DOC in terms of the level of institutionalization and legally binding force, apart from the dynamic changes in the security situation in the South China Sea. The chapter believes that when evaluating the role of the DOC mechanism in a specific period, it should be closely concerned with the basic security situation in the South China Sea, focusing on the specific context in which the DOC mechanism exists, and whether China and ASEAN have effectively responded to the changes in the situation and whether they have played a positive role in stabilizing the situation and managing the crisis through institutional cooperation.

Since the end of the Cold War, there have been three major security crises in the South China Sea. The first is the Mischief Reef incident at the turn of the century, and the 2001 China–U.S. plane collision in the South China Sea. The second is the Huangyan Island dispute between China and the Philippines in 2012, and the Hai Yang Shi You 981 standoff between China and Vietnam. The third is the 2016 South China Sea arbitration case. The commonality of these three crises is that the claimant countries escalated frictions over sovereignty disputes, which led to the heating up of the situation in the South China Sea, but eventually brought under control peacefully and did not lead to conflicts or wars. At the same time, political, economic, domestic, and other crises have superimposed on them, which together constitute the policy context for the option of institutional cooperation between China and ASEAN countries.

The response of the DOC implementation mechanism to the crisis situation is an important indicator variable, which can be verified in terms of crisis response and situation stabilization. Crisis response

---

[14]Hu Bo, "Short-term troubles and long-term worries coexist in the maritime situation around China," *World Knowledge* 15 (2021): 29–30; Zhu Feng and Hu Bo, ed., "The future stability of the situation in the South China Sea depends on the establishment of regional rules," *World Knowledge* 16 (2018): 18–21.

mainly examines the efficiency and choice of the countries involved in the crisis and the relevant claimant countries in responding to the crisis, while situation stabilization focuses on results, and examines whether the response has effectively prevented the escalation and deterioration of the situation. As the security situation in the South China Sea is constantly changing, China and ASEAN countries' perceptions of institutional cooperation are also changing, and their crisis response and situation stabilization in different periods are naturally different. This needs a comprehensive consideration when evaluating the institutional effectiveness of the DOC.

(ii) *Institutional Strategy*

The institutional strategy of China and ASEAN countries directly affects the institutional effectiveness of the DOC, but it is often inseparable from the policy context mentioned previously. These two factors should be analyzed together. China and ASEAN countries have different perceptions of institutional rules and multilateral diplomacy in different periods, which are driven by both norm evolution and practical interests. Therefore, it is necessary to analyze the changes and differences in their institutional strategies. Regarding the progress of the implementation mechanism of the DOC, the institutional process has been advancing, which shows that both China and ASEAN countries have formed a relatively stable preference for institutional cooperation, which is the basis for future COC and order construction. But at the same time, it should be noted that geopolitical competition and preference for prioritizing national interests also affect this preference for institutional cooperation, resulting in a nonlinear development of the institutional process of the DOC.

The institutional strategy under the framework of the implementation of the DOC can be examined from three aspects, namely institutional composition, frequency of dialogue, and scope of topics. In terms of institutional composition, after the signing of the DOC in 2002, China and ASEAN countries have decided to establish ASEAN–China Senior Officials' Meeting on the Implementation of the DOC (SOM-DOC) and ASEAN–China Joint Working Group on the Implementation of the DOC (JWG-DOC) in 2003, to promote the implementation of the DOC by holding regular meetings. During this period, a number of auxiliary institutions were successively established, which could reflect the strategic preferences of China and ASEAN countries. In terms of the frequency of dialogue, there are differences between China and ASEAN countries in different periods based on the security situation in the South China Sea and the needs of all parties. The mechanism stipulates that the JWG-DOC will meet at least once a year and submit reports to the SOM-DOC regularly. It is worth noting that the frequency of dialogue in the two periods is significantly different from the regular level. One is the suspension of dialogue between 2007 and 2009, and the other is the particularly intensive dialogue and consultation between 2014 and 2016. These two phases correspond exactly to the stagnation and acceleration of institutional progress. From the perspective of the scope of topics, the implementation mechanism of the DOC basically follows the directions of cooperation in marine environmental protection, marine scientific research, maritime navigation and traffic safety, search and rescue, and combating transnational crimes as determined in the DOC. Among them, the progress of marine environmental protection and marine scientific research has been the most smooth and visible, as compared to the relatively slow progress in other fields. By examining these three indicators in different periods, it is possible to comprehensively study and evaluate the institutional strategy to implement the DOC and its changes in different security situations.

(iii) *Institutional Cooperation Tension*

Institutional cooperation is the most distinctive feature of the development of relations between China and Southeast Asian countries since the end of the Cold War. China is one of the most staunch supporters of ASEAN Centrality. This is not only reflected in the fact that China has joined all regional cooperation mechanisms led by ASEAN, and is the first major power other than ASEAN members to join the Treaty of Amity and Cooperation in Southeast Asia, and supports ASEAN in maintaining its core position in the Asia-Pacific regional cooperation framework. It is also manifested in a deeper level consistency of normative recognition. Although the centrality of ASEAN has been weakened under the impact of major power competition in recent years, China's emphasis on ASEAN has not decreased but increased. Deepening institutional cooperation and integration of interests with ASEAN has become a priority direction and strategic choice of China's diplomacy.[15] Conversely, ASEAN's demand for institutional cooperation with China is also increasing. On the one hand, ASEAN's own institutional construction has made steady progress. By implementing normative influence internally, ASEAN has buffered the pressure of external forces to politicize the norms of freedom of navigation.[16] On the other hand, ASEAN continues to promote cooperation with China in different institutions to maintain the stability of the security order in the Asia-Pacific region after the end of the Cold War.

The institutional cooperation of the implementation mechanism of the DOC has both continuity and tension in different periods. Continuity stems from a major underlying logic of the institutional strategies of China and ASEAN, namely the ASEAN Way. It is a decision-making process characterized by a high degree of consensus, which is based on ASEAN's informality, consensus-building and non-confrontational trading style. The specific manifestation in the process of consultation on the COC is to steadily and orderly promote the consultation on the COC through the continuous accumulation and expansion of consensus, by tactics of "sorting out consensus," "from easy to difficult," and "consensus by negotiation."[17] The tension manifests itself as the tension within institutional cooperation and the tension between institutional cooperation and the geopolitical

---

[15] Wu Lin, "The Impact of China–US institutional competition on ASEAN's centrality: Taking the ASEAN Regional Forum (ARF) as an example," *Diplomatic Review* 5 (2021): 88–117.
[16] He Jiajie, "ASEAN's normative influence and its role in the South China Sea issue," *World Economics and Politics* 7 (2021): 127–152.
[17] "The Eighth Senior Officials Meeting on the Implementation of the Declaration on the Conduct of Parties in the South China Sea," October 29, 2014, *China Daily*, https://world.chinadaily.com.cn/2014-10/29/content_18823024.htm.

competition of major powers. These two tensions jointly affect the development of the implementation mechanism of the DOC. When the two tensions are well controlled, the institutional cooperation of the implementation mechanism of the DOC is easier to make a breakthrough; if they are not effectively controlled, the logic of competition is ahead of the logic of cooperation, and the effectiveness of the implementation mechanism of the DOC is difficult to fully play.

IV. The Evolution and Effectiveness of the Implementation Mechanism of the DOC

From the birth of the DOC to the continuous enrichment and development of the implementation mechanism of the DOC, the three factors, namely the regional security situation, institutional strategy, and institutional cooperation tension, have been running through, providing a comprehensive evaluation framework to analyze the institutional cooperation between China and ASEAN countries in handling the South China Sea issue. Due to the different performances of these three factors in different periods, the mechanisms for implementing the DOC need to be examined in the historical process. This chapter divides its historical process into four stages, namely the birth of the DOC, the launch and delay of the implementation of the DOC, the recovery and acceleration of institutionalization, and the entry into the substantive stage of the COC consultation.

(i) *The Birth of the DOC (1997–2002)*

The historical significance of the birth of the DOC needs to be interpreted by going back to the security situation in the South China Sea at the turn of the century. The outbreak of the dual crises of the South China Sea security crisis and the Southeast Asian financial crisis was an important background for the birth of the DOC. Under these two crises, ASEAN countries were under unprecedented dual pressure on the economy and security. On the one hand, economically, the financial crisis sweeping across Southeast Asia had led to severe economic recession in many countries. The IMF's reform requirements did not save these countries in time, and increased their concerns about the loss of sovereignty caused by the intervention of international organizations. On the other hand, the Mischief Reef incident had aggravated the attention within ASEAN on the South China Sea issue. In March 1995, ASEAN foreign ministers held a closed-door meeting and issued a statement entitled "Recent Developments in the South China Sea." Vietnam, which had not yet joined ASEAN at that time, also expressed support for this. The South China Sea issue gradually became an important issue of concern to ASEAN. With the economic crisis, the South China Sea claimant countries in ASEAN had no time to take into account the South China Sea issue, which made them more worried about China taking advantage of the South China Sea. However, instead of taking advantage of others' dangers, China showed an "unexpected" friendly willingness and ability to respond to crises and stabilize the situation with a cooperative attitude, which played a key role for China and ASEAN countries to embark on the road of institutional cooperation. In 1996, China was accorded full Dialogue Partner of ASEAN. In December 1997, President Jiang and the ASEAN leaders had the first ASEAN–China Informal Summit in Kuala Lumpur, Malaysia, and issued a Joint Statement, in which China expressed confidence in ASEAN's economic future, agreed to implement Manila Framework Group as soon as possible to promote regional financial stability, and ASEAN countries also appreciate China's regional financial aid package. The statement also clearly stated that the South China Sea disputes should be resolved through friendly consultations and negotiations.[18] The escalation of political relations had directly brought about the improvement of political mutual trust, creating conditions for the security situation in the South China Sea to "turn crisis into stability" and institutional dialogue on the South China Sea issue.

---

[18]Chinese Ministry of Foreign Affairs, "The joint statement of the summit of the People's Republic of China and ASEAN: China–ASEAN Cooperation in the 21st Century," December 16, 1997, https://www.mfa.gov.cn/web/gjhdq_676201/ gjhdqzz_681964/lhg_682518/zywj_682530/199712/t19971216_9386047. shtml.

The institutional dialogue between China and ASEAN countries had just started, and there were two real tensions in its institutional process. One was internal disputes, and the other was mutual testing. There was debate within ASEAN over how to talk to China. The Philippines and other countries advocated that on the basis of the 1992 ASEAN Declaration on the South China Sea and the 1995 Joint Communiqué of the 28th ASEAN Ministerial Meeting, they should first reach a consensus on the COC within ASEAN, and then negotiate with China in a collective capacity to reach the final COC. However, there was disagreement within ASEAN countries over the geographical scope of the COC's application,[19] and overlapping institutions within ASEAN also made such discussions confusing and ineffective. At this time, China and Southeast Asia were still at the stage of approaching each other and "discovery of neighbors."[20] Therefore, China also had domestic debates on whether to conduct consultations in a mutilateral way, the content and goals of consultations, etc. During this period, the coordination and dialogue between China and ASEAN around the COC showed the characteristics of mutual testing.

In the end, the common demands and real tensions to resolve the South China Sea issue through a mechanism led to the birth of the DOC, rather than a one-step approach to the COC. On November 4, 2002, the sixth ASEAN–China Summit was held in Phnom Penh, Cambodia. After the meeting, China and ASEAN foreign ministers and their representatives signed the DOC. As the first political document on the South China Sea issue signed by China and ASEAN countries, the DOC clearly committed for the first time the principles, paths, rules, measures, and goals for dealing with the South China Sea issue. The principle is the principle of international law; the path is the

---

[19]Liu Zhongmin, "Development trends of Southeast Asian countries' South China Sea policies after the Cold War and reflections on China's countermeasures," *Studies in Nanyang Issues* 2 (2008): 25–34.

[20]Brantly Womack, "The New Normal of China's relations with Southeast Asia," Presentation at Seminar on "Changing Asia 2019: Perspectives on Regional and Global Cooperation" at China foreign Affairs University on October 26–27, 2019.

consultation and negotiation of directly related sovereign states; the rule is self-restraint (including actions not to inhabit now uninhabited islands, reefs, beaches, sand, or other natural formations) and constructive handling disagreements; the measures include trust-building and maritime cooperation; the goal is to approach the COC based on consensus.[21] In other words, the DOC confirmed some basic problems in dealing with the South China Sea issue, but did not reach an agreement on the content of the COC. Combining with China's response to the dual crises mentioned above, and the real tensions faced by China and ASEAN countries in the initial institutional cooperation, it can be found that the birth of the DOC was actually the result of the political choices and real tensions of all parties, and it was also at that time the best choice for China and ASEAN countries under the security situation of the South China Sea. It is precisely because of the DOC that the institutional cooperation on the South China Sea issue between China and ASEAN countries has been started.

(ii) *The Launch and Delay of the Implementation Mechanism of the DOC (2003–2010)*

The birth of the DOC only started the institutional cooperation between China and ASEAN countries in the South China Sea, and the formulation of COC based on consensus is the ultimate goal. In 2003, the implementation mechanism was officially launched, but the subsequent development was not continuous enough, and the process of institutional cooperation gradually fell into a state of stagnation. To trace the roots, the rising of external intervention, the mutual constraints of the institutional strategies of regional countries, and the lack of endogenous motivation for institutional cooperation had all played a role in restricting institutional cooperation.

In 2003, China and ASEAN countries decided to hold regular SOM-DOC, and set up JWG-DOC to deal with specific issues.

---

[21] Chinese Ministry of Foreign Affairs: Declaration on the Conduct of Parties in the South China Sea.

The rapid follow-up of the mechanisms for implementing the DOC stems from the rapid development of China–ASEAN relations in the early 21st century. Politically, in 2003, China established a strategic partnership with ASEAN and took the lead in joining the Treaty of Amity and Cooperation in Southeast Asia as a dialogue partner of ASEAN. In terms of security, China and ASEAN launched non-traditional security cooperation in 2004. Economically, China proposed the establishment of the China–ASEAN Free Trade Area in 2000, and signed the ASEAN–China Framework Agreement in 2002, officially launching the process of establishing the Free Trade Area. On the issue of joint oil and gas development in the South China Sea, CNOOC had successively signed the Joint Maritime Seismic Understanding with PETRON and PetroVietnam, starting the cooperation of the joint development of oil resources in the disputed waters of the South China Sea among China and claimant countries.[22]

The initial operation of the mechanism was quite smooth, including the establishment of two major institutions, SOM-DOC and JWG-DOC, and the launch of specific cooperation and work plans. In December 2004, China and ASEAN countries held the first SOM-DOC in Kuala Lumpur, Malaysia. The meeting established JWG-DOC, and adopted the document on its terms of reference, specifying its composition and responsibilities. The task of JWG-DOC is to develop specific policy measures for the implementation of the DOC and to identify actions that complicate or escalate disputes. JWG-DOC can nominate experts to provide technical support or policy advice, hold meetings at least once a year, and submit a report to SOM-DOC after each meeting. China and ASEAN countries agreed that the establishment of them was an important step toward ensuring peace and stability in the South China Sea and would create a favorable context for resolving disputes over sovereignty in the South China Sea. In August 2005, the first JWG-DOC

---

[22]State Information Office, "China's insistence on negotiations to settle disputes between China and the Philippines in the South China Sea," White Paper, July 2016, http://www.scio.gov.cn/ztk/dtzt/34102/34818/index.htm.

was held in Manila, Philippines. All parties discussed the draft guidelines for the implementation of the DOC proposed by ASEAN countries. In February 2006, the second JWG-DOC was held in Sanya, China. The meeting agreed to focus on six areas of cooperation, reached a consensus on specific cooperation projects, and adopted an annual work plan. In May, the second SOM-DOC was held in Siem Reap, Cambodia. However, when discussing the crucial issue of implementing the draft guidelines of the DOC, differences emerged within ASEAN as well as between China and ASEAN countries, and the internal tension of institutional cooperation reappeared. Within ASEAN, the Philippines advocated first reaching a unified draft of guidelines among ASEAN countries and then negotiating with China, but some countries expressed different opinions. China also raised questions about the approach. Negotiations on the guidelines were temporarily stalled due to disputes and disagreements.

Since 2007, the security situation in the South China Sea had undergone major changes, which made the implementation mechanism of the DOC with internal tensions encounter greater obstacles. This is reflected in the stagnation of the mechanisms for implementing the DOC between 2007 and 2009. The change in the situation came from two aspects. First, some claimant countries stepped up their claims to the South China Sea. In February 2009, the Philippine House of Representatives passed House Bill No. 3216, which amended Act No. 3046, entitled "An Act to Define the Baselines of the Territorial Sea of the Philippines." This bill put China's Huangyan Island and some islands and reefs of the Nansha Islands within the baseline of the territorial waters of the Philippines, triggering protests from China and Vietnam. Second, the deepening of U.S. involvement made the situation in the South China Sea increasingly complicated. In March 2009, the U.S. spy ship Flawless sailed into the South China Sea and used sonar and other equipment to monitor the activities of Chinese submarines. At the China–ASEAN Summit held in November, then-premier Wen Jiabao clearly stated that "(the South China Sea issue) should be resolved through friendly consultation and negotiation by the sovereign countries directly concerned, and external forces should not intervene under any pretext."[23] In January 2010, when the China–ASEAN Free Trade Area was officially established, then U.S. Secretary of State Hillary Clinton delivered a U.S. Asia-Pacific policy speech in Hawaii, which changed its prudent attitude since 1995, pointing out that the relationship between the United States and its allies in the Asia-Pacific region is the key to U.S. engagement in Asia-Pacific affairs. At the ASEAN Regional Forum held in July 2010, Hillary Clinton stated that the United States has national interests in freedom of navigation, open access to Asian maritime commons, and respect for international law in the South China Sea, and expressed the United States' willingness to promote multilateral negotiations. In this regard, China reiterated its position of not internationalizing the South China Sea issue, and said that the implementation framework of the DOC can play a positive role in dispute resolution.

In order to reduce the negative impact of changes in the security situation in the South China Sea on the implementation of the DOC, China and ASEAN countries restarted the cooperative mechanism in the first half of 2010. In April and December, two JWG-DOC meetings were held. All parties reaffirmed the importance of the DOC mechanism and had active and candid discussions on continuing to promote the follow-up process. In October, the ASEAN–China leaders' summit agreed to continue negotiations on the COC, which provided the political impetus for the resumption of the mechanism.

In general, the development of the mechanisms for implementing the DOC experienced twists and turns during this period. On the one hand, China–ASEAN relations were improving rapidly, and the construction of the free trade area was in full swing. In particular, the implementation of the U.S. Asia-Pacific rebalancing strategy and changes in the South China Sea policy indicated that the implementation of the DOC would not only test the determination of regional countries to cooperate in solving the South China Sea issue and the

---

[23]"Wen Jiabao's speech at the China–ASEAN (10+1) Leaders' Summit," November 18, 2011, http://www.gov.cn/govweb/ldhd/2011-11/18/content_1997289.htm.

resilience of institutional cooperation but would also face severe geopolitical challenge from outside the region.

(iii) *The Recovery and Acceleration of Institutionalization (2011–2016)*

Since 2011, China has increased its investment in the mechanisms for implementing the DOC, and its willingness to jointly maintain stability in the South China Sea with ASEAN countries through institutional cooperation has increased significantly. China's emphasis on the strategic position of ASEAN and the clarification of institutional strategies are the main driving forces for the implementation mechanism of the DOC to accelerate the in-depth development toward practical cooperation. On July 20, 2011, China and ASEAN countries reached an agreement on the implementation of the DOC guidelines at the SOM-DOC held in Bali, Indonesia. The document defined the guidelines and basic consensus for carrying out cooperation, projects, and activities under the implementation framework of the DOC. Compared with the DOC, this guideline clarified that its next step was trust-building, and promoting practical cooperation in the South China Sea was the core of it.[24] At the meeting, Liu Zhenmin, then Assistant Minister of Foreign Affairs of China, expounded China's position of actively supporting cooperation in the South China Sea, suggested that all parties should shift their focus to practical cooperation under the framework of the DOC, and put forward a series of cooperation initiatives, including holding a seminar on the freedom of navigation in the South China Sea, establishing three specialized technical committees for (a) marine scientific research and environmental protection, (b) navigation safety and search and rescue, and (c) combating transnational crimes at sea, and promising to continue

---

[24]Chinese Ministry of Foreign Affairs, "Guidelines for implementing the Declaration on the Conduct of Parties in the South China Sea," August 12, 2011, https://www.fmprc.gov.cn/wjb_673085/zzjg_673183/yzs_673193/dqzz_673197/nanhai_673325/201108/t20110812_7491672.shtml.

to undertake the three confirmed cooperation projects, which received positive responses from all parties.

Since then, China and ASEAN countries have accelerated the pace of institutionalization to promote maritime pragmatic cooperation, which is embodied in the frequency of dialogues and the improvement of institutions. In 2014, SOM-DOC was held twice within a year for the first time; in 2015, SOM-DOC was again held twice within a year; in 2016, SOM-DOC was held three times in succession in April, June, and August of that year. In terms of institutions, in 2014, the 8th SOM-DOC approved the first consensus document of the COC consultation, and established the Joint Maritime Search and Rescue Hotline Platform among the technical departments of China and ASEAN countries and the Hotline for Senior Officials in Response to Maritime Emergencies among the ministry of foreign affairs of China and ASEAN countries, hold sand table exercise of China–ASEAN joint maritime search and rescue, and promoted the application of satellite systems in navigation and search and rescue in the South China Sea. In 2015, the 9th SOM-DOC reviewed and adopted the second consensus document to negotiate the COC, the terms of reference of expert group and other important documents. In 2016, the 13th SOM-DOC reviewed and approved the Guidelines for Hotline Communications among Senior Officials of the Ministers of Foreign Affairs of ASEAN member states and China in Response to Maritime Emergencies and the Joint Statement on the Application of the Code for Unplanned Encounters at Sea in the South China Sea, and decided to submit these documents as an outcome to the China–ASEAN Summit for publication. The acceleration of the institutional process has created conditions for all parties to carry out maritime pragmatic cooperation. Since 2012, cooperation in the fields of marine scientific research and environmental protection, navigation safety and search and rescue, and combating transnational crimes at sea has been carried out successively.

It is worth noting that the acceleration of the institutional process during this period occurred simultaneously with the increasing complexity of the security situation in the South China Sea, and the complexity of the situation was mainly manifested in the strategic interaction of some claimant countries and external forces and the intra-ASEAN divisions and regional tensions triggered by their sovereignty claims. Unlike the previous stage of the crisis where institutionalization was hindered, both China and ASEAN realized the importance of strengthening crisis response and stabilized the situation through clearer institutional strategies.[25] The South China Sea issue did not escalate into a large-scale conflict.

The change in the situation first occurred in 2012, when the Philippines attempted to hold joint military exercises with the United States in the South China Sea, while cooperating with Vietnam to put pressure on ASEAN. The confrontation between China and the Philippines on Huangyan Island occurred from April to July 2012. Serious disagreements within ASEAN over the South China Sea issue resulted and the ASEAN Foreign Ministers' Meeting held on July 9, 2012, failed to issue a joint communiqué for the first time in history. On July 20, the ASEAN foreign ministers urgently reached a six-point principle on the South China Sea issue, namely, (a) fully implement the DOC and relevant statements, (b) implement the guidelines for follow-up actions of the DOC, (c) reach the COC as soon as possible, (d) fully abide by the United Nations Convention on the Law of the Sea (hereinafter referred to as UNCLOS), (e) all parties continue to exercise restraint and refrain from the use of force, and (f) resolve disputes peacefully in accordance with UNCLOS and other international laws. ASEAN has ensured unity in times of crisis and reaffirmed the DOC's priority in addressing the South China Sea issue.

On January 22, 2013, the South China Sea issue was submitted to the Hague Arbitration Tribunal, and at the same time, it was continuously urged to reach a legally binding COC as soon as possible, which made the focus of the South China Sea issue deviate from the original track. In this context, SOM-DOC and JWG-DOC were held more intensively than before. In August and November 2014, Foreign Minister Wang Yi and Premier Li Keqiang proposed and advocated respectively for the first time the "dual track" approach for

---

[25]Liu Ruonan, "Responding to the South China Sea Crisis: The measures and limits of ASEAN's 'self-repair'," *Diplomatic Review* 4 (2018): 25–53.

dealing with the South China Sea issue at a series of meetings on East Asia cooperation. The "dual track" approach means that disputes related to the South China Sea should be addressed properly through negotiations and consultations among countries directly concerned, and China and the ASEAN countries should work together to safeguard peace and stability in the South China Sea.[26] The "dual track" approach clarified the Chinese government's policy to resolve the South China Sea issue through consultation and negotiation, and boosted confidence for the implementation of the DOC.

In 2015, the involvement of the United States in the South China Sea arbitration case with the Philippines triggered an escalation of the regional situation. On the one hand, the United States used regional mechanisms to publicly express its concerns about the situation in the South China Sea. On the other hand, it created the issue of "freedom of navigation," sent ships into the waters of the South China Sea, and strengthened defense relations with some claimant countries. The situation in the region was under extreme tension. The implementation mechanism of the DOC also responded positively and played a role at this time. In 2016, SOM-DOC was held for three historic times, and all parties agreed to speed up the completion of the COC framework. Meanwhile, Duterte, who was elected as the new president of the Philippines in June 2016, began to develop positive relations with China and pushed the South China Sea issue to return to the right track of institutional cooperation.

To sum up, the security situation in the South China Sea has undergone profound changes during this period, with increased complexity and increased risk of conflict escalation. However, facing a more complex regional situation, the institutionalization of the implementation mechanism of the DOC has been continuously strengthened, showing strong crisis response capabilities. China's clearer and firmer "dual-track" approach and ASEAN's institutional resilience in bridging internal differences ensure the main channel status of the

---

[26]"Wang Yi, "Dealing with the South China Sea issue with a 'dual-track' approach," August 9, 2014, *People's Daily Online*, http://politics.people.com.cn/n/2014/0809/c70731-25435555.html.

implementation mechanism of the DOC in handling the South China Sea issue. This also shows that the institutional inertia of the DOC implementation mechanism acts as a stabilizer.

(iv) *The Substantive Stage of the COC Consultation (2017–2022)*

Under the Duterte administration, the Philippines was actively seeking to ease relations with China, and China–U.S. relations were showing a warming trend. In addition, the Chinese government set a clear timetable for the COC consultations and promoted the progress of the DOC implementation mechanism to achieve a series of positive results. On May 18, 2017, the 14th SOM-DOC reviewed and approved the COC framework, which was adopted at the China–ASEAN Foreign Ministers' Meeting held in August of that year. At the meeting, Foreign Minister Wang Yi expounded China's "three-step" vision for advancing the COC consultations, namely: The first step was to initiate the substantive consultation within a year after all necessary preparatory work was done. Second, the thinking, principle, and plan for the next stage COC consultation should be discussed at the JWG-DOC at the end of August. Third, with preparations basically ready and on the condition that there was no major outside interference and the South China Sea situation was generally stable, leaders of China and ASEAN member states would officially announce the start of the next step to negotiate on the text of the COC at the China–ASEAN Leaders' Summit in November.[27] The "three-step" vision gained warm response and support from ASEAN countries, and the consultation on the text of the COC was successfully launched in 2017. At the 15th SOM-DOC held in June 2018, all parties agreed to form a single draft negotiating text as soon as possible on the basis of the established COC framework. At the China–ASEAN Leaders' Summit on

---

[27]Chinese Ministry of Foreign Affairs, "Wang Yi: China–ASEAN strategic partnership enters a new stage of comprehensive development," August 6, 2017, https://www.mfa.gov.cn/web/gjhdq_676201/gjhdqzz_681964/lhg_682518/xgxw_682524/201708/t20170806_9385837.shtml.

November 14, China and ASEAN countries agreed to complete the first reading of the text within 2019. Premier Li Keqiang attended the meeting and stated that China was ready to work with ASEAN countries toward concluding COC consultations in three years on the basis of consensus.[28] In July 2019, the China–ASEAN Foreign Ministers' Meeting announced that the first reading of the single draft negotiating text of the COC had been completed ahead of schedule and that it was entering the second reading. The 18th SOM-DOC held in October spoke highly of the progress and expressed the hope to complete the consultations by the end of 2021.

However, the outbreak of the COVID-19 epidemic interrupted the progress. Judging from the process of institutional development, the impact of the epidemic on the security situation in the South China Sea was significant. The development of the implementation mechanism of the DOC was divided into two phases: pre-pandemic and post-pandemic. The pre-pandemic COC consultations progressed rapidly, and the clear timetable ensured a high degree of integration and cooperation among the DOC implementation mechanism, the China–ASEAN Foreign Ministers' Meeting, and the China–ASEAN Leaders' Summit. The China–ASEAN cooperation mechanism provided positive institutional support for the implementation mechanism of the DOC. Under the influence of this process, the security situation of the South China Sea tended to be relatively stable. But after 2020, as the pandemic overlapped with intensified U.S.–China competition, the situation in the South China Sea evolved into unrest,[29] and the negotiation process of the COC slowed down. According to the plan, consultations on the COC should be completed in 2021, and China and ASEAN countries should communicate and interact more frequently in order to achieve the set goals. The epidemic created difficulties for consultations. In 2020, only one special meeting

---

[28]"Li Keqiang's Speech at the 13th East Asia Summit," November 16, 2018, Xinhuanet: http://www.xinhuanet.com/politics/leaders/2018-11/16/c_11237 20563.htm.

[29]Liu Lin, "The situation and development trend of the South China Sea outlook," *Asia-Pacific Security and Ocean Research* 2 (2021): 72–90.

of JWG-DOC was held, and there was no reading of the COC text. Nonetheless, China and ASEAN countries still expressed their strong willingness to continue to promote the implementation mechanism of the DOC to approach the COC. In November 2020, Premier Li Keqiang stated at the East Asia Summit that the negotiations on the COC should be steadily advanced, making it an upgraded and enhanced version of the DOC, which is more substantive, more effective, and more operable.[30] ASEAN countries also expressed the need to reach a substantive and effective COC as soon as possible. Since 2021, the implementation mechanism of the DOC was reverted through a flexible way combining offline and online. In June 2021, the 19th SOM-DOC was held in Chongqing, China. In May 2022, the 36th JWG-DOC was held in Siem Reap, Cambodia. All parties agreed to take the opportunity of the 20th anniversary of the signing of the DOC to advance various work under the implementation framework of the DOC. On November 3, at the 2022 Forum on Maritime Cooperation and Governance, Foreign Minister Wang Yi proposed to promote regional maritime governance according to local conditions, affirmed the role of the DOC as a stabilizer, and reiterated the position on accelerating the negotiation process of the COC and the establishment of rules for maritime interaction in the common interest of all.[31]

In general, the negotiation on the COC has entered a substantive stage in this period and has made breakthrough progress. At present, all parties are actively preparing for the second reading of the text. The positive progress is due to the strengthening of political relations between China and ASEAN countries, China's determination to follow the path of dealing with the South China Sea issue through

---

[30]Chinese Ministry of Foreign Affairs, "Li Keqiang's Speech at the 15th East Asia Summit," November 15, 2020, https://www.mfa.gov.cn/web/gjhdq_676201/gjhdqzz_681964/dyfheas_682566/zyjh_682576/202011/t20201115_9386679.shtml.

[31]Chinese Ministry of Foreign Affairs, "Coordinating Security Development and Promoting Ocean Governance," November 3, 2022, https://www.mfa.gov.cn/web/wjbz_673089/zyjh_673099/202211/t20221103_10799809.shtml.

institutional rules, and the efforts of all parties to uphold peace and cooperation in the South China Sea. At the same time, it should be noted that the impact of the epidemic and the competition between major powers is still ongoing. The intertwining of these two factors may hinder the progress of the implementation mechanism of the DOC and weaken the current momentum for institutional cooperation. This is the biggest obstacle facing the current implementation mechanism of the DOC.

V. Conclusion

After the end of the Cold War, the situation in the South China Sea has been in crisis, but overall peace and stability have been maintained. China and ASEAN countries have played an active and important role in it. The DOC was signed in 2002 and the implementation mechanism of the DOC established in the following two decades has built a platform for all claimants to build consensus, formulate rules, and carry out cooperation. It is the institutional guarantee that the overall stability of the South China Sea can be achieved. On the occasion of the 20th anniversary of the signing of the DOC, it is necessary to conduct a dynamic and systematic clarification and evaluation of the institutional cooperation between China and ASEAN countries in the South China Sea. By constructing an effectiveness evaluation framework with the South China Sea security situation, institutional strategy, and institutional cooperation tension as the main indicators, this study attempts to analyze how the implementation mechanism of the DOC was established and developed in the form of institutional cooperation, how to respond to and shape the regional security situation, how to choose the institutional strategy, and how the internal tensions of the mechanism have affected the development of the implementation mechanism of the DOC.

The study found that the effectiveness and limitations of the implementation mechanism of the DOC were different in different historical stages. At the establishment stage, China's active response to the dual economic and security crises in Southeast Asia laid the foundation for political mutual trust for the signing of the DOC;

however, the institutional choices of China and ASEAN countries were still in the tension of internal debate and mutual testing. In the end, they reached a compromise document namely the DOC, rather than forming the COC in one step. After the implementation mechanism of the DOC was launched, the development of institutional cooperation was not smooth, and there was a period of stagnation. This was because of changes in external intervention and prominent internal institutional tensions, which made regional countries oscillate between institutional cooperation and unilateral actions. The risk of another crisis was mounting and it erupted after 2011. Facing the complex regional situation, China and ASEAN countries adjusted their institutional strategies in a timely manner. In 2014, China proposed the "dual track" approach and vigorously promoted practical maritime cooperation within the framework of the DOC, strengthening the capacity of the DOC implementation mechanism in terms of strategy, functions, and scope of issues. Although the crisis escalated during this period, the institutionalization of the implementation mechanism of the DOC was also advancing rapidly, and the regional turmoil caused by the South China Sea arbitration case was stably controlled. After 2017, the COC negotiation entered a substantive stage and made positive progress. However, the uncertainty of the security situation in the South China Sea under the influence of the epidemic and the competition between major powers, the institutional choices of China and ASEAN countries, and the institutional resilience of the implementation mechanism of the DOC has formed a new test.

The summary above has two implications for shaping the regional order in the future. First, crises in the South China Sea are not uncommon. The key to upholding lasting peace in the South China Sea is not to eliminate the crisis completely but to make good use of the existing institutional framework to enhance the dynamic perception of the security situation in the South China Sea, and to improve the capability of crisis response and crisis prevention. The implementation mechanism of the DOC should actively play this role. Second, although the epidemic and major power competition have made the security situation in the South China Sea more complicated, the prospect of institutional cooperation in the DOC is still mainly in the hands of China and ASEAN countries. History has proved that the institutional strategies of China and ASEAN countries and the institutional resilience of the implementation mechanism of the DOC have played a more critical role in crises. China should firmly follow the path of rule-based governance in the South China Sea, ensure security with the COC, and promote development through cooperation; ASEAN countries should also strengthen communication and coordination with China, maintain their normative status in regional security, and jointly promote the South China Sea to become a sea of peace, friendship, and cooperation.

Chapter 6

Roads toward Sustainable Peace through the Declaration on the Conduct of Parties in the South China Sea

Pou Sothirak

*The Cambodian Center for Regional Studies,
Phnom Penh, Cambodia
pousothirak@gmail.com*

Abstract

Achieving sustainable peace in the South China Sea requires both the Association of Southeast Asian Nations (ASEAN) and China to overcome tensions created over the issues of sovereignty and maritime claims in the South China Sea among all claimant states which have been considered the most complex regional flashpoint. Failure to prevent tensions and without effective ways to restrain the disputes in the South China Sea, hard-earned peace in this region can erode and conflict is becoming eminent. In this regard, ASEAN and China have a collective duty to collaborate to promote a friendly, peaceful, and harmonious environment in the South China Sea and to enhance regional stability, economic growth, and prosperity in order to ensure that the South China Sea is indeed a sea of peace and stability. Recognizing these challenges, ASEAN and China have made strenuous efforts overtime to prevent the escalation of tensions from brewing up into conflict including adopting the Declaration on the Conduct of Parties in the South China Sea (DOC) in 2002, and working together, despite slow progress, toward the conclusion of the Code of Conduct in the South China Sea (COC). This chapter will reflect, after 20 years of DOC, on the effort made by ASEAN and China in developing the DOC and COC while assessing their merits and discussing their deficits. The chapter will then highlight priorities for an effective implementation of the DOC before concluding with a set of considerations for ASEAN and China to work together to address their differences to conclude the COC negotiations, so as to ensure sustainable peace in the South China Sea.

Keywords: ASEAN, China, South China Sea, Declaration of the Conduct of Parties in the South China Sea (DOC), Code of Conduct in the South China Sea (COC), Sustainable Peace

I. Introduction

Achieving sustainable peace in the South China Sea requires both the Association of Southeast Asian Nations (ASEAN) and China to overcome tensions created over the issues of sovereignty and maritime claims among all claimant states which have been considered as the most complex regional flashpoint in the region. In this regard, ASEAN and China have a collective duty to collaborate to promote a friendly, peaceful, and harmonious environment in the South China Sea and to enhance regional stability, economic growth, and prosperity in order to ensure that the South China Sea is indeed a sea of peace and stability.

Recognizing these challenges, ASEAN and China have made strenuous efforts over time to prevent the escalation of tensions from brewing up into conflict. In so doing, they pin their extended energies to work on developing an acceptable regional Code of Conduct in the South China Sea (COC) in the hope that these codes can guide them to manage and improve the situation to keep the South China Sea free from pressure and tension.

ASEAN and China have been investing several years in drafting the Guidelines for the Implementation of the Declaration on the Conduct of Parties in the South China Sea (DOC)[1] and have endeavored to fulfill their obligation to work toward a binding code of conduct. Paragraph 10 of the DOC reads: "The Parties concerned reaffirm that the adoption of a code of conduct in the South China Sea would further promote peace and stability in the region and agree to work, on the basis of consensus, towards the eventual attainment of this objective."

Working on the basis of consultation and consensus to realize these codes have never been easy or efficient. After two decades, the implementation of the DOC is still a work in progress and the binding COC is still in drafting mode, working itself through a rigid negotiation process between ASEAN and China, as divergences remain.

As 2022 marks the 20th anniversary of the signing of the DOC, it is important to reflect on the effort made by ASEAN and China in developing the DOC and COC while assessing their merits and discussing their deficits. This chapter will then highlight priorities for an effective implementation of the DOC before concluding with a set of considerations for ASEAN and China to work together to address their differences to conclude the COC negotiations, so as to ensure sustainable peace in the South China Sea.

II. The Development of the DOC

Since 2002, ASEAN and China have reached an agreement on the Terms of Reference of the ASEAN–China Joint Working Group (JWG) on the Implementation of the Declaration on the Conduct of

---

[1] Association of Southeast Asian Nations, "Declaration on the Conduct of Parties in the South China Sea," May 14, 2012, https://asean.org/declaration-on-the-conduct-of-parties-in-the-south-china-sea-2/.

Parties in the South China Sea (DOC). ASEAN and China have also adopted the Guidelines to Implement the DOC in 2011. The ASEAN–China JWG was formed and has held many meetings to date. Progress has been recorded in general terms on how to implement the DOC, and initial consultations on a Code of Conduct (COC) have also commenced.

In December 2004, the ASEAN–China Senior Officials' Meeting (SOM) on the implementation of the DOC agreed to establish the ASEAN–China Joint Working Group on the Implementation of the DOC (ASEAN–China JWG). The Terms of Reference of "The ASEAN–China JWG" stipulated that the JWG shall meet regularly at least twice a year and submit a report and recommendations to the ASEAN–China SOM at the end of each meeting.[2]

ASEAN and China adopted the Guidelines for the Implementation of the DOC in 2011 which stated that the "progress of the implementation of the agreed activities and projects under the DOC shall be reported annually to the ASEAN–China Ministerial Meeting (PMC)" and the JWG began to adopt annual work plans to explore various activities of mutual interest such as confidence building projects on marine environmental protection, marine scientific research, search and rescue, and combating transnational crime.

In May 2012, ASEAN and China adopted the Terms of Reference of the ASEAN–China JWG on the Implementation of the DOC[3] with a primary objective to study and recommend measures to translate the provisions of the DOC into concrete cooperative activities that will enhance mutual understanding and trust.

During mid-September 2013, the 9th ASEAN–China JWG met in Suzhou, Jiangsu province, China during which time China agreed to begin consultations with ASEAN on COC. China's Foreign

---

[2] "Terms of Reference on the ASEAN–China Joint Working Group on the Implementation of the Declaration on the Conduct of Parties in the South China Sea," https://asean.org/terms-of-reference-of-the-asean-china-joint-working-group-on-the-implementation-of-the-declaration-on-the-conduct-of-parties-in-the-south-china-sea/.

[3] *Ibid.*

Ministry reportedly mentioned that both sides agreed to follow the "step by step and to reach consensus through consultation" and to continue to steadily push forward the COC process through the full and effective implementation of the DOC.[4]

The 12th ASEAN–China JWG on the DOC met in Thailand in late October 2014. At the 17th ASEAN–China Summit held in Nay Pyi Taw, Myanmar on November 13, 2014, the 8th ASEAN–China SOM on the DOC, and the 12th JWG welcomed the positive outcome of the Implementation of the DOC in Bangkok, Thailand, from October 26 to 29, 2014 and continued to maintain the momentum of regular official consultations to work toward the early conclusion of the COC.[5] Meanwhile, then Chinese Premier Li Keqiang in remarks at the East Asia Summit in Nay Pyi Taw noted that with respect to the COC an "early harvest has been achieved."[6]

According to the Chairman's Statement at the 26th ASEAN Summit in Malaysia on April 27, 2015, ASEAN leaders shared serious concerns, expressed by some leaders, on the land reclamation being undertaken in the South China Sea. They tasked their Foreign Ministers to urgently address this matter constructively including under the various ASEAN frameworks such as ASEAN–China relations, as well as the principles of peaceful co-existence. They also reaffirmed the importance of maintaining peace, stability, security, and freedom of navigation in and overflight over the South China Sea, ensured the full and effective implementation of the DOC in its

---

[4]Ministry of Foreign Affairs of the People's Republic of China, "The Sixth Senior Officials Meeting and the Ninth Joint Working Group Meeting on the Implementation of the 'Declaration on Conduct of Parties in the South China Sea,' Suzhou, China," September 15, 2013, http://www.fmprc.gov.cn/mfa_eng/zxxx_662805/t1079289.shtml.
[5]Ministry of Foreign Affairs of the People's Republic of China, "Chairman's Statement of the 17th ASEAN–China Summit," November 13, 2014, http://www.fmprc.gov.cn/mfa_eng/zxxx_662805/t1215668.shtml.
[6]Ministry of Foreign Affairs, People's Republic of China, "Li Keqiang Expounds on China's Principled Position on South China Sea in East Asia Summit," November 13, 2014, http://www.fmprc.gov.cn/mfa_eng/topics_665678/lkqzlcxdyhzldrxlhybdmdjxzsfw/t1211375.shtml.

entirety, refrained from resorting to threat or use of force, and called on all parties to resolve their differences and disputes through peaceful means, in accordance with international law, including the 1982 United Nations Convention on the Law of the Sea (UNCLOS).[7]

III. The Development of the COC

ASEAN issued its first statement on the South China Sea disputes in 1992 and endorsed the idea of a COC in 1996.[8] Although ASEAN and China subscribe to the idea that any disputes involving sovereignty over features, such as islands and rocks in the South China Sea, can only be solved through direct negotiations between the claimant parties; however, ASEAN maintains that any disagreements among the claimants must not resort to the use of force or the threat of force to support any individual claim in the absence of the resolution of sovereignty disputes. As such, since 2002, ASEAN has sought to obtain China's consent to a binding COC.[9]

China and ASEAN have been holding talks for years to achieve the COC as a regional framework that establishes rules and standards and contains a set of regional norms in the South China Sea to avoid conflicts in the disputed waters. The Single Draft for the COC was adopted at the 51st ASEAN–China Foreign Ministers in Singapore on August 2, 2018[10] at which time Singapore Foreign Minister Vivian

---

[7]Chairman's Statement of the 26th ASEAN Summit, "Our People, Our Community, Our Vision," April 27, 2015, https://asean.org/wp-content/uploads/2012/05/26th-Chairman-Statement-of-the-26th-ASEAN-Summit.pdf.

[8]Asia Maritime Transparency Initiative, "A Blueprint for a South China Sea Code of Conduct," October 11, 2018, https://amti.csis.org/blueprint-for-south-china-sea-code-of-conduct/.

[9]Carlyle A. Thayer, "ASEAN, China and the Code of Conduct in the South China Sea," *The SAIS Review of International Affairs* 33(2) (2013): 75–84.

[10]Joint Communiqué of the 51st ASEAN Foreign Ministers' Meeting, Singapore, August 2, 2018, https://asean.org/wp-content/uploads/2018/08/51st-AMM-Joint-Communique-Final.pdf.

Balakrishnan called it a milestone and Chinese Foreign Minister Wang Yi hailed this as a "breakthrough" for the COC negotiation.[11]

The adoption of the Single Draft of the COC verified that progress has been made and that China and ASEAN countries have been capable of maintaining peace and stability in the South China Sea, in addition to agreeing on regional rules followed by all parties through negotiations. The draft text has served as the basis of future COC negotiations ever since.

In July 2019, the first reading of the COC Single Draft Negotiating Text was reached ahead of schedule.[12] The Draft is intended to serve as the basis for the adoption of COC. The Parties to the Draft acknowledge that the COC does not address nor affect the Parties' position on legal questions relating to the settlement of disputes, maritime boundaries, or the permissible maritime entitlements of the Parties under international law of the sea, enshrined in the 1982 UNCLOS. Regional experts, however, pointed out that the progress on drafting and adopting the COC was likely to be tardy and unlikely to be finalized within the stipulated time frame of 2021.[13]

Due to the outbreak of the COVID-19 pandemic, formal consultation has stalled since the completion of the first reading. At the 19th SOM on the Implementation of the DOC in the South China Sea held in Chongqing, China, on June 7, 2022, a consensus on the negotiation of the COC was reached and both sides agreed to resume as soon as possible the second reading of the Single Draft COC Negotiating Text and strive for the early conclusion of COC

---

[11]"ASEAN, China debuts COC 'single draft'," *The Jakarta Post*, https://www.thejakartapost.com/seasia/2018/08/02/asean-china-debuts-coc-single-draft.html.

[12]Statement of the Embassy of the People's Republic of China in the Kingdom of Thailand, "The First Reading of the Single Draft Negotiating Text of the Code of Conduct (COC) in the South China Sea Completed Ahead of the Schedule," https://www.mfa.gov.cn/ce/ceth//eng/zgyw/t1685674.htm.

[13]"South China Sea Code of Conduct," *The Diplomat*, August 3, 2018, https://thediplomat.com/2018/08/a-closer-look-at-the-asean-china-single-draft-south-china-sea-code-of-conduct/.

negotiations.[14] On July 1, 2022, the 26th ASEAN–China Senior Officials' Consultation was held virtually, during which time the Vietnamese Deputy Minister of Foreign Affairs and head of the SOM Vietnam said that ASEAN would continue cooperating with China to build the COC in accordance with international law, including the 1982 UNCLOS.[15]

Even during the difficult time of the pandemic, ASEAN and China remained committed to the full and effective implementation of the DOC and to sustaining the COC process in a flexible and pragmatic manner when they met and exchanged views during the 19th SOM on the Implementation of the DOC held in Chongqing, China on June 19, 2021.[16]

China promised to work with ASEAN countries on the adoption of a consensus-based COC in the South China Sea to maintain peace, cooperation, security, and stability in the region. This is why at the present time the situation in the South China Sea remains relatively stable, and there has never been any problem with the freedom of navigation and overflight. Accordingly, State Councilor and the then Chinese Foreign Minister Wang Yi has recently mentioned that China–ASEAN security cooperation has been making steady progress, with the deepening of military and security exchanges and productive cooperation has been carried out in non-traditional security areas such as counter-terrorism, climate response, cybersecurity, combating transnational crime, and disaster preparedness and reduction. With the

---

[14] Ministry of Foreign Affairs of the People's Republic of China, "The 19th Senior Officials' Meeting on the Implementation of the Declaration on the Conduct of Parties in the South China Sea held in Chongqing," June 7, 2021, https://www.fmprc.gov.cn/eng/wjbxw/202106/t20210608_9134301.html.

[15] "China Agrees to Resume Negotiations on COC in South China Sea," *Hanoi Times*, July 2, 2022, https://m.hanoitimes.vn/china-agrees-to-resume-negotiations-for-coc-in-south-china-sea-313001.html.

[16] Ministry of Foreign Affairs of the People's Republic of China, "The 19th Senior Officials' Meeting on the Implementation of the Declaration on the Conduct of Parties in the South China Sea held in Chongqing," June 7, 2021, https://www.fmprc.gov.cn/eng/wjbxw/202106/t20210608_9134301.html.

full implementation of the DOC in sight and positive progress in the consultation of the COC, differences and disputes are being effectively managed by both ASEAN and China.[17]

IV. The Merits of the DOC

The adoption of the DOC in Phnom Penh, Cambodia in 2002, has been known to be the first political document among China and ASEAN member states to address the South China Sea issue at the regional level, strengthening collective efforts in seeking common ground, reserving differences, and engaging in dialogue and consultation in order to put aside disputes. The signing of the DOC was a major step in creating a mechanism for dealing with the South China Sea issue. It serves to effectively enhance political mutual trust among regional countries and lay a solid foundation for the further development and upgrading of the China–ASEAN relations.[18]

The DOC, signed by China and the members of ASEAN reaffirms freedom of navigation and overflight, peaceful settlement of disputes, and self-restraint in the conduct of activities in the South China Sea. During a virtual workshop on the commemoration of the 20th Anniversary of the DOC in July 2022, Chinese Foreign Minister Wang Yi declared that the DOC has been a framework enabling China and ASEAN to consolidate political mutual trust and build vibrant relations, and by acting in compliance with the DOC over the past two decades, China and ASEAN have jointly maintained peace

---

[17]Ministry of Foreign Affairs of the People's Republic of China, "Upholding Peace, Development, Independence and Inclusiveness and Renewing the Firm Commitment to Open Regionalism," Speech by State Councilor and Foreign Minister Wang Yi at the ASEAN Secretariat, July 11, 2022. https://www.fmprc.gov.cn/mfa_eng/wjb_663304/wjbz_663308/2461_663310/202207/t20220712_10718689.html.

[18]Zong Haihe, "DOC: The Cornerstone for South China Sea Peace and Stability," *Global Times*, June 16, 2022, https://www.globaltimes.cn/page/202206/1268287.shtml.

and stability as well as ensured freedom and safety of navigation in the South China Sea.[19]

With the DOC, China and ASEAN have been able to maintain peace and stability in the region and facilitate communication and negotiations between the two sides. The DOC is the embodiment of political goodwill between ASEAN member states and China. In particular, the DOC has served as a platform for all claimant states to communicate and exchange views. It has also served as a tool to impose moral constraints on concerned parties and provided a reference point when tensions between the claimant states arose.[20] Furthermore, the DOC has contributed to the promotion of political confidence, cooperative activities, peaceful settlement of disputes, friendly negotiation and consultation, and maritime cooperation.[21]

A Chinese scholar recognized that the DOC has contributed to promoting the consideration of key principles of international law when it comes to peaceful settlement of disputes in the South China Sea because the document represents "the collective commitment of China and ASEAN Member States to promote peace, stability and mutual trust, as well as peaceful settlement of disputes in the South China Sea in accordance with the universally recognized principles of international law."[22]

Another Chinese scholar said that the purpose of the DOC is to promote confidence-building measures, engage in practical maritime

---

[19] Ministry of Foreign Affairs of the People's Republic of China, "Carrying Forward the DOC Spirit and Forging Regional Consensus to Jointly Build a Sea of Peace, Friendship and Cooperation," Remarks by State Councilor and Foreign Minister Wang Yi at the Opening Ceremony of the Workshop on Commemoration of the 20th Anniversary of the DOC, July 25, 2022, https://www.fmprc.gov.cn/mfa_eng/wjb_663304/wjbz_663308/2461_663310/202207/t20220725_10727703.html.

[20] Mingjiang Li, "Managing Security in the South China Sea: From DOC to COC," *Kyoto Review of Southeast Asia*, Issue 15, March 2014, https://kyotoreview.org/issue-15/managing-security-in-the-south-china-sea-from-doc-to-coc/.

[21] Li Jianwei, "The Important Role of the DOC on Regional Peace and Stability," *China Daily*, July 2, 2022, https://www.chinadaily.com.cn/a/202207/26/WS62dfad45a310fd2b29e6e7f6.html.

[22] *Ibid.*

cooperation, and set the stage for the discussion and conclusion of a formal and binding COC.[23]

Twenty years have passed since the signing of DOC. The DOC is the first political document regarding the South China Sea issue and a milestone document demonstrating the political will between ASEAN and China to promote a peaceful, friendly, and harmonious environment in the South China Sea for the enhancement of stability, economic growth, and prosperity in the region.

The DOC has been developed to instill the basic principles and common norms for all parties to handle the South China Sea issue. Since its signing in Phnom Penh, Cambodia in 2002, all signatories have aspired to abide by the stipulation of the DOC and worked together to maintain peace and stability as well as freedom and safety of navigation in the South China Sea, in addition to committing to the full and effective implementation of the DOC in its entirety.

According to Professor Carl Thayer, the DOC calls for cooperation in five areas: marine environmental protection; marine scientific research; safety of navigation and communication at sea; search and rescue operations; and combating transnational crime, including but not limited to trafficking in illicit drugs, piracy and armed robbery at sea, and illegal traffic in arms.[24] Therefore, to gain a greater appreciation of what the DOC has been able to accomplish for ASEAN and China, more serious research should be done to assess whether there have been concrete results yielded from these five areas of cooperation up until the present day.

V. The Deficits of the DOC

Notwithstanding the acknowledgment that the DOC has contributed by and large to the maintenance of the overall stability and forged

---

[23] *Ibid.*
[24] Carlyle A. Thayer, "ASEAN and China Set to Agree on Single Draft South China Sea Code of Conduct," *The Diplomat*, July 20, 2018, https://thediplomat.com/2018/07/asean-and-china-set-to-agree-on-single-draft-south-china-sea-code-of-conduct/.

several cases of cooperation in the South China Sea, as shown by the tripartite joint seismic study among China, Vietnam, and the Philippines from 2005 to 2008, there are observers who claim that the DOC has not been able to fulfill all its obligations because so far not a single claimant state has strictly abided by the DOC. In addition, there have been too few bilateral or multilateral cooperative projects that took place in the South China Sea, and the COC process has been too slow with less-than-expected results.[25]

Despite 20 years of its existence, the DOC has not fully fulfilled its mission of building greater trust between the claimant states and preventing the disputes in the South China Sea from escalating, making it known as "troubled waters."[26] The text in the DOC itself provided little information on the implementation of confidence-building measures and other forms of cooperation in the South China Sea, and it lacked the scope, specific modalities, and policy measures to push for mutual cooperation among the claimants.

Over the years, maritime disputes have flared up repeatedly as the claimants violate the DOC's Article 5 by not restraining their activities that would complicate or escalate disputes. The claimants have been asserting a combination of sovereignty, resource-related sovereign rights, and jurisdictional claims to the maritime areas located in the South China Sea to build military facilities on its occupied islands and reefs, and reclaim land to allow further construction.

The aforementioned assertion leads to a fundamental shortcoming of the DOC which instills no legal power to restrain any claimant party's behavior in the South China Sea. The DOC also lacks mechanisms to monitor and evaluate all the 10 articles stipulated in the document, let alone any compliance mechanism to enforce what had been stipulated, even with the DOC implementation guidelines

---

[25]Hendra Manurung, "South China Sea Territorial Dispute: A Lesson for Association of Southeast Asia Nations (ASEAN)," SSRN, August 5, 2017, https://papers.ssrn.com/sol3/papers.cfm?abstract_id=3026333.

[26]Nien-Tsu Alfred Hu, "South China Sea: Troubled Waters or a Sea of Opportunity?," *Ocean Development and International Laws* 41(3) (2010), https://doi.org/10.1080/00908320.2010.499312.

concluded at the China–ASEAN Foreign Ministers' Meeting in July 2011.[27]

After 20 years and with many joint statements regarding the progress of their negotiations, China and ASEAN are still unable to finalize the legally binding document of the COC.[28]

Perhaps of all the weakness of the DOC, it is the slow progress on the negotiations of the COC in the South China Sea that stands in the way for China and ASEAN to claim their stride with respect. ASEAN and China are still struggling to bridge their differences to bring the long-awaited code of conduct to an acceptable conclusion.

The main challenge to the inactivity of the COC negotiations is the fact that ASEAN claimant states want to ensure regional peace and security by upholding the international law and multilateralism, while China wishes to resolve the disputes through bilateral mechanisms with parties most directly involved to minimize the participation of other extra-regional parties in the dispute settlement.[29]

Despite the challenges, both parties have made some progress in the COC negotiations as evidenced by the approval of a draft COC framework in 2017, a Single Draft Negotiating Text in 2018, and the First Reading and Second Reading of the Single Draft Negotiating Text in 2019.[30] Moreover, at the conclusion of the 33rd ASEAN Summit in November 2018, an expression of keen interest in specifying a three-year time frame to conclude an effective COC in the South China Sea was revealed between ASEAN and China, following

---

[27] *Ibid.*

[28] Viet Hoang, "The Code of Conduct for the South China Sea: A Long and Bumpy Road," *The Diplomat*, September 20, 2020, https://thediplomat.com/2020/09/the-code-of-conduct-for-the-south-china-sea-a-long-and-bumpy-road/.

[29] Aristyo Rizka Darmawan, "The US–ASEAN Summit and the South China Sea Code of Conduct," *Asia and the Pacific Policy Society*, June 8, 2022, https://www.policyforum.net/the-us-asean-summit-and-the-south-china-sea-code-of-conduct/.

[30] Ian Storey, "As ASEAN and China Discuss a Code of Conduct for the South China Sea, America Looks on Sceptically," *ISEAS Yusuf Ishak Institute*, October 24, 2019, https://www.iseas.edu.sg/media/commentaries/as-asean-and-china-discuss-a-code-of-conduct-for-the-south-china-sea-america-looks-on-sceptically-by-ian-storey/.

a proposition from China during then Chinese Premier Li Keqiang's 44th Singapore Lecture on November 13 of that year.[31]

VI. Considerations for a Full and Effective Implementation of the DOC

For the DOC to be able to serve as the beacon of stability in stabilizing the situation in the South China Sea and managing differences over time, it must be fully implemented. This means that the political expression in the DOC made 20 years ago must prevail to instill deeper mutual trust, forge greater cooperation in the maritime domain, and ensure that the adoption of the COC must be forthcoming.

(i) *Instill Deeper Mutual Trust*

Hegemonic perceptions of China in the South China Sea remain a lingering concern among some ASEAN member states; likewise, the suspicion by China toward some countries in ASEAN for allowing or even facilitating the involvement of external powers, namely the United States, in the South China Sea are intrinsic factors creating deep mutual distrust between the two sides.[32]

It is within this situation that China and ASEAN must focus their utmost attention on building mutual confidence, chasing away lingering pessimism, and developing friendly and cooperative behavior among and between them while taking serious steps to implement the DOC in its entirety. This is the first priority that must be done to overcome the constraints that the DOC lacks legal power to restrain

---

[31]Tommy Chai, "ASEAN–China Code of Conduct to Conclude in Three Years?," *Foreign Brief*, November 16, 2018, https://foreignbrief.com/asia-pacific/southeast-asia/asean-china-code-of-conduct-to-conclude-in-three-years/.

[32]Nguyen Hung Son, "Three Priority Measures in Maintaining Peace and Stability in the South China Sea," *Kyoto Reviews of Southeast Asia*, March 2014, https://kyotoreview.org/issue-15/three-priority-mesures-in-maintaining-peace-and-stability-in-the-south-china-sea/.

any claimant state's behavior in the pursuit of any unfounded claim in the South China Sea and has no effective mechanisms to monitor, let alone enforce, compliance with international law.

To promote mutual trust in the South China Sea, ASEAN and China should be encouraged to engage in frank discussion and open dialogue to address common security challenges, especially maritime issues. Both sides must avoid acts of provocation which can lead to miscalculation among parties concerned for peace, security, and stability in the South China Sea. They must improve all communication channels and provide better clarification on issues related to individual countries' historical interpretations so as to minimize domestic patriotic sentiment and allow diplomacy to prevail over the narrow nationalistic interest.

As the text of the DOC provides no clear measures on the specific implementation to build confidence, ASEAN and China should proceed with the spirit of trust and strengthened confidence, committing to working together at the comfort level by the parties involved in order to fully implement the DOC and achieve consensus in the formulation of the COC as soon as possible so as to ascertain the process of building a sound legal regime to help regulate crisis and manage tension in the South China Sea effectively.

(ii) *Forge Greater Cooperation in the Maritime Domain*

To achieve the goal of making the South China Sea a "sea of peace, stability, security, friendship, and prosperity," more intense cooperation between China and ASEAN in the maritime domain must be promoted within the confinement of greater trust and proper management of the various functional cooperation.

China's concept of setting aside sovereignty disputes for joint exploration of Nansha Islands[33] emanated from former Chinese leader Deng Xiaoping on how to solve maritime disputes with the

---

[33]Ellen T. Tordesillas, "China's Concept of Setting Aside Sovereignty Dispute for Joint Exploration of Spratlys," August 1, 2017, https://verafiles.org/articles/chinas-concept-setting-side-sovereignty-dispute-joint-explor.

idea of *"setting aside dispute and pursuing joint development"* should be applied to forge deeper engagement between China and ASEAN in the maritime cooperation. However, for joint development, or other forms of functional cooperation to take center stage in the maritime domain, there must be an enhanced political will from the heads of State/Government of the countries that are bordering the South China Sea to agree on cooperative joint projects and promote maritime cooperation in such areas as marine environmental protection, marine scientific research, safe maritime navigation, maritime search and rescue, anti-transnational crime operations, or joint oil and gas exploration.[34]

Over the years, we have observed keen interest from China in the pursuit of maritime cooperation. After the adoption of the DOC in 2002, the Chinese leaders expressed their desire to make the South China Sea a "sea of peace, friendship and cooperation," and in March 2005, representatives from national oil companies of China, the Philippines, and Vietnam signed a Tripartite Agreement for Joint Marine Seismic Undertaking in the Agreement Area in the South China Sea in Manila. Continued effort made by China with regard to maritime cooperation has continued, for example, during the ASEAN Regional Forum's Foreign Ministers' Meeting, then Chinese Foreign Minister Yang Jiechi stated that "China and ASEAN countries should make full use of this opportunity to promote practical cooperation in the South China Sea and work together to turn the South China Sea into a sea of peace, friendship and cooperation."[35]

For ASEAN, on the other hand, Indonesia is probably the leader in maritime cooperation which has been eager to develop confidence

---

[34] Yann-huei Song, "Maritime Cooperation in the South China Sea: Three Possible Ways to Help Achieve the Goal of Making the SCS a "Sea of Peace, Friendship and Cooperation," Institute of European & American Studies, November 6, 2020, http://www.csarc.org.cn/yann-huei-song-maritime-cooperation-in-the-south-china-sea-three-possible-ways-to-help-achieve-the-goal-of-making-the-scs-a-sea-of-peace-friendship-and-cooperation/.

[35] Mingjiang Li, "Managing Security in the South China Sea: From DOC to COC," *Kyoto Review of Southeast Asia*, Issue 15, March 2014, https://kyotoreview.org/issue-15/managing-security-in-the-south-china-sea-from-doc-to-coc/.

building and strengthen cooperation among ASEAN member countries in the maritime domain to tackle a range of non-traditional security issues such as illegal fishing, transnational crimes, maritime environment, and fisheries, just to name a few. Since 1990, Indonesia has initiated a peaceful cooperative informal workshop on managing potential conflicts in the South China Sea, known as the SCS Workshop. This initiative is considered one of the important Confidence-Building Measures that is useful to promote maritime cooperation in the South China Sea and help manage potential conflicts and maintain stability and peace in the South China Sea.[36] Therefore, Indonesia should be encouraged to continue the SCS Workshop by stimulating greater interest among all other ASEAN member states toward any form of maritime functional cooperation and to strengthen its effectiveness, as well as to find more innovative ways to support or cover the cost of convening the SCS Workshop.

Even with such a leading role by China in promoting maritime cooperation, for example, by launching the ASEAN–China Maritime Cooperation Fund and establishing the China–Southeast Asia Research Centre for the South China Sea and so on, these initiatives have made little progress due mainly to the lack of trust among regional countries about China's motives, which in turn prevents cooperation to come forward and common interest to prevail. For functional cooperation to work properly in the maritime domain, China must reaffirm its commitment to properly manage differences with all countries who share the South China Sea and to overcome any hurdle that causes negative perceptions of China among some ASEAN countries. Attention should be paid to promoting political trust, upholding the spirit of fairness, exploiting maritime resources through orderly cooperation based on the principles of reasonableness, and together tackling other forms of common concern such as carrying out search, rescue, and disaster prevention at sea in order to make the South China Sea a sea of peace, friendship, and cooperation.[37]

---

[36] *Ibid.*
[37] Sam Bateman, "Building Cooperation for Managing the South China Sea without Strategic Trust," *Asia & the Pacific Policy Studies* 4(2) (2017): 251–259.

VII. Consideration for the COC Process

In September 2013, ASEAN and China started the "consultation" process on the COC by holding the first Senior Official Meeting on the COC in Suzhou, China[38] and five years later, the Single Draft for COC was reached in 2018. It has been nine years now since the process of COC started and despite constant reassurance by both ASEAN and China, the COC negotiation process remains excruciatingly slow and difficult to conclude.

Perhaps from a philosophical point of view, this tardiness has to do with the non-conversion of ASEAN and China's geostrategic interests on the South China Sea, or perhaps ASEAN and China's legal perspectives on the South China Sea cannot be made compatible. However, the slowness of the COC tends to lie in a lack of collective wisdom that can enforce mutual understanding between the two sides to agree on the format and substance of the COC that can serve as an honest jury to settle the differences among stakeholders in the South China Sea without prejudice and one-sidedness.

Emotion aside, the slow process can be attributed to how China intends to proceed with the negotiation. In August 2013, Chinese Foreign Minister Wang Yi proposed four views on the COC process. First, it is unreasonable to expect a quick fix. Second, the process should observe maximum consensus and respect the comfort level of each claimant party. Third, external interferences should be eliminated. Fourth, negotiations should proceed in a step-by-step manner with the top priority being to implement the DOC, especially promoting maritime cooperation and the fact that the COC process should go hand in hand with the implementation of the DOC.[39]

---

[38] Mingjiang Li, "Managing Security in the South China Sea: From DOC to COC," *Kyoto Review of Southeast Asia*, Issue 15, March 2014, https://kyotoreview.org/issue-15/managing-security-in-the-south-china-sea-from-doc-to-coc/.

[39] Carlyle A. Thayer, "New Commitment to a Code of Conduct in the South China Sea?" *National Bureau of Asian Research* 9 (2013), https://www.nbr.org/publication/new-commitment-to-a-code-of-conduct-in-the-south-china-sea/.

From this view, all parties agreed to start the COC process on the principles of observing consensus and adopting a gradual approach. For sure, the COC process will be significantly slow and laborious, contrary to the expectations of many regional states and external powers such as the United States.

Technically speaking, there are remaining challenges for a binding and credible COC which must be overcome by both ASEAN and China. These challenges include: the geographical scope has not been clear and agreed upon; the COC's legal status remains undefined; there is an absence of practical arrangement for duty to cooperate in maritime cooperation; the applicability of international norms for the COC remains doubtful; and the divergent view on the role of third parties remains unsettled.[40]

Moving forward in the negotiation process to wrap-up the COC, the following considerations should be taken into account:

- In drafting the COC, ASEAN and China should be mindful of the DOC's limitations and ensure that the COC squarely addresses them and avoid, whenever possible, the ambiguity in language that is quite common in the DOC.
- Spell out clearly dispute settlement mechanisms based on peaceful means and suggest a practical management regime to settle disagreements related to jurisdiction over water, seabed, and airspace without resorting to the threat or use of force, as well as to exercise self-restraint and pay due regard to the rights of other parties in the conduct of their legal activities in the South China Sea.
- The COC should contain a practical mechanism to guarantee compliance and enforcement that are needed to ensure the binding aspect of the code and the adherence to international law.
- The COC needs to anticipate the evolving developments on the ground that might outpace the drafting process of the code,

---

[40]Carlyle A. Thayer, "A Closer Look at the ASEAN-China Single Draft South China Sea Code of Conduct," *The Diplomat*, August 3, 2018, https://thediplomat.com/2018/08/a-closer-look-at-the-asean-china-single-draft-south-china-sea-code-of-conduct/.

thereby possibly rendering it irrelevant. Therefore, the COC should not be developed on the basis of compromising the territorial and maritime interests of any claimant states, nor at the expense of the sanctity of international law.
- Lastly, the COC should not only contain overarching rules and principles but also have clear-cut procedural guidelines that can help parties trapped in any situation that might lead to misunderstanding or tension to resort to the de-escalation of potentially eruptive disputes between and among them.

It is also important to keep in mind that the COC, as we all envisage, will not and cannot settle the overlapping claims of sovereignty and jurisdiction in the South China Sea. The claimants directly concerned will have to settle their disputes by themselves, or by going to the International Court of Justice.

The region still needs China that would support ASEAN to play a constructive role in the South China Sea disputes by managing conflicting interests honestly and by following the spirit of the DOC, exploring rules-based governance of the South China Sea, and actively advancing the consultations on the COC in the South China Sea with the spirit of mutual trust and understanding.

VIII. Conclusion

China and ASEAN signed the DOC in 2002 in Phnom Penh, Cambodia. The COC is known to be a milestone document that embodies the collective commitment of ASEAN member states and China to promote peace, stability, and mutual trust in the South China Sea.

There has been a long-standing ASEAN position in seeking to play a moderating role in managing the South China Sea disputes. During a visit to Beijing in September 2012, the Prime Minister of Singapore said, "The South China Sea is a major issue in the heart of ASEAN's own region. For ASEAN not to address it would severely damage its credibility." He also added that "ASEAN must not take sides on the various claims but it has to take and state a position which is neutral, forward-looking, and encourage the peaceful resolution of the issue."[41]

The DOC stipulates that all signatory states should resolve disputes through peaceful means and refrain from the conduct of activities that would escalate tensions. The DOC, which is not binding, serves as a guiding template for the COC, which is supposed to be a binding one. There is a recognition that moving from DOC to COC is critically important for the region to contain and defuse the current tensions in the South China Sea. At the same time, there is an acceptance that ASEAN is one of the key instruments to help resolve disputes over the South China Sea. However, for the COC to be more meaningful, the inadequacies of the DOC and factors that have delayed its full implementation must be overcome.[42]

The roads to sustainable peace for the South China Sea require the full implementation of the DOC which can truly play its role in safeguarding peace and stability in the South China Sea. All parties must strictly abide by the spirit of the DOC. Its duties should involve more than imposing moral constraints on relevant parties and transpire beyond collective efforts to maintain the overall stability in the South China Sea. It must be able to fulfill its three intended purposes: promoting confidence-building measures, engaging in practical maritime cooperation, and setting the stage for the discussion and conclusion of the formal and binding COC.

While the COC is not going to resolve the disputes, a legally binding COC with effective compliance and enforcement mechanisms can bring peace and reduce tensions in the region. However, the negotiation process is expected to be slow and arduous due to the complexity and difficulty in getting all parties to agree upon a set of rules-based governance that defines the legal status and the

---

[41] Prime Minister's Office of Singapore, "Speech by Prime Minister Lee Hsien Loong at Central Party School," September 6, 2012, https://www.pmo.gov.sg/Newsroom/speech-prime-minister-lee-hsien-loong-central-party-school-english-translation.

[42] Mingjiang Li, "Managing Security in the South China Sea: From DOC to COC," *Kyoto Review of Southeast Asia*, Issue 15, March 2014, https://kyotoreview.org/issue-15/managing-security-in-the-south-china-sea-from-doc-to-coc/.

applicability of international norms, with clarity over the geographical scope and with an effective dispute management procedure in place.

No doubt, sustainable peace in the South China Sea demands that ASEAN countries and China reaffirm their commitment enshrined in the DOC and ramp up their efforts in speeding up the COC negotiations.

© 2025 World Scientific Publishing Company
https://doi.org/10.1142/9789811296031_0007

Chapter

7

Provisional Arrangements under UNCLOS: A Comparative Analysis for the South China Sea Code of Conduct

Aristyo Rizka Darmawan

Faculty of Law Universitas, West Java, Indonesia
aristyodarmawan@ui.ac.id

Abstract

For many decades the South China Sea has been a significant security challenge in Southeast Asia. The complex dispute and the surrounding geopolitical tension have hampered a successful conflict settlement mechanism. Therefore, all parties must strive to maintain peace and security in this disputed area. In this regard, the Association of Southeast Asian Nations (ASEAN) and China established the Declaration on the Conduct of Parties in 2002 and negated the Code of Conduct (COC). The United Nations Convention on the Law of the Sea (UNCLOS) also considered creating a provisional arrangement in the disputed marine area. Therefore, this chapter aims to analyze the legal framework for cooperation in the South China Sea and the lessons from previous agreements in a disputed and undelimited maritime area. First, the chapter discusses how the COC fits the provisional arrangement regulated under the UNCLOS. It analyzes the similarities and differences for the COC to be considered the provisional agreement under UNCLOS. Second, the study also examines existing provisional arrangements as a lesson for the ASEAN–China COC. It explores the obligations of third parties not involved in the dispute. The analysis is hoped to provide recommendations for policymakers and COC negotiators.

Keywords: South China Sea dispute, COC, UNCLOS, Maritime boundaries negotiation, China-ASEAN relations

I. Introduction

Since the Declaration of Conduct (DOC) on the China Sea was established in 2002, the South China Sea has remained a major dangerous conflict in Asia. Although the declaration has not settled the dispute, it has helped establish common principles and trust between claimants.[1] This chapter aims to promote a peaceful, friendly, and harmonious environment to enhance stability, economic growth, and prosperity in the South China Sea. The declaration is more a principle than a guideline for all claimants.[2] Therefore, there should be a follow-up and detailed mechanism to implement the principles to achieve its goals. One follow-up after the DOC is the negotiation of the South China Sea Code of Conduct (COC). Although the negotiation is ongoing, the COC would regulate detailed conflict management in the disputed area.

Undelimited maritime boundaries and overlapping areas are important issues for neighboring countries. It raises conflict and tension regarding daily law enforcement, resource exploration, and exploitation. There are often standoffs between two neighboring law enforcement institutions. These institutions claim to enforce their national law in an area overlapping with its neighbors. Also, small

---

[1]Carlyle A. Thayer, "ASEAN, China and the code of conduct in the South China Sea," *The SAIS Review of International Affairs* 33 (2013): 75–84.
[2]Leszek Buszynski, "ASEAN, the declaration on conduct, and the South China Sea," *Contemporary Southeast Asia: A Journal of International and Strategic Affairs* 25 (2003): 343–362.

friction and standoff between law enforcement agencies sometimes escalate tension between neighboring states. Therefore, countries with maritime disputes should maintain their relationship to minimize conflicts.

The United Nations Convention on the Law of the Sea (UNCLOS) has some principles regarding the importance of maritime boundary delimitation.[3] The UNCLOS does not state the law enforcement in unresolved maritime boundaries. However, it regulates coastal states' obligations in the undelimited exclusive economic zone and continental shelf. It has introduced mechanisms to minimize tension in unresolved maritime boundaries.[4]

This chapter aims to explore how the international legal framework fits with the ongoing South China Sea COC negotiation. After the introduction, the second section discusses the obligation in unresolved maritime boundaries under UNCLOS. The section analyzes how UNCLOS obligates coastal states and the limitations enforced in an undelimited maritime area. Moreover, it discusses how the obligation under UNCLOS can fit with the ongoing negotiation of the COC. The third section explores and analyzes states' practices in implementing the obligations. It examines how several states govern their agreements in unresolved maritime boundaries. The conclusion presents the lesson from UNCLOS on provisional measures and state practices for the South China Sea COC negotiation.

II. Code of Conduct as Provisional Arrangement under UNCLOS

There are debates on the possibility of the ongoing South China Sea COC being a provisional agreement regulated under UNCLOS. In Articles 73(3) and 83(3), UNCLOS has regulated the obligation of

---

[3]David Anderson, "Rights and Obligations in Areas of Overlapping Maritime Claims," presented at the Center for International Law Roundtable Conference National University of Singapore, June 27–28, 2013, Singapore.
[4]British Institute of International and Comparative Law (BIICL), Report on the Obligations of States under Articles 74(3) and 83(3) of UNCLOS in respect of Undelimited Maritime Areas.

coastal states in undelimited contiguous and exclusive economic zones.[5] One of the articles states that:

"Pending an agreement on the delimitation of maritime boundaries, the States concerned, in a spirit of mutual understanding and cooperation, should make every effort to enter into interim arrangements which are practical and, during this transitional period, do not jeopardize or hinder the achievement of a final agreement."

The two articles do not give clear obligations for coastal states in undelimited maritime boundaries. They do not limit the coastal states' law enforcement in a disputed maritime area. The main obligation is to avoid escalations and create mutual trust and a provisional agreement.

The obligation under these articles is broad and could be implemented differently according to the need of each coastal state. An example is the issue of the agreement as to whether it is legally binding. The legal status of the provisional arrangement depends on the agreement between the two countries. When the provisional arrangement is an international agreement or a treaty, it is binding as law. A temporary arrangement stated less formally, such as a Memorandum of Understanding (MoU), is not binding as law for both parties. However, the binding nature is not determined by the arrangement's title but by the interpretation of the two countries. Even an informal document could contain binding commitments. The tribunal court may determine the regulatory document's legal status. In this case, it is interpreted objectively based on the wording and circumstances surrounding the conclusion indicating whether the party intended the instrument legally. The ongoing COC is still debated regarding its possibility to be a legally binding document depending on the parties' decision. Many Association of Southeast Asian Nations (ASEAN) parties to the COC demand a legally binding document to ensure its

---

[5]David Anderson, "Rights and Obligations in Areas of Overlapping Maritime Claims," presented at the Center for International Law Roundtable Conference National University of Singapore, June 27–28, 2013, Singapore.

compliance and effectiveness. However, China seems to be against creating such a legally binding document.[6]

Marine resource exploration and exploitation in the delimited maritime boundaries is also an important issue besides law enforcement.[7] Escalation often erupts between two countries regarding how they catch fish or explore oil and gas on the continental shelf. For instance, fisheries issues often involve disputes among fishermen and law enforcement authorities. The same happens concerning the issues of exploration and exploitation of continental shelf. UNCLOS does not explain how the interim arrangements between the two countries should be implemented. Anderson and van Logchem suggested possible forms of agreement. The first form is cooperative agreements or cooperation to grant exploration and exploitation permits in undefined border areas. The second form is moratoriums on certain activities such as partial or complete drilling. The third form is arrangements regarding notifications when granting activity permits in undefined border waters accompanied by a consultation forum between the two countries.

Oil and gas exploration in the disputed area sometimes causes further escalations between countries.[8] An example is a case between Guyana and Suriname, where Suriname used military force to take threat actions against activities from Guyana, which granted licenses to Canadian oil exploration company CGX Inc. In one of its demands before the International Court of Justice, Guyana requested compensation for Suriname's military actions. Guyana considered Suriname's actions more of a military threat than law enforcement. The International Court of Justice ruled that Suriname's actions constituted more of a threat and a violation of the United Nations Charter

---

[6]Shannon Tiezzi, "Why China is Not Interested in a South China Sea Code of Conduct," *The Diplomat*, February 26, 2014, https://thediplomat.com/2014/02/why-china-isnt-interested-in-a-south-china-sea-code-of-conduct/.
[7]Mark J. Valencia, Jon M. Van Dyke, and Noel A. Ludwig, *Sharing the Resources of the South China Sea*, BRILL, 2021.
[8]Emily Meierding, "Joint development in the South China Sea: Exploring the prospects of oil and gas cooperation between rivals," *Energy Research & Social Science* 24 (2017): 65–70.

and International Law. However, the court refused to comply with the demands for compensation submitted by Guyana because the losses suffered could not be proven.[9]

The debates on the possibility of the ongoing South China Sea COC to be a provisional agreement under UNCLOS lie in the parties' decisions. There are at least two arguments why the COC is not intended to become a provisional agreement under UNCLOS. First, COC only aims to create mutual trust, not technical cooperation.[10] Although it does not aim to create a confidence-building measure, it could fit with the provisional agreement under UNCLOS. Articles 73(3) and 84(3) do not regulate strict obligations on concluding the provisional agreement.[11] The articles only guide how parties could create mutual trust and prevent disputes in the undelimited maritime boundaries. Therefore, the party states should regulate their provisional agreement according to their needs. An example is whether the provisional agreement would be legally binding. The parties should also determine whether the arrangement would be based on a specific time frame or last until the final boundary delimitation is concluded.

Second, the party states in a provisional agreement should only be the parties to the boundary delimitation. However, Indonesia is involved in the COC negotiation, but it is not a party to the South China Sea dispute. The country does not claim maritime features and has no pending delimitation in the South China Sea. Article 74(3) does not state that a provisional agreement is only created by the parties to the undelimited maritime boundaries. The article states "the States concerned" and not state parties to the dispute or undelimited maritime boundaries. Therefore, Indonesia has a significant interest in the dispute, even when it is not a party to the undelimited maritime

---

[9]International Court of Justice, "Award in the Arbitration regarding the delimitation of maritime boundary between Guyana and Suriname (Guyana v. Suriname)," (2007), para 163.
[10]Carlyle A. Thayer, "ASEAN, China and the Code of Conduct in the South China Sea," *The SAIS Review of International Affairs* 33 (2013): 75–84.
[11]Enrico Milano and Irini Papanicolopulu, *State Responsibility in Disputed Areas on Land and at Sea*, Max-Planck-Institut für ausländisches öffentliches Recht und Völkerrech, p. 622

boundaries. Although it is not a claimant to the dispute, its involvement does not mean the COC cannot be a provisional agreement regulated under UNCLOS.

The ongoing COC could become a provisional agreement regulated under Articles 74(3) and 83(3) when the concerned party states create such an agreement.

III. States Practice on the Provisional Arrangement

(i) *Indonesia–Malaysia*

The Indonesian and Malaysian governments have agreed to make a guideline for the treatment of law enforcement officers to fishers in undetermined border waters. This aims to avoid negative impacts on the undelimited border waters between Indonesia and Malaysia and refers to Article 74(3) of UNCLOS. The guidelines are contained in an agreement officially named Memorandum of Understanding on the Common Guidelines Concerning Treatment of Fishermen by Maritime Law Enforcement Agencies of the Republic of Indonesia and Malaysia. This agreement is hoped to stop the arrests of Indonesian and Malaysian fishers in the UMBA area.

The common guideline was established to determine law enforcement on fisheries issues between Indonesia and Malaysia and ensure the welfare of fishers from both parties. The Indonesia–Malaysia guidelines have four main principles.[12] First, the main priority is maintaining good relations, close cooperation, and mutual understanding between the two countries. Second, every action and maneuverer by law enforcement agencies at sea must avoid violence and be performed without using armed force. Third, the acts or omissions based on this memorandum of understanding shall not affect existing bilateral agreements on maritime boundaries, bilateral negotiations conducted on maritime boundary delimitation, sovereignty issues,

---

[12]Memorandum of Understanding between the Government of the Republic of Indonesia and the Government of Malaysia in Respect of the Common Guidelines Concerning Treatment of Fishermen by Maritime Law Enforcement Agencies of the Republic Of Indonesia and Malaysia, Article 1.

including the position taken in interpretation, application of international law, and territorial maritime claims in written or otherwise, and end of maritime boundary delimitation. Fourth, impartial treatment must be extended to fishers according to fundamental human rights.

One important principle is that this guideline only regulates the agreed-upon provisions and does not impact the ongoing maritime boundary delimitation agreement negotiation process. The guideline does not concern whether the dispute is resolved through negotiation between the two countries or an international tribunal process.

(ii) *Norwegian–Russia (Barents Sea)*

Before Norway and Russia concluded their maritime boundary delimitation agreement in 2007 and 2010, they had previously agreed on joint management.[13] Data from the Norwegian government showed that since 1980, Norway and Russia agreed not to explore and exploit petroleum resources in their undelimited waters. This was based on the provisional arrangement or a moratorium.[14] Furthermore, in 1982 the Norwegian Minister of Oil and Energy conveyed to the Norwegian parliament that international law obligates states to prevent conflicts in undelimited maritime boundaries.[15]

Negotiations for the boundaries of the continental shelf between Norway and Russia began in 1970. Technology had not allowed the two countries to exercise exploration rights on their continental shelf in the Barents Sea. The parties had much experience in offshore exploitation of oil and gas. For instance, hydrocarbon production in the Norwegian sector of the North Sea, the first area of the Norwegian

---

[13]Agreement between the Russian Federation and Norwegia Mengenai Delimitasi Batas Maritim di Varangerfjord Area (signed July 11, 2007, entered into force July 9, 2008) 2526 UNTS 33; and *Treaty between Norway and the Russian Federation Concerning Maritime Delimitation and Cooperation in the Barents Sea and Arctic Ocean* (signed September 15, 2010, entered into force July 7, 2011) 2791 UNTS.
[14]Dokumen Pemerintah Norwegia Prop. 43 S (2010–2011), requesting the consent of the Storting (Parliament) to ratification of the 2010 agreement referred to in the previous note, 9.
[15]Stortingstidene, 1981–1982, 2678 (translation from Norwegian by RR Churchill).

continental shelf to be exploited, did not begin until the early-mid 1970s. This explains that the parties did not recognize the obligation of restraint until the 1980s when they considered exercising rights on their continental shelf in the Barents Sea, estimated to have considerable hydrocarbon potential.[16]

Norway and Russia had complied with mandatory restraint in undetermined border waters.[17] However, a Russian drilling vessel drilled 1.5 nm deep within the disputed area in 1993. This area lies between the equidistance line recommended by Norway as the boundary and the sectoral line advocated by Russia or the Soviet Union.[18] Norway and Russia conducted several seismic tests in the disputed area. Although the two countries have protested against each other's actions, such seismic testing may not constitute a breach of the restraint obligation.

(iii) *United States–Canada (Gulf of Maine)*

The Gulf of Maine is one of the most dynamic marine areas worldwide. It is filled with cold marine waters and characterized by complex geomorphology comprising deep valleys and shallow banks. This semi-enclosed sea is one of the most biologically critical marine ecosystems. The Gulf of Maine is located in the United States adjacent to Canada.[19] The bay has a maritime border between the United States and Canada that has not been officially agreed upon by the two countries. As a result, there are often problems regarding law enforcement authority and granting permits for natural resource exploration and exploitation. In 1969, the United States proposed a moratorium on exploration and exploitation at Georges Bank, the disputed area in the

---

[16]British Institute of International and Comparative Law (BIICL), "Report on the Obligations of States under Articles 74(3) and 83(3) of UNCLOS in respect of Undelimited Maritime Areas."
[17]*Ibid*.
[18]D Scrivener, "Oil, fish and strategy: The USSR, Svalbard and the Barents Sea," *Aberdeen Studies in Defence Economics* 27 (1987): 14.
[19]Gulf of Maine Council on the Marine Environment, "About Gulf of Maine," http://www.gulfofmaine.org/2/gomc-home/the-gulf-of-maine/.

Gulf of Maine, but this was rejected by Canada. However, both countries implemented legal restraint and issued exploration licenses only to be carried out in the undisputed part of Georges Bank. The policy did not allow drilling activities anywhere in Georges Bank.[20] Such restraints probably aimed to make negotiations on maritime boundaries easier.

(iv) *United States–Mexico (Gulf of Mexico)*

The United States and Mexico demarcated most of their maritime boundaries in the Gulf of Mexico, as stated in two treaties in 1970[21] and 1978.[22] However, the agreement highlights two undetermined areas of the continental shelf beyond 200 nm, known as the "Western Gap" and "Eastern Gap" or "Donut Hole."[23] In 2000, the United States and Mexico reached a continental shelf agreement, each beyond 200 nm in the Western Gap. The agreement also established a 1.4 nm buffer zone along the continental shelf boundary line to conserve hydrocarbons. The deposits that may straddle boundaries and prevent exploitation by one party would prejudice the rights of the other's non-living resources. The agreement provided a 10-year moratorium on drilling and exploitation activities in this area, later extended until 2014. In 2012, the parties signed the Transboundary Hydrocarbon Agreement 225 to commence unitizing and

---

[20]Case concerning Delimitation of the Maritime Boundary in the Gulf of Maine Area (Canada/USA), [1984] ICJ Rep 246 at 279–281. See also the US memorial, paras 139–140 and 143; and TL McDorman, Salt Water Neighbors: International Ocean Law Relations between the United States and Canada (OUP 2009), 134–135.

[21]Perjanjian Perbatasan Maritim antara Amerika Serikat dengan Meksiko (completed 4 May 1978, entered into force November 13, 1997) 2143 UNTS 405.

[22]Agreement between the United States of America and Mexico. *The Delimitation of the Continental Shelf in the Western Gulf of Mexico beyond 200 Nautical Miles* (completed June 9, 2000, entered into force January 17, 2001) 2143 UNTS 417.

[23]British Institute of International and Comparative Law (BIICL), "Report on the Obligations of States under Articles 74(3) and 83(3) of UNCLOS in respect of Undelimited Maritime Areas."

co-developing the Western Gap. They ended the moratorium on buffer zones when it entered into force in July 2014.

(v) *Indonesia–Australia*

In the Australian Exclusive Economic Zone (EEZ), there are five agreed fishing operation areas for traditional Indonesian fishermen in Australian waters, namely Ashmore Reef (Sand Island), Browse (Burselan Island), Cartier Island (New Island), Scott Island, and Seringapatam Island.[24]

Among the five coral islands, Ashomore Reef is the largest. This island is located at the northernmost tip and is approximately 120 kilometers to the south of the island of Rote, East Nusa Tenggara province. In addition to regulating the Australian waters that Indonesian traditional fishermen may enter, the Australia–Indonesia Memorandum of Understanding regarding the Operations of Indonesian Traditional Fishermen in Areas of the Australian Fishing Zone and Continental Shelf — 1974, known as the MoU Box or the MoU Box 1974, which consists of three pages of documents plus a map, also regulates the marine biological resources that may be caught. These biological resources include lola shellfish, sea cucumbers, abalone, green snails, and all types of shellfish in the five fishing operation areas above. The countries in the MoU are also interested in that traditional Indonesian fishermen are second to get fresh water at the two designated locations on Ashmore Reef. Australia also provides fishermen to rest with their boats in these territorial waters.[25]

The MoU Box 1974 also provides recognition of limited fishing rights and the legal framework for Indonesian traditional fishermen to operate fishing in certain water areas that have been agreed upon in

---

[24]Akhmad Solihin, "Konflik illegal fishing di wilayah perbatasan Indonesia–Australia." *Journal Marine Fisheries* 1 (November 2010): 31.

[25]James J. Fox and Sevaly Sen, *A Study of Socio-Economic Issues Facing Traditional Indonesian Fisheries Who Access the MOU Box*. A Report for Environment Australia, Research School of Pacific and Asian Studies. (Canberra: The Australian National University dan FERM), hlm. 11.

Australia. The MoU is a tangible manifestation of the commitment of the governments of the two countries to accommodate traditional Indonesian fishermen who have been fishing for hundreds of years in Australian waters.[26]

The scope of discussion of the MoU Box 1974 includes the following: First, what is meant by traditional fishermen in this agreement are fishermen who have taken fish and organisms in Australian waters from generation to generation using a method that has become a tradition for decades.[27] In addition, what is meant by "exclusive fishing zone?" (Exclusive Fishing Zone is a zone of waters measured 12 miles to the sea starting from the base of the Australian territorial sea).

Second, the Government of the Republic of Indonesia has understood that in relation to fishing activities within the exclusive Australian fishing grounds and exploration for the extraction of natural resources associated with the Australian continental shelf, in each case adjacent to Indonesian waters.[28] The Australian Government complies with the rules and refrains from applying its laws regarding fishing operations against traditional fishermen in accordance with joint decisions.

Third, the Government of the Republic of Indonesia understands that every crew member in Australian waters, whether fishing or exploiting natural resources, must comply with the laws of Australian waters.

Fourth, the Australian Government understands that the Government of the Republic of Indonesia will use its best efforts to notify all Indonesian fishermen who may be operating in areas adjacent to Australia in connection with the foregoing agreement.

---

[26] Genewati Wuryandari, "Menerobos Batas Nelayan Indonesia di Perairan Australia: Permasalahan dan Prospek"; *Ibid.*, hlm. 12.

[27] Memorandum of Understanding between the Government of Australia and the Government of the Republic of Indonesia Regarding the Operations of Indonesian Traditional Fishermen in Areas of the Australian Exclusive Fishing Zone and Continental Shelf, 1974), Article 1.

[28] *Ibid.*, Article 2.

Fifth, both the Indonesian and Australian governments have agreed to facilitate the exchange of information regarding the activities of traditional Indonesian fishing vessels operating in the western part of the Timor Sea. The Government of the Republic of Indonesia understands that the Australian government until February 28, 1975 refrained from applying its laws, relating to fisheries, to Indonesian traditional fishermen in the areas concerned with fishing areas and the Australian EEZ.

IV. Conclusion

At least two conclusions could be drawn from the preceding analysis. First, the COC could be considered a provisional measure under UNCLOS Article 74(3). UNCLOS does not regulate the provisional agreement. It only suggests that party states should enter into practical interim arrangements but does not regulate the agreement formation. Therefore, party states should negotiate and create a provisional agreement that fits their specific conditions. For instance, they should decide whether the agreement is legally binding and how long it should last. There are also issues regarding the involvement of Indonesia as a non-claimant country in the South China Sea dispute. However, Article 74(3) does not limit involvement in a provisional agreement only to the disputing parties. The article uses "states concerned" and not "state parties to the dispute" to be involved in provisional measures. Therefore, the ongoing COC negotiation could be a provisional measure under Article 74(3).

This chapter has analyzed previous provisional measures negotiated by several countries in their undelimited or disputed maritime boundaries. The analysis showed diverse practices according to each maritime border's specific conditions and needs. Indonesia and Malaysia agreed upon the limitations of law enforcement in unresolved maritime boundaries. This aimed to avoid escalations between law enforcement institutions and to protect marine resources. Moratoriums or joint exploitation and exploration could be implemented in other undelimited maritime boundaries and continental shelf with vast minerals, oil, and gas. These provisional agreements depend on negotiations by parties and could become a lesson for the ongoing COC negotiation. There are many options on how countries could regulate their provisional agreements to avoid escalations and tensions in disputed areas.

© 2025 World Scientific Publishing Company
https://doi.org/10.1142/9789811296031_0008

Chapter

8

The Underlying Economics of Conflict and Peace in the South China Sea

Mana Southichack

Lao Intergro Sole Co., Ltd.
manasouth9@gmail.com

Abstract

The economic dynamics underlying the South China Sea (SCS) disputes are pivotal to understanding the region's stability. The SCS, a crucial maritime area, supports approximately one-third of global shipping, holds substantial hydrocarbon reserves, and ranks among the world's most productive fishing zones. These economic assets drive the territorial disputes involving China and four ASEAN member states (Brunei, Malaysia, the Philippines, and Vietnam). The 2002 Declaration on the Conduct of Parties in the South China Sea (DOC), although non-binding, seeks to manage these disputes through peaceful means. Despite its limitations, the DOC has played a significant role in maintaining dialogue and reducing conflict risks. The document's inability to fully prevent unilateral actions underscores the necessity of establishing a binding Code of Conduct (COC). Furthermore, cooperative initiatives in marine resource management and environmental conservation are critical for long-term peace and stability in the region. These measures are essential to sustain the socioeconomic development of East and Southeast Asia, ensuring that the SCS continues to serve its vital economic functions without escalating conflicts.

Keywords: South China Sea, Economic Cooperation, ASEAN-China Relations, Maritime Disputes, Regional Stability.

I. Introduction

In consonance with the occasion of the 20th anniversary of the signing of the Declaration on the Conducts of Parties in the South China Sea (DOC), which took place in 2002 in Phnom Penh, Cambodia, by the People's Republic of China (for convenience, China) and 10 ASEAN (Association of Southeast Asian Nations) countries, this chapter aims to discuss how to contribute to sustaining peace in the region. While the South China Sea (SCS) issues are multifaceted, this chapter focuses on the economics as the underlying force of conflict and possible solutions for peace.

The SCS, an area of approximately 1.4 million square miles (3.5 million square kilometers), is the center of regional peace and stability critical for sustaining socioeconomic development in the East and Southeast Asian regions. This vast body of the sea can either directly or indirectly affect the lives of more than a billion people in the economically vibrant Asian region through various economic functions it serves. About a third of global shipping passes through the SCS annually.[1]

---

[1] A total of USD14 trillion of goods were shipped worldwide in 2019, according to the International Chamber of Shipping: "Shipping Fact — Shipping and World Trade: Driving Prosperity," https://www.ics-shipping.org/shipping-fact/shipping-and-world-trade-driving-prosperity/ (Accessed September 5, 2022).

The area has 190 trillion cubic feet (5.38 trillion cubic meters) of natural gas and 11 billion barrels of oil in "proved and probable" reserves, with more to be uncovered.[2] The SCS is one of the world's five most productive fishing ground, where 12% of the world's total catches were produced in 2015.[3]

Sustained socioeconomic development requires continual peace and stability. However, conflicts arising from the overlapping claims involving four ASEAN member countries (Brunei, Malaysia, the Philippines, Vietnam) and China are the region's major destabilizing factor. Deadly clashes of naval forces over territorial claims in the SCS took place in 1974 and 1988 between China and Vietnam.

Since the 1988 Sino-Vietnamese naval clash, conflicts arising from the overlapping claims among countries sharing the SCS have been relatively small and, in decades, have not escalated to disrupt trade flow in any significant way. Nevertheless, the fluidity of the situation in the SCS involving fishing activities, hydrocarbons exploration, drilling activities, or attempts to establish a settlement by any claimant have been major points of past conflicts and will continue to be flashpoints for instabilities in the East and Southeast Asian region. The SCS affairs are complex, sensitive, and potentially perilous, requiring close attention and meticulous care.

As an attempt to maintain peace and stability, in 1992, ASEAN proposed the Code of Conduct (CoC) as a way of establishing rules and norms, which China agreed to in 1999. In association with the CoC, the DOC was adopted in 2002 in Phnom Penh, Cambodia. The final step to ensure peace and stability in the region is for the parties to finalize the CoC, which has yet to be realized.

---

[2]U.S. Energy Information Administration (February 2013): "South China Sea," https://www.eia.gov/international/analysis/regions-of-interest/South_China_Sea (Accessed August 9, 2022).
[3]Asia Maritime Transparency Initiative: https://amti.csis.org/coc-blueprint-fisheries-environment/#:~:text=The%20South%20China%20Sea%20is,global%20fish%20catch%20in%202015 (Accessed August 8, 2022).

II. Background on Conflicts and Efforts to Maintain Peace

The territorial claims of the SCS go back centuries and have had many turns following major global and geopolitical events.[4] However, claimants at the present, since several decades after World War II, include four ASEAN member countries (Brunei, Malaysia, the Philippines, Vietnam) and China. In this contending sea, there are two major archipelagos, Xisha (the Paracel) and Nansha (the Spratly) Islands. China's naval forces have occupied some Xisha Islands since 1955, one year after Vietnam defeated France's Colonial Forces in Dien Bien Phu which led to France's withdrawal that ended its colonial rule in Indochina.[5] In January 1974, China took complete control of Xisha Islands, which are also claimed by Vietnam. Nansha Islands are wholly claimed by China and Vietnam, mostly by the Philippines, and partially by Malaysia and Brunei.

History aside, the territorial dividing lines between countries sharing the body of water in the SCS have never been formally and jointly established among these competing claimants, resulting in the present's unsettled overlapping territorial claims. The area contains small islands but without a permanent settlement of human (indigenous) population, creating an open range for interest parties to claim sovereignty, and making it more difficult to resolve territorial claims.[6]

Further complicating the problem is the Exclusive Economic Zones (EEZs) as stipulated in the 1982 United Nations Convention

---

[4] *China & US Focus:* "Understanding the South China Sea Disputes, South China Sea Timeline," https://www.chinausfocus.com/south-china-sea/ (Accessed August 25, 2022); Wikipedia: "Timeline of the South China Sea Dispute," https://en.wikipedia.org/wiki/Timeline_of_the_South_China_Sea_dispute#1000_BCE%E2%80%932nd_century_CE (Accessed August 25, 2022).
[5] Indochina comprised Cambodia, Laos, and Vietnam.
[6] Among the hundreds of islands in the SCS, the largest and most contentious islands, due to overlapping claims involving six ASEAN countries, include Nansha (the Spratly) Islands, Xisha (the Paracel) Islands, Dongsha (Pratas) Islands, and Zhongsha Islands (Macclesfield Bank and Scarborough Shoal). See Beina Xu, "South China Sea Tensions," May 14, 2014, https://www.cfr.org/backgrounder/south-china-sea-tensions (Accessed August 16, 2022).

on the Law of the Sea (UNCLOS).[7] An EEZ extends 200 nautical miles outward from the coast of each state's sea territory, within which a country can claim exclusive rights to exploit marine and hydrocarbon resources. These EEZs belonging to claimants overlap in some areas and are left for the neighboring countries to agree on a settlement.[8] Furthermore, making the settlement more problematic is that the small islands, some of which are claimed by more than one party, are used to define territorial sea and, hence, EEZs. From a small naturally formed island, a claimant gets 12 nautical miles of territorial sea, further extending the overlapping areas in the EEZs.[9]

Indonesia, while not a party of the SCS claimants, is a party of conflicts in this area of the sea through its EEZ in the Natuna Island area. With increased foreign intrusions into its EEZ around the Natuna Island, located at the south edge of the disputed area, Indonesia had recently strengthened its defense position there and, in 2017, renamed the waters the North Natuna Sea. In December 2019, "dozens" of Chinese fishing vessels entered Indonesia's EEZ in this area escorted by China's coastguard.[10]

III. Nature of Conflicts and Incidents

Conflicts took place in various forms, from official protests to boat ramming, to water cannon shooting, to coast guards or naval forces shooting at fishing boats, and to military-to-military clashes. Serious military-to-military clashes in the SCS took place from the late 1970s to late 1980s between China and Vietnam. In January 1974, with the political support of North Vietnam, China fought a one-day naval war and took over the remaining Vietnamese positions in Xisha Islands

---

[7]The UNCLOS establishes a legal framework for maritime jurisdiction. It includes a definition of territorial seas, exclusive economic zones, and continental shelves.
[8]J. Rennie Short, "Trouble Waters: Conflict in the South China Sea Explained," *The Conversation*, May 24, 2016, https://theconversation.com/troubled-waters-conflict-in-the-south-china-sea-explained-59203 (Accessed August 31, 2022).
[9]*Ibid.*
[10]International Crisis Group: "Competing Visions of International Order in the South China Sea," Asia Report No. 315, November 21, 2021, Brussels, Belgium.

from South Vietnam.[11] March 14, 1988 marked the last clash of naval forces between China and Vietnam, which took place at Chigua (Johnston) Reef in a group of Nansha Islands.[12] The clash resulted in at least 66 deaths of Vietnam's naval personnel.[13] After that, incidents mostly involved fishing vessels and naval vessels (e.g., coast guard, navy); standoffs at oil rig and gas rig between support vessels, fishing vessels, and naval vessels; and a few skirmishes between naval forces.

Fast forward to the 2010–2020 period, there were a total of 73 maritime incidents reported, according to the data compilation of the Center for Strategic and International Studies.[14] Most incidents involved China, with 62 incidents (85%); followed by Vietnam, with 43 incidents (59%); the Philippines, with 22 incidents (30%); and Indonesia, with 10 incidents (14%). Malaysia had the fewest incidents over this same period, just once in 2016 with the Philippines near the Siling (Commodore) Reef in the disputed Nansha (Spratly) Islands, and another in 2019 with China over a gas rig Malaysia deployed at the Nankang, Zhongkang, and Beikang (Luconia) Shoal.[15]

Maritime incidents increased considerably in 2015 and 2016, from an average of 4.6 times annually between 2010 and 2014, to 17 in 2015 and 16 in the following year before dropping to 6 incidents in 2017 (Figure 1). Most incidents in 2015 involved China and Vietnam and, in 2016, between China and Vietnam and the Philippines. While

---

[11] At the time Vietnam was separated into North Vietnam and South Vietnam. The two consolidated with the end of the Vietnam War in April 1975. The brief naval war was an attempt by South Vietnam naval forces to expel Chinese forces from the area of the Paracel Islands, https://en.wikipedia.org/wiki/Battle_of_the_Paracel_Islands (Accessed August 23, 2022).

[12] Peace Research Institute Oslo: "14 March 1988: East Asia's Last Interstate Battle," July 24, 2015, https://blogs.prio.org/2015/07/14-march-1988-east-asias-last-interstate-battle/ (Accessed August 23, 2022).

[13] International Crisis Group, *op. cit.*

[14] Center for Strategic and International Studies: "Are Maritime Law Enforcement Forces Destabilizing Asia?" https://csis-ilab.github.io/cpower-viz/csis-china-sea/ (Accessed July 23, 2022).

[15] Center for Strategic and International Studies, https://csis-ilab.github.io/cpower-viz/csis-china-sea/ (Accessed July 23, 2022).

The Underlying Economics of Conflict and Peace in the South China Sea   167

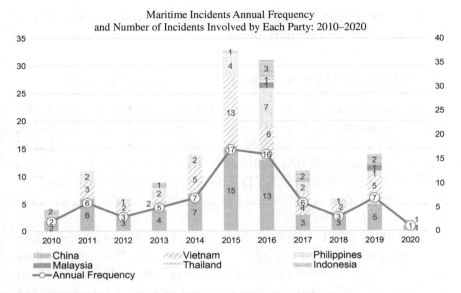

Figure 1. Maritime incidents in the South China Sea: 2010–2020.
Data source: https://csis-ilab.github.io/cpower-viz/csis-china-sea/ (Accessed July 23, 2022).

most incidents involved coast guard (naval force) ships and fishing boats, some involved deadly gunshots by naval authorities causing injuries and deaths.[16] Other incidents involved protests over gas and oil rigs, boat ramming between surveillance vessels and fishing vessels,

---

[16]As examples, according to information compiled by the Center for Strategic and International Studies:
- September 22, 217, a Philippines navy patrol ship opened fire at six Vietnamese fishing vessels (30 nautical miles from Bolinao) killing two fishermen.
- July 22, 2017, an Indonesian naval ship shot at two Vietnamese fishing vessels (132 nautical miles southeast of Con Dao Island) wounding four crew members, two of which severely injured.
- July 8, 2016, Thai naval force opened fire at Vietnamese fishing vessels in the Gulf of Thailand, which resulted in two fishing vessels to sink, two fishermen injured, one missing, and 18 arrested.
- September 11, 2015, a Thai marine vessel opened fire at four Vietnamese fishing vessels (at a location where Vietnam declared to be in waters between Vietnam and

as well as coast guards or naval forces water cannon shooting at fishing boats and other non-military boats.

IV. Efforts to Maintain Peace in the South China Sea

As an attempt to maintain peace and stability in the SCS, in 1992, ASEAN proposed the CoC as a way of establishing rules and norms, which China agreed to in 1999. Negotiations following that led to the DOC, signed in 2002 in Phnom Penh, Cambodia, between China and the 10 ASEAN countries. The final step to ensure peace and stability in the region is for the parties to finalize the CoC that has yet to be realized.

Not until 2011 was a draft of guidelines for implementation adopted. The consultations on the CoC began in 2013, and in July 2018 China and ASEAN agreed on the Single Draft Negotiating Text for the CoC.[17] All parties want peace and security. China wants the disputes to be exclusively between China and ASEAN claimants with minimal involvement from extra-regional powers in the disputed area.[18] ASEAN wants the CoC "to ensure peace and security in the dispute area and to uphold international law."[19] However, the Single Draft Negotiating Text is a compilation of proposals from nine governments, not a negotiated consensus, that included uncompromising demands.[20] This suggests that China and ASEAN still have some distance before both sides can reach an agreement somewhere between their differences.

Malaysia while Thailand insisted the location lies 40 km within Thailand's waters) fatally injuring one fisherman.
- May 9, 2013, the Philippines coastguard opened fire at Taiwanese fishing vessels (approximately 170 nautical miles off the southern tip of Taiwan) resulting in one Taiwanese fisherman being fatally injured.

[17] International Crisis Group, *op. cit.*
[18] *Asia & The Pacific Policy Society*, "The US-ASEAN summit and the South China Sea Code of Conduct," https://www.policyforum.net/the-us-asean-summit-and-the-south-china-sea-code-of-conduct/ (Accessed August 29, 2022).
[19] *Ibid.*
[20] *Ibid.*

V. Economic Services of the SCS and Their Role in Sustaining Peace

The SCS has the potential to affect the lives of more than a billion people, either directly or indirectly, in the economically vibrant and growing East and Southeast Asian regions (collectively referred to as East Asian region) through the various economic functions it serves. Much of the economic development, modernization, and industrialization that have taken place in the region in the past decades have been made possible by the SCS in three major ways. They include its function as shipping channels for international trade; fishery grounds for food and income of hundreds of millions of people in the region; and natural resources, particularly hydrocarbons, for industrial development. These three major economic functions of the SCS largely underpin conflicts among parties of the SCS.

Shipping channel: The SCS serves a critical role as a trade route connecting the East and Southeast Asian regions with the rest of the world via the Taiwan and Luzon Straits in the northeast, the Sunda and Lombok Straits in the south, and the Malacca Strait in the southwest. Nearly half of the world's oil tankers pass through the SCS, where more than half of the world's top 10 shipping ports are located. Among all the economies relying on the SCS for shipping, Southeast Asian countries are most heavily dependent on the SCS for their trade. Goods that were shipped through the SCS between the 2008 and 2016 period accounted for between 53% (Malaysia) and up to 100% (Cambodia) of their total international trade.[21] Over this same period, more than 80% of the total trade of Indonesia, Vietnam, and Myanmar passed through the SCS, while it was more than 70% for the Philippines, Brunei, and Thailand (see Figure 2). Over this same period, 40% of China's total trade passed through the SCS, while it was more than 40% for Chinese Taiwan and South Korea, almost 29% for India, 26% for Australia, and less than 6% for the United States.

---

[21]China Power Project, Center for Strategic and International Studies, https://chinapower.csis.org/much-trade-transits-south-china-sea/ (Accessed July 27, 2022).

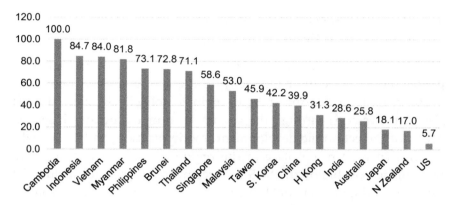

Figure 2. Share in total trade that passed through the SCS by selected economies: Annual Average 2008–2016.

Data source: China Power Project, Center for Strategic and International Studies. https://chinapower.csis.org/much-trade-transits-south-china-sea/ (Accessed July 27, 2022).

Similarly, when the monetary values of imports and exports that passed through the SCS are compared, East Asian economies are among the top. China, with USD1,472 billion of imports and exports shipped through the SCS in 2016, was the largest shipper that relied on the SCS, followed by the European Union (USD890 billion), and the next nine are East Asian economies (see Figure 3).

Maintaining an open sea for shipping is in the interest of every country in the region because any major physical conflict in the SCS would disrupt trade and the economy of countries in the region most heavily. A simulation by Cosar and Thomas (2020) predicts that a complete shutdown of the SCS, which forces shipping in the Pacific and Indian oceans to go south of Australia, would result in a GDP loss of 6.2%–12.4% for countries in the East and Southeast Asia and the Pacific.[22] Should a large-scale military conflict erupted and pro-

---

[22] Kerem Cosar and D. Benjamin Thomas, "The Geopolitics and International Trade in Southeast Asia," Working Paper 28048, November 2020, National Bureau of Economic Research.

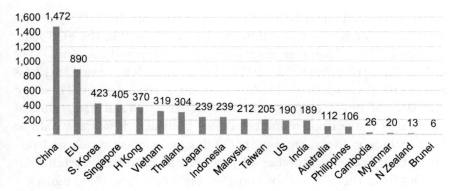

Figure 3. Value of trade that passed through the SCS by selected economies: 2016 (USD Billion).

Data source: China Power Project, Center for Strategic and International Studies. https://chinapower.csis.org/much-trade-transits-south-china-sea/ (Accessed July 27, 2022).

longed, the potential losses for the entire East Asia region are clear. It will not only entail the human cost and destruction to structures and the environment but resources will also have to be diverted to conduct war at the expense of the citizen's welfare, adding to the loss from trade disruption. Also, even just rising tensions alone could raise military spending by each party. Inevitably, this would have to occur at the expense of societal welfare as more resources would be diverted to military spending, and the effect would be greater for smaller countries than for larger ones.

Fishery: It is crucial to understand the importance of fishery to recognize conflicts in the SCS. The SCS is one of the world's five most productive fishing zones, where more than half of the world's fishing vessels and 3.7 million people are employed.[23] From the SCS, total

---

[23]Asia Maritime Transparency Initiative, Center for Strategic and International Study, https://amti.csis.org/coc-blueprint-fisheries-environment/ (Accessed August 8, 2022).

catch accounted for 12% of the world's total in 2015.[24] Over the 1950–2014 period, it was estimated that total catch in the SCS zone averaged 7.76 million tons annually with an estimated value of USD9 billion (in 2010 prices).[25] In 2014, the total catch increased to 12.63 million tons, valued at USD18.69 billion (in 2010 prices). These are estimates of direct employment in fisheries and farm gate value of catches. If the seafood value chains are considered, which would at least include delivery, storage, packaging, wholesale, retail, and restaurant services, the number of jobs and income that started with catches from the SCS will be considerably larger than these figures.

Given the importance of fisheries in providing employment and income, directly and indirectly, as well as in providing food and nutritional security for the population in the region, especially those living in the coastal areas, it is unsurprising why most incidents in the SCS involved fishing vessels. As income and population increased, demand for seafood has also increased. In response to the increased demand, fishing activities in the SCS and catches increased rapidly between the 1980s and early 1990s. However, the total catch stagnated at around 10 million tons annually from the mid-1990s, regardless of fishing efforts that had increased with more equipment, longer stay at the sea, and at farther distances from the shores.[26] This level of catches was also achieved by harvesting smaller fish.[27] After a period of catch stagnation, harvest increased as indicated in Sumaila's estimate in 2018. Overfishing has depleted fish stocks by about 70%–95% since the 1950s and caused considerable damage to marine environment.[28]

---

[24] *Ibid.*
[25] U. Rashid Sumaila, "Comparative Valuation of Fisheries in Asian Large Marine Ecosystems with Emphasis on the East China Sea and South China Sea LMEs," *Deep Sea Research Part II: Topical Studies in Oceanography* 163 (2019): 96–101.
[26] Daniel Pauly and Cui Liang, "The Fisheries of the South China Sea: Major Trends since 1950," *Marine Policy* 121 (2020): 103584.
[27] *Ibid.*
[28] Asia Maritime Transparency Initiative, Center for Strategic and International Study, *op. cit.* See also Rachael Bale, "One of the World's Biggest Fisheries Is on the Verge of Collapse: Major Disputes in the South China Sea Are Putting Critical Habitat — And the Food Supply of Millions — At Risk," National Geographic, August 29,

As fish stocks in the coastal areas depleted due to overfishing, fishing vessels needed to go farther offshore and stay longer in the sea. This resulted in two major problems. First, it increased chances of encounter and competition among fishermen from different countries for more productive fishing areas, which often led to physical conflicts. Second, as overfishing extended farther offshore, it increased damage to the ecological systems in the fishing grounds, threatening sustainability for both human and marine habitats.

Besides a growing population and demand for seafood that has led to overfishing and environmental degradation in the SCS, the unsettled sovereign demarcation (or undefined ownership) with overlapping claims is also the source of the problem since fish stock management enforcement by any claimant is unacceptable by the other.

A joint stewardship of marine resources is an area of opportunity for claimants of the SCS to cooperate to promote peace and cooperation for mutual benefits and minimize conflicts. Marine lives move around the area freely regardless of the boundaries that claimants of the SCS will eventually settle. Thus, a joint effort to steward marine lives and environment is one critical area that can promote peace and continual development in the region.

Natural resources: Natural resources at issue in the SCS are hydrocarbons. The area is rich in hydrocarbon deposits, one of the major reasons for the existence of competing claims among countries bordering the SCS. There are 190 trillion cubic feet (5.38 trillion cubic meters) of natural gas and 11 billion barrels of oil in "proved and probable" reserves in the SCS, according to an estimate of the U.S. Energy Information Administration; however, most are unexploited.[29]

As economies in the region continue to develop and industrialize, demand for hydrocarbon energy naturally increases. Thus, securing as much of a resource-rich area as possible in the SCS is in the interest

---

2016, https://www.nationalgeographic.com/animals/article/wildlife-south-china-sea-overfishing-threatens-collapse (Accessed September 3, 2022).
[29]U.S. Energy Information Administration, *op. cit.*

of every country bordering the SCS. However, exploiting hydrocarbons in much of the areas is impossible due to disputing claims. For example, an oil rig deployed by Vietnam in its oil and gas block 06-01 around Vanguard Bank withdrew and left after more than four months (June 16–October 23, 2019) of a standoff with China's patrolling coastguard and other vessels. An oil rig deployed by China in a disputed water involving China and Vietnam ended after a 2.5-month (May 1–July 15, 2014) standoff between 120 Chinese vessels and Vietnamese coastguard and fishing vessels.

VI. Conclusion

The SCS problems involve multifaceted issues — history, geopolitics, economics, and national defense. The territorial claims of the SCS go back centuries and have had many turns following major global and geopolitical events. In the more recent history of the SCS conflicts, competing claims have led to deadly military clashes between China and Vietnam, one in 1974 in Xisha Islands and another in 1988 in Nansha Islands. After that, many more small incidents mostly involving fishing vessels, some deadly, have occurred among competing claimants.

Since the end of the Vietnam War in 1975 and the Sino-Vietnamese conflicts that lasted from 1979 through 1991, the East Asian region has remained relatively calm, allowing the economies in the region to sustain growth and industrialization. With a rapid economic expansion, demand for resources has also grown rapidly. Beyond the need for more resources to feed economic growth, the SCS also has logistical and defense values. This necessarily makes the vast SCS area of 3.5 million square kilometers rich with marine and hydrocarbon resources — an attractive real estate for grab. Overlapping claims by four ASEAN member countries (Brunei, Malaysia, the Philippines, Vietnam) and China have created conditions risking a potentially large-scale conflict in the SCS destroying hope for sustained socioeconomic advancement for the entire region.

So long as conflicts can be kept small and non-military, the SCS can continue to serve its shipping lane function as it has been. However, without a clear and mutually agreed designation of national boundaries among competing claimants, or without a clear framework of cooperation for mutual benefits that countries sharing the waters can agree, especially among competing claimants, regarding fishery and hydrocarbon exploration and exploitation, risks of conflicts will remain as they are.

However complex and difficult to settle the differences between the competing claimants, all parties have in common the desire for peace and stability in the SCS, a requirement for sustaining industrialization, modernization, and socioeconomic development to catch up with the developed world. The entire East Asian region also has a long history complicated by the legacy of colonialism and geopolitics. Given such complexities involving the SCS unsettled territories and a wide range of possibilities of conflicts to break out, patience, and compromises will definitely be necessary.

History aside, without a compromise from concerned parties in the disputed areas, the only alternative is physical challenge for control and China clearly has the upper hand. If peace and stability is a mutual desire of all parties of the SCS, a compromise settlement seems to be the only middle ground to seek. Trust is necessary and it can only be gradually built. Without it, the SCS problems will not be intra-regional, but extra-regional and more difficult. China, as the most powerful country among all the parties of the SCS, needs to gain trust from other countries in the region. Joint programs on fish stock management, marine environmental stewardship, hydrocarbon exploitation, and joint patrol on piracy and other illegal activities are areas offering opportunities for trust building.

Finally, it does not matter how much China wants to keep out non-party (to the SCS) great powers, the United States cannot be kept out of the SCS equation. It is in the interest of China to conform with the UNCLOS, gain trust from its ASEAN neighbors of its peaceful stance, and prevent its neighbors from perceiving the need to draw in non-party great powers to intervene to counterbalance China's assertiveness.[30] Meanwhile, the United States should not expect China to respect the UNCLOS while it is unwilling to do the same.

---

[30]International Crisis Group, *op. cit.*

Chapter 9

Together for Sustainable Peace of the South China Sea

Bounphieng Pheuaphetlangsy, Sounanda Bolivong, and Haknilan Inthalath

*Strategic and International Studies Division,
Institute of Foreign Affairs, Ministry of Foreign Affairs
of the Lao PDR, Vientiane, Laos
ifamofalaos@gmail.com*

Abstract

The South China Sea is claimed to be one of the most important geographical locations in the world. The region holds abundant natural resources including rich marine life and large oil and natural gas reserves. Natural resource endowment in the South China Sea is unfortunately a double-edged sword. While it has supported the livelihoods in the region for centuries, its rich natural resources have been a trigger for disputes among claimants and the intervention of external actors. As a result, the ASEAN and China have joined hands to draw up regional roles and norms to govern activities in the South China Sea. Following that, the Declaration on the Conduct of the Parties (DOC) was signed by the ASEAN member states and China in 2002. Although the DOC has played a role in maintaining and promoting peace, stability, and security in the South China Sea to some extent, it was widely criticized for its ineffectiveness in achieving the stated objectives. To this end, the achievements and challenges associated with the DOC implementation are discussed in the chapter, and the journey from DOC to the Code of Conduct of the South China Sea has also been explored along with a series of recommendations that have been provided on how to further maintain and promote sustainable peace, stability, and development in the South China Sea.

Keywords: Declaration, DOC, Code of Conduct, COC, South China Sea, Peace, Party, Dispute, Conflict & Maritime

I. Introduction

The South China Sea, which stretches from Singapore and the Strait of Malacca in the southwest to the Strait of Taiwan in the northeast, plays a critical role in the socio-economic development of the region and the world. It is rich in marine life including various species of fish, which is the major source of protein for millions of people in Southeast Asia. In addition, large oil and natural gas reserves have been discovered under the floor of the South China Sea.[1] It is estimated that there are approximately 11 billion barrels of oil reserves and 190 trillion cubic feet of natural gas reserves in the South China Sea.[2] Moreover, the South China Sea is one of the busiest trading routes in the world, with over USD5.3 trillion of

---

[1] Britannica, "South China Sea," *Britannica*, n.a., https://www.britannica.com/place/South-China-Sea/Economic-aspects (Accessed September 2, 2022).
[2] *U.S. Energy Information Administration*, "South China Sea," *EIA*, October 15, 2019, https://www.eia.gov/international/analysis/regions-of-interest/South_China_Sea (Accessed September 2, 2022).

trade carried through its waters annually, which accounts for nearly one-third of the global maritime trade.[3]

It is claimed by scholars that its strategically important geographical location in combination with its abundant natural resources, especially its gigantic oil and natural gas reserves are the underlying factors triggering disputes among the claimant states in the South China Sea, which has become an ongoing regional issue for several decades. It seems that there is no exit strategy for such conflicts among concerned parties. However, since the South China Sea issue became a hotspot for regional and international communities, in the 1990s ASEAN member states initiated the idea of working with China to formulate regional roles and norms for governing the marine activities in the South China Sea. Following that, historically in 2002, the Declaration on the Conduct of the Parties (DOC) was signed by the ASEAN member states and China in Cambodia after a long journey of negotiations. It is the first political document between ASEAN and China, which sets fundamental principles and norms for the parties concerned. The DOC was aimed at maintaining and promoting peace, stability, and security in the region through promoting confidence-building measures, engaging in practical maritime cooperation, and setting a platform for dialogue.[4] The DOC has played a critical role in maintaining and promoting peace, stability, and security in the South China Sea over the past two decades. However, critics assert that the DOC was ineffective in achieving its set objectives. This chapter discusses the achievements and challenges of the

---

[3]David Uren, "Southeast Asia Will Take a Major Economic Hit if Shipping is Blocked in the South China Sea," *The Strategist*, December 8, 2020, https://www.aspistrategist.org.au/southeast-asia-will-take-a-major-economic-hit-if-shipping-is-blocked-in-the-south-china-sea/ (Accessed November 3, 2022).

[4]Mingjiang Li, "Managing Security in the South China Sea: From DOC to COC," Kyoto Review of Southeast Asia," March 2014, https://kyotoreview.org/issue-15/managing-security-in-the-south-china-sea-from-doc-to-coc/ (Accessed November 15, 2022).

DOC implementation over the past 20 years and provides recommendations on how to maintain and further promote sustainable peace, stability, and development in the South China Sea.

II. Achievements of the DOC

The year 2022 marks the 20th anniversary of the DOC, and looking back 20 years ago, it can be seen that the DOC has made various achievements. The first achievement is indicated by the fact that, as noted previously, the DOC has created fundamental principles for peace, stability, and maritime security in the South China Sea, particularly settlement of disputes by peaceful means through diplomatic consultations and negotiations in accordance with the international law including the United Nations Convention on the Law of the Sea (UNCLOS 1982).[5] In addition, the DOC has created platforms, for instance, the Senior Officials' Meeting (SOM-DOC) and the Joint Working Group Meeting on the implementation of the DOC (JWG-DOC), which have become the key platforms for dialogue between ASEAN and China regarding the South China Sea issue. So far, 19 SOM-DOC meetings and 36 JWG-DOC meetings have been fruitfully organized. Apart from that, hotline communication among foreign senior officials of ASEAN member countries and China was set up. Through these existing mechanisms, ASEAN and China are able to communicate on a regular basis.[6] As a result, political mutual trust and understanding between both parties have been enhanced to a great extent, creating a concrete foundation for further development and uplifting ASEAN–China relations to a new height.

---

[5]ASEAN, "The Declaration on Conduct of the Parties in the South China Sea," https://asean.org/declaration-on-the-conduct-of-parties-in-the-south-china-sea-2/ (Accessed October 25, 2022).

[6]Hong Liang, "In Commemoration of the 20th Anniversary of the DOC: Managing Differences and Building Consensus to Jointly Open Up New Prospects for Cooperation on the Governance of the South China Sea," *Chinese People's Institute of Foreign Affairs*, http://www.cpifa.org/en/cms/book/366 (Accessed November 15, 2022).

Respectively, in 2020, ASEAN–China relations have been upgraded to Comprehensive Strategic Partnership for Peace, Security, Prosperity and Sustainable Development.

Since the DOC was signed in 2002, efforts to avoid using force to settle conflicts have been witnessed. When the situation in the South China Sea intensifies, the fundamental principles stipulated in the DOC are a reference that the concerned parties have referred to in order to guide the conduct of their activities that would prevent the circumstance from being further escalated.[7] Moreover, the DOC has opened up opportunities for maritime cooperation not only among the claimant countries but also the whole ASEAN member states and China. It has identified five areas of cooperation namely maritime environmental protection, marine scientific research, safety of navigation and communication at sea, search and rescue operations as well as measures to deal with non-traditional maritime security issues like drug trafficking, piracy, and arm robbery at sea.[8] Specifically, to act as guidance for maritime environmental cooperation, the leaders of ASEAN and China issued the Declaration for a Decade of Coastal and Marine Environmental Protection in the South China Sea (2017–2027) on the occasion of the 20th ASEAN–China Summit in the Philippines and the 15th anniversary of the signing of the DOC on November 13, 2017.

In addition to the existing multilateral cooperation frameworks, under the guidance of the DOC, bilateral dialogue mechanisms have also been established among the directly concerned parties. For example, three working groups on consultation of maritime issues have been established between China and Vietnam. Similarly, a bilateral consultation mechanism on the South China Sea issue has been set up

---

[7]Jianwei Li, "The Important Role of the DOC on Regional Peace and Stability," *China Daily*, July 26, 2022, https://www.chinadaily.com.cn/a/202207/26/WS62dfad45a310fd2b29e6e7f6.html (Accessed November 7, 2022).
[8]ASEAN, Priority Areas of Cooperation, https://asean.org/our-communities/asean-political-security-community/peaceful-secure-and-stable-region/situation-in-the-south-china-sea/priority-areas-of-cooperation/ (Accessed November 16, 2022).

between China and the Philippines, and possibilities for more bilateral mechanisms are being explored. The efforts made at both bilateral and multilateral frameworks have made a significant contribution to creating an enabling environment for dispute settling and for the relevant parties to interact in a calmer and less aggressive manner toward each other in the South China Sea.[9] This demonstrates the achievements made by the implementation of the DOC, especially the principle of self-restraint over the past two decades.

III. Challenges Associated with Implementing the DOC

As discussed previously, the signing of DOC is a significant step for the claimant states in their efforts to foster practical cooperation and manage conflicts at the sea, creating the environment and enabling circumstances necessary for them to ultimately settle their disputes through peaceful means. However, the parties have encountered challenges in putting the DOC into practice for more tangible outcomes because of a wide range of factors.

From a legal perspective, the DOC lacked the legal power to impose restrictions and penalties for misconduct of the parties in the South China Sea since it is a non-legally binding document.[10] To this end, it seems that not a single claimant state has strictly adhered to or abided by the DOC due to its non-legally binding nature. Although a political proclamation can be a significant document, it typically does not offer the same level of clarity as a statute regarding official conduct. Additionally, since the DOC does not specify where the activities in the South China Sea take place in their exclusive,

---

[9]Hong Liang, "In Commemoration of the 20th Anniversary of the DOC: Managing Differences and Building Consensus to Jointly Open Up New Prospects for Cooperation on the Governance of the South China Sea," *Chinese People's Institute of Foreign Affairs*, http://www.cpifa.org/en/cms/book/366 (Accessed November 15, 2022).

[10]Li Mingjiang, "Managing Security in the South China Sea: From DOC to COC," *Kyoto Review of Southeast Asia*, March 2014, https://kyotoreview.org/issue-15/managing-security-in-the-south-china-sea-from-doc-to-coc/#:~:text=As%20the%20embodiment%20of%20political%20goodwill%20of%20all,all%20claimant%20states%20in%20the%20South%20China%20Sea (Accessed November 7, 2022).

uncontested maritime zones, it is frequently criticized for its geographic ambiguity.[11] In addition, the DOC also lacked the tools necessary to oversee, much less enforcement and compliance.

Extrinsically, the political mutual trust between the disputed parties is still at a minimum level despite efforts that have been made to build mutual trust over the past years, and there are a handful of nations that are less eager to implement the DOC. A significant barrier to cooperation in the South China Sea has been the absence of strong political will, which is necessary for cooperation between the claimant states in disputed regions. The South China Sea's coastline governments have long been troubled by the disputes over the region's territories and energy resources, and tensions are rising among the parties. As a result, the parties are wary and distrustful of one another, making cooperation in the South China Sea particularly challenging.[12]

Furthermore, the South China Sea issue has grown into one of the key battlefields for strategic competition between major powers. For instance, the increasing presence of the United States and its allies in the South China Sea as part of its Indo-Pacific Strategy and an effort to counterbalance China's influence may be regarded by some claimant states as the destabilizing force in the South China Sea's peace and stability. This causes hostility between China and other claimants and could strrain ties between China and ASEAN nations[13] despite the freedom of navigation in different seas granted by the UNCLOS 1982.[14] In recent years, the U.S. has conducted guard operations within 12 miles of the disputed islands in the South China

---

[11] *ASEAN Today*, "Progressing from the DOC to the COC: A Difficult Route to Navigate," November 13, 2018, https://www.aseantoday.com/2018/11/progressing-from-the-doc-the-coc-a-difficult-route-to-navigate/ (Accessed November 7, 2022).

[12] Wu Shicun, "DOC Implementation and Cooperation at Sea," *China-Southeast Asia Research Center on the South China Sea*, September 2, 2020, http://www.csarc.org.cn/publications/doc-implementation-and-cooperation-at-sea/ (Accessed November 7, 2022).

[13] *Ibid.*

[14] Zewei Yang, "The Freedom of Navigation in the South China Sea: Ideal or a Reality?" *Beijing Law Review* 3 (2012): 137–144.

Sea region.[15] The increasing U.S. military activities in the region have inevitably triggered tension between the U.S. and China as well as among the claimant parties. This has significantly complicated the DOC compliance and arguably, diverted the claimant parties' attention away from the DOC.

IV. The Journey from DOC to COC

Despite some drawbacks, the DOC has been a pillar in ASEAN and China's activities relating to the South China Sea disputes over the past two decades. However, the DOC is not an end in itself. In other words, it is not the final target to resolve disputes. Given the continuous rising tensions among claimants, it is crucial to establish regional rules to maintain long-term peace, stability, and order in the South China Sea. Rather than replacing the DOC, the Code of Conduct (COC) is an upgraded version of the DOC. In the DOC, the parties agreed to cooperate further in order to eventually achieve the COC in the South China Sea. This agreement set the stage for future rule-making and mechanism-building in the South China Sea. Since its introduction in 2013, the COC consultations have made steady progress and kept up a positive pace. Through the process, the parties have increased their level of trust and built consensus to some extent. In fact, the consultation is a component of the South China Sea confidence-building measures in and of itself, bringing some hope for effective cooperation to ensure regional peace and stability. Consequently, a draft Framework of COC and a single draft negotiating text (SDNT) were revealed by ASEAN and China in 2017 and 2018 respectively. In the following year, the anticipated COC's First Draft was released.[16] These illustrate some positive development and

---

[15] Adhit Prayoga, Jonni Mahroza and Surryanto Djoko Waluyo, "Indonesian Defense Strategy to Encounter Challenges in the Indo-Pacific (Case Study: Hegemonic War of China and the United States of America in the South China Sea)," *International Journal of Social Science and Human Research* 4 (2021): 2880–2889.

[16] Viet Hoang, "The Code of Conduct for the South China Sea: A Long and Bumpy Road," *The Diplomat*, September 28, 2020.

progress of the COC negotiation. Nevertheless, the emergence of the COVID-19 pandemic, to some extent, interrupted ASEAN and China's objectives and plans, including the COC negotiation process, which considerably has been slowed down as a result of the halt in face-to-face meetings.[17] Despite the pandemic, ASEAN and China advocated for a resumption of COC negotiations through virtual platforms such as the ASEAN Political-Security Community (APSC) Council Meeting,[18] demonstrating a positive sign for the realization of the COC.

Nonetheless, the road to COC negotiation is a long and bumpy one. There were clear divergent interests not only between ASEAN member states and China but also among ASEAN member states themselves, which has complicated the negotiation process.[19] The South China Sea situation on the ground and policy talks also differed significantly. There were still conflicts among fishermen as well as between coastguards and fishermen from claimant states.[20] Thus, these problems might easily undermine the DOC's diplomatic intentions. It is true that despite these encouraging tendencies, there have been heated discussions on matters like whether or not the COC should have legal power. While there are some countries that desire to make the COC legally binding, the others are reluctant and uncertain about the legality of the COC.[21]

---

[17] Kei Koga, Four Phases of South China Sea Disputes 1990–2020. In: *Managing Great Power Politics. Global Political Transitions*, Singapore: Palgrave Macmillan, 2022, pp. 43–160.
[18] VNA, "Foreign Ministers Reiterate ASEAN's Resolve to Resume COC Talks," *Vietnam Plus*, November 10, 2020, https://en.vietnamplus.vn/foreign-ministers-reiterate-aseans-resolve-to-resume-coc-talks/190117.vnp (Accessed November 7, 2022).
[19] Kei Koga, Four Phases of South China Sea Disputes 1990–2020. In: *Managing Great Power Politics. Global Political Transitions*, Singapore: Palgrave Macmillan, 2022, pp. 43–160.
[20] The Free Library, "Philippines Bends to Diluted S. China Sea Code of Conduct," n.d., https://www.thefreelibrary.com/Philippines+bends+to+diluted+S.+China+Sea+code+of+conduct.-a077236142 (Accessed November 8, 2022).
[21] Joeal Calupitan, "Philippines: Framework of South China Sea Pact Possible Soon," *AP News*, February 21, 2017, https://apnews.com/ (Accessed November 10, 2022).

In the meantime, the Code of Conduct continues to be the best option for disputing parties to follow when resolving the South China Sea conflict in an ASEAN-Way.[22] If the COC is realized, it has the potential to develop into a framework for resolving disputes that establish marine and territorial delineation. Through the development of consensus rules and the promotion of trust between parties, they are intended to handle crises and jointly uphold peace and stability in the South China Sea. This would eventually lead to the peaceful resolution of disputes in the region.[23]

V. The Relationship between the COC and the DOC

As noted earlier, the COC is not a replacement for the DOC but rather an upgraded version of the Declaration. The DOC serves as the foundation and institutional framework for the creation of the COC, which aims to achieve the broadest possible consensus and accommodate all parties. In fact, China and the ASEAN member countries are promoting COC consultation within the framework of comprehensively and effectively implementing the DOC and have used the same working team to achieve the purpose. The need for a Code of Conduct that draws claimants back from the edge and lays out clear procedures for settling disputes is urgent in the South China Sea and that is what the COC is intended to. The core purpose of the COC is to manage disputes to avoid conflicts by direct negotiation among the claimants. Therefore, this document would be a major step towards peacefully managing the South China Sea disputes.[24]

---

[22]Yasintha Selly Rossiana, "The South China Sea Dispute: Code of Conduct Implementation as the Dispute Settlement," *Jurnal Diplomasi Perthanan* 8 (2022): 15–30.

[23]Luo Liang, "A Guide to the South China Sea COC," *China US Focus*, September 15, 2017, https://A Guide to the South China Sea COC — CHINA US Focus (Accessed November 9, 2022).

[24]Gregory Poling, "South China Sea Code of Conduct Still a Speck on the Horizon," *Asia Maritime Transparency Initiative*, September 6, 2018, https://amti.csis.org/south-china-sea-code-conduct-still-speck-horizon/ (Accessed November 22, 2022).

The DOC and COC are not able to be separated from one another. This is because COC implementation should learn from the DOC's lessons so that it could be a more effective document that ensures peace and security in the region. In fact, the COC should uphold the same principles of the DOC including but not limited to developing trust and confidence building measures, freedom of navigation, resolving territorial and jurisdictional disputes by peaceful means, refraining from engaging in activities that could lead to conflict escalation and undertaking cooperative activities between concerned parties.[25]

VI. Principles or Legal Frameworks under the COC

As noted previously, the COC's scheme is a work in progress. The consultation process for the COC in the South China Sea started in 2013. The COC is considered an upgraded version of the DOC, which was signed by China and ASEAN countries in 2002. The efforts made beginning from the discussion through ASEAN–China Joint Working Group on South China Sea (JWGSCS), which was established according to the decision made in the ASEAN–China Senior Officials' Meeting on the implementation of the DOC convened in Kuala Lumpur on December 7, 2004. The main task of the ASEAN–China JWG is to study and recommend measures to translate the provisions of the DOC into concrete cooperative activities that will enhance mutual understanding and trust.[26]

To further ensure the DOC implementation, the Statement of the ASEAN foreign ministers released in Phnom Penh, Cambodia, July 20, 2012, "ASEAN's Six-Point Principles on the South China Sea"

---

[25]ASEAN, Declaration on the Conduct of Parties in the South China Sea, May 14, 2012.

[26]ASEAN, Terms of Reference of the ASEAN-China Joint Working Group on the Implementation of the Declaration on the Conduct of Parties in the South China Sea, *Statement*, December 7, 2014, https://asean.org/terms-of-reference-of-the-asean-china-joint-working-group-on-the-implementation-of-the-declaration-on-the-conduct-of-parties-in-the-south-china-sea-2/ (Accessed November 22, 2022).

was issued.[27] More significantly, the 1st formal consultations on COC were held at the 6th ASEAN–China SOM and the 9th JWGSCS. In 2017, the ASEAN–China framework for COC was endorsed and followed by the First reading of the Single draft negotiating text of COC in 2019. The Single draft of negotiating text of COC is the latest framework that ASEAN and China have been working on and its final draft is expected to be a resolution with more binding effects and serve better for regional peace and stability. However, there are also growing opinions that one should not anticipate the framework agreement between ASEAN and China to result in the COC that is legally binding. Even though the framework agreement is a crucial first step in establishing the tone for subsequent negotiations, it will be difficult to create a legally enforceable COC.[28]

VII. Will the COC Make a Difference?

For COC to be effective, it must address the DOC's shortcomings and provide clear legal mechanisms for preventing conflicts and managing its geography scope. Most importantly, trust building among concerned parties should be further enhanced so that it can prevent the external influence.

With regard to those challenging circumstances, it is probably reasonable to infer from the DOC process that the COC process will not be simple and straight-forward. There will probably be tense negotiations over the COC's drafting. Furthermore, there are reasons to think that, even if the dispute were to be settled, the COC might not be sufficient to maintain the South China Sea's peace and stability even though over the years, the COC has been illustrated some positive sign in cooperation in the South China Sea, which will potentially lead to more cooperation in the future. Different claimant parties

---

[27]ASEAN, "Statement of the ASEAN Foreign Ministers, 20 July 2012," https://asean.org/wp-content/uploads/images/AFMs%20Statement%20on%206%20Principles%20on%20SCS.pdf (Accessed November 22, 2022).

[28]Wei-Chin Lee, "Can It Contain China's Territorial Assertions?" *Asia and the Pacific Policy Society*, August 17, 2017, https://www.policyforum.net/cracking-code-conduct/ (Accessed November 22, 2022).

have adopted or have publicly agreed on some guidelines and standards for handling the South China Sea conflict. The DOC and other ASEAN–China treaties provide excellent illustrations of these concepts. The parties have all agreed to a peaceful resolution of the conflict. In handling and resolving the disputes, they have agreed to comply with the international laws including the UNCLOS 1982. They also agreed to use a bilateral strategy where there are only two countries involved in the issue and a multilateral strategy when there are more. Claimant governments are willing to cooperate to resolve the conflict despite frequent clashes and arguments.[29]

Moreover, The COC also represents a constructive confidence-building step to prevent the disputes from further escalating, which seems to be enhanced from the DOC. The framework offers all concerned parties a starting point for continuous dialogue and shows a collective willingness to manage the disputes. This can be seen that despite minor instability, the South China Sea has mostly stayed calm and stable over the past 20 years, and the DOC is to be commended for this. This historic declaration, which has paved the way on numerous fronts, should give China and the ASEAN Member States every reason to be proud. As the result, the DOC and the upcoming COC are crucial procedures for examining how the UNCLOS 1982 and general international law are applied in the area. They ought to be viewed as the main tools for resolving the South China Sea conflicts. Most crucially, publications that discuss how to resolve maritime conflicts, practice forbearance, and improve military confidence-building are completely outside the scope of the UNCLOS. In this way, the DOC and the COC would advance both the law of the sea in the modern era as well as regional peace and security. After 20 years of operation, the DOC has shown to be one of the best methods for combining the rich expertise of neighboring nations in addressing challenges. A high-quality COC is expected to be concluded soon, and the South China Sea will continue to be a sea of peace, friendship,

---

[29]Mingjiang Li, "Managing Security in the South China Sea: From DOC to COC, Kyoto Review of Southeast Asia," March 2014, https://kyotoreview.org/issue-15/managing-security-in-the-south-china-sea-from-doc-to-coc/ (Accessed November 15, 2022).

and cooperation as long as COC is broadly accepted, and more essentially provided that concerned parties firmly adhered to the spirit of COC and deepen their dialogue and cooperation for the vision of building a community with a shared future for all.[30]

VIII. Recommendations

To maintain stable peace and achieve a prosperous future in the South China Sea, some recommendations have been provided as follows:

(1) The claimant states shall commit to handling any disputes over the waters, the seabed, and airspace amicably and without using force, as well as to acting with restraint and respect for the rights of the other parties when conducting their activities in the South China Sea, adhering to the DOC and the principles of international laws including the UNCLOS 1982.
(2) ASEAN and China should engage in initiatives such as joint training and exercise sessions among regional maritime law enforcement agencies to promote best practices and reduce the risk of maritime incidents in order to increase the safety of navigation, communication, and search and rescue in the South China Sea.
(3) ASEAN and China should explore opportunities for collaboration in combating transnational crime, including but not limited to human trafficking, piracy, armed robbery at sea, and the trafficking of drugs and weapons.
(4) More importantly, ASEAN and China should support the immediate start of talks between the involved parties on environmental protection, fishery management, oil and gas development, and other marine economic development initiatives in the South China Sea.
(5) ASEAN and China should strengthen cooperation on maritime scientific research through hosting regular scientific workshops

---

[30]Zong Haihe, "DOC: The Cornerstone for South China Sea Peace and Stability," *Global Times*, June 16, 2022, https://www.globaltimes.cn/page/202206/1268 287.shtml (Accessed November 22, 2022).

and research trips inviting experts from the region and beyond. In this connection, promote joint conferences, historical research, and cooperation in marine archaeology to increase public awareness of the South China Sea as a common space and resource used for centuries by people from the surrounding area and beyond. Crucially, invest on initiatives to educate the public about the importance of and dangers to the marine environment.

(6) ASEAN and China should learn from other regions' successful experiences with regional cooperation, including the Mediterranean. In order to explore maritime cooperation in the North Sea, the Mediterranean Sea, and the Baltic Sea, European nations have adopted the strategy of "narrowing claims and extending cooperation" from the end of the 1960s. The South China Sea region's nations can benefit from European countries' regional maritime cooperation networks. China and the ASEAN states can draw from Europe's successful experience and seek a workable solution to maritime cooperation in line with the actual circumstances and present needs of the region based on the consensus and practices already established in the area.

(7) It is vital that existing mechanisms, including the Senior Officials' Meeting and the Joint Working Group Meeting on the implementation of the DOC be reviewed and further built on and enhanced so as to ensure that both ASEAN and China remain regularly communication in order to minimize the risk of maritime incidents.

(8) Along with working together multilaterally, the claimant states should seek high-level bilateral dialogues as a way to enhance political trust among disputed parties. For instance, the recent talks between President Xi Jinping and Secretary-General Nguyen Phú Trọng in November 2022 signified a positive and special relationship between the two countries despite some challenges associated with the South China Sea issue. The bilateral talks between state leaders could potentially lessen the tension in the South China Sea and at the same time, help achieve a win–win cooperation rather than confrontation.

Chapter 10

The DOC and Dispute Management in the South China Sea: Maintaining Dialogue, Maximizing Convergences

Kuik Cheng-Chwee

*Centre for Asian Studies (iKAS),
Institute of Malaysian and International Studies (IKMAS),
National University of Malaysia (UKM), Malaysia
cckuik@gmail.com*

Abstract

The Declaration on the Conduct of Parties in the South China Sea (DOC), signed by ASEAN member states and China in 2002, plays a pivotal role in managing the complex territorial disputes in the region. Despite its nature as a non-legally binding political declaration, the DOC facilitates dialogue, manages expectations, and promotes cooperation among the claimants. While the DOC has not effectively restrained unilateral actions or prevented rising tensions, it remains a significant framework for continuous negotiation and risk mitigation. Over the past two decades, the DOC has provided a foundational platform for further engagement, leading to incremental progress towards establishing a Code of Conduct (COC). The DOC's importance lies in its ability to maintain regional stability and support ASEAN-China dialogue, even amidst increasing international uncertainties. Although the DOC faces criticism for its limitations, it has enabled ASEAN and China to explore peaceful dispute management strategies, emphasizing the necessity for ongoing dialogue and practical cooperation. The chapter underscores the need to further develop and expand the DOC's promises and potential to achieve sustainable peace and stability in the South China Sea.

Keywords: South China Sea, DOC, ASEAN-China relations, dispute management, Code of Conduct, regional stability.

I. Introduction: The Politics and Promises of Dispute Management

Leaders and policy practitioners talk *settlement* but often think and act *management* when it comes to territorial disputes. While the peaceful and durable settlement of territorial disputes is always desirable, this goal may not be achievable for such disputes as the multi-nation disputes in the South China Sea (SCS). Since the 1970s, four Southeast Asian states — Brunei, Malaysia, the Philippines, and Vietnam, alongside China — have been embroiled in the SCS disputes, one of the most complex territorial and maritime issues in Asia. In addition to these claimants, numerous countries within and outside Asia — littoral states, user countries, and big powers — view their stakes in the SCS as increasing profoundly, whether over maritime resources and security, or out of concern for the freedom of navigation in the disputed waters.[1] Since the 2010s, the SCS has evolved from a territorial issue

---

[1] Sam Bateman and Ralf Emmers, eds. *Security and International Politics in the South China Sea*, Routledge, 2008; International Crisis Group, *Stirring up the South China Sea (III): A Fleeting Opportunity for Calm*, ICG, 2015; C. J. Jenner and Tran Truong Thuy, eds., *The South China Sea: A Crucible of Regional Cooperation or Conflict-Making Sovereignty Claims?* Cambridge University Press, 2016; Ian Storey and Cheng-Yi Lin, eds., *The South China Sea Dispute: Navigating Diplomatic and Strategic Tensions*. 1st ed., ISEAS–Yusof Ishak Institute, 2016.

to big-power rivalries, primarily between the United States and China, but also between China and tier-two powers in Asia and beyond.[2]

As the complexity of the SCS issue grows and big power rivalries intensify, these disputes are not expected to be resolved in the near- or even mid-term. When peaceful settlement does not look feasible in the foreseeable future, peaceful dispute management is widely viewed as the next best scenario for all claimants, littoral states, and other stakeholders (including industrial actors, as well as inter-governmental and international entities) in the SCS. Peaceful dispute management encompasses handling the disputes with the bottom-line goals of avoiding conflict, allowing negotiation, and preserving the core stakes of regional stability and wider cooperation while enabling individual countries and actors to protect their own sovereignty or maritime interests.

The Declaration on the Conduct of Parties in the South China Sea (DOC), signed in November 2002 by the Association of Southeast Asian Nations (ASEAN) member states and China, is a major mechanism enabling the peaceful management of the multi-country disputes. The DOC was the product of three years of negotiations from 2000 to 2002 by a working group of the ASEAN-China Senior Officials' Meeting (SOM). Being more a political declaration than a legally binding document, it was a watered-down version of the original goal of a Code of Conduct (COC) to manage the SCS disputes in the post-Cold War era.[3]

---

[2]Bill Hayton, *The South China Sea: The Struggle for Power in Asia*. Yale University Press, 2014; Malaysian Ministry of Defence, *Defence White Paper: A Secure, Sovereign and Prosperous Malaysia*, Percetakan Nasional Malaysia Berhad, 2020; Thi Ha Hoang, "Pitfalls for ASEAN in negotiating a code of conduct in the South China Sea," *ISEAS Perspective* 57 (2019b): 1–8.

[3]Leszek Buszynzki, "ASEAN, the declaration on conduct, and the South China Sea," *Contemporary Southeast Asia* 25(3) (2003): 343–362; Hong Thao Nguyen, "The 2002 Declaration on the Conduct of Parties in the South China Sea: A Note," *Ocean Development & International Law* 34(3–4) (2003): 279–285; Ian Storey, "Slipping away? A South China Sea code of conduct eludes diplomatic efforts," *East and South China Seas Bulletin* 11 (2013): 1–7; Ian Storey, "Assessing the ASEAN–China Framework for the Code of Conduct for the South China Sea," *ISEAS Perspective* 62

When the DOC was signed, it was considered the best compromise both sides could arrive at. For Southeast Asian states, the DOC stabilized regional security and restored international confidence in ASEAN in the wake of the 1997–1998 Asian financial crisis and enabled the smaller states to focus on their domestic development. For China, the DOC helped win the political trust of its Southeast Asian neighbors, reduced the likelihood of interference by external powers in the disputes, and preserved Chinese sovereignty. For ASEAN and China, the DOC helped preserve regional stability and strengthen ASEAN–China dialogue relations, while paving the way for further cooperation in economic, diplomatic, and other domains. While signing the DOC in November 2002, both sides entered into the ASEAN–China Free Trade Agreement (ACFTA). In October 2003, China acceded to the Treaty of Amity and Cooperation (TAC), ASEAN's non-aggression pact, and the ASEAN–China "Strategic Partnership for Peace and Prosperity" was also established.

Twenty years after the DOC was implemented, its assessments are mixed, ranging from negative and dismissive to positive, sanguine, and cautiously optimistic. This chapter argues that the DOC is largely ineffective but still significant and indeed, instrumental in the core functions of peaceful dispute management, i.e., maintaining dialogue, managing expectations, mapping cooperation, and mitigating risks. Put differently, while the DOC has been ineffective in restraining claimant countries (especially the stronger ones) from undertaking unilateral actions to maximize their territorial and commercial interests, it has still served as a baseline for further negotiations, a platform for reducing tensions and exploring practical collaboration, as well as a vehicle for promoting the realization of the COC, while cultivating fallback options amid increasing international uncertainty. As an avenue for peaceful dispute management, the DOC has been constrained

---

(2017): 1–7; Carlyle A. Thayer, "ASEAN, China and the Code of Conduct in the South China Sea," *SAIS Review of International Affairs* 33(2) (2013): 75–84; Carlyle A. Thayer, "ASEAN's Long March to a Code of Conduct in the South China Sea," *Maritime Issues*, 2017, http://www.maritimeissues.com/politics/aseans-long-march-to-a-code-of-conduct-in-the-south-china-sea.html.

by politics at various levels, but its promises and potential must be further developed and expanded.

II. Minding the Gaps: The Origin and Nature of the DOC

Far from being the legally binding code as originally envisaged, the eventual DOC falls short of constituting a credible regime for providing security and cooperative management in the South China Sea.[4] Indeed, the DOC has suffered from several gaps since its inception: between a loose declaration and a binding regime, between desirability and feasibility, and a functional lag (lengthy process, but limited progress). These gaps are rooted in the nature of the DOC as a political (rather than legal) document, where signatory parties pledge to build up confidence and trust, to recognize the freedom of navigation and overflight in the South China Sea, as well as to cooperate on certain marine activities and manage the dispute through international law and peaceful means, but without binding commitment.

While the signing of the DOC is attributable to the above-mentioned three-year negotiations from 2000 to 2002 by the ASEAN–China SOM working group, its origins can be traced further back. ASEAN first expressed a desire to negotiate a COC through the ASEAN Declaration of the South China Sea on July 22, 1992. The 1992 declaration was issued in the wake of naval clashes between China and Vietnam on Chigua (Johnson) Reef in the Nansha (Spratly) archipelago in March 1988, as well as China's promulgation of the Law on the Territorial Sea and the Contiguous Zone in February 1992, which laid Beijing's claims to the entire SCS based on its "historical right" to the area.

---

[4]Sam Bateman and Ralf Emmers, eds. *Security and International Politics in the South China Sea*, London: Routledge, 2008; Leszek Buszynzki, "ASEAN, the declaration on conduct, and the South China Sea," *Contemporary Southeast Asia* 25(3) (2003): 343–362; Ralf Emmers, "ASEAN, China and the South China Sea: An opportunity missed," *IDSS Commentaries*, (2002): 1–3.

Numerous developments in the 1990s — most notably incidents at sea and the creation of informal dialogue arrangements and official diplomatic mechanisms — led to further talks on the COC among the ASEAN member states and China. In early 1995, China occupied and constructed a guard post on Meiji (Mischief) Reef (which is claimed by the Philippines), about 217 km (135 miles) off the coast of the Philippines' Palawan Island. In late 1998, China was found to be expanding its structures on Meiji Reef. These incidents — known as "Meiji Reef 1" and "Meiji Reef 2" — heightened regional anxieties about China's intentions and deepened regional efforts to strengthen alignments and cultivate a stable balance of power in Southeast Asia. The incidents also pushed the Philippines and some ASEAN states to emphasize dialogue and confidence-building measure (CBM) activities with China to avoid similar occupations by the Chinese and to restrain Beijing from the use of force in the SCS.[5]

Since the early 1990s, several Track-1 (inter-governmental) and Track-2 (non-governmental) mechanisms were created, which provided avenues for these interactions and dialogues to take place. These included the Track-2 Indonesian-sponsored South China Sea Workshops, which allowed frank discussion of potential areas of disagreement in an informal setting, and the Track-1 ASEAN-based mechanisms, most notably the 1995 ASEAN–China SOM, and to an extent, the ASEAN Regional Forum (ARF, created in 1994).[6] Used in conjunction with the conventional bilateral channels, these mechanisms have become the consultative platforms for the ASEAN states and China to discuss the contents of the envisaged COC.

In the beginning, China was cautious and suspicious of such multilateral security arrangements and processes, largely out of concern

---

[5] Leszek Buszynzki, "ASEAN, the declaration on conduct, and the South China Sea," *Contemporary Southeast Asia* 25(3) (2003): 343–362; Lai To Lee, *China and the South China Sea Dialogues*, Praeger, 1999.

[6] Ramses Amer, "The South China Sea: Achievements and challenges to dispute management," *Asian Survey* 55(3) (2015): 618–639; Nian Peng and Ngeow Chow Bing, "Managing the South China Sea dispute: Multilateral and bilateral approaches," *Ocean Development & International Law* 53(1) (2022): 37–59.

that they might be detrimental to its sovereignty, especially over such issues as Taiwan and the SCS. Although China joined the ARF and agreed to embark on the annual ASEAN–China consultation on political and security issues at the senior official level, Beijing's involvement in these multilateral forums was apprehensive and passive, intending primarily to ward off developments that might challenge its sovereignty and jeopardize its interests. Over time, however, China's perceptions of multilateralism changed, realizing that forums such as the ARF and the ASEAN–China SOM might not necessarily be harmful and instead could be used as diplomatic platforms to promote its foreign policy agenda.[7]

It is through these ASEAN-based multilateral platforms — side-by-side with bilateral channels — that ASEAN states and China have been engaging in talks surrounding the COC and other dispute management efforts. The pace and direction of the talks have been shaped not only by the differences between ASEAN states and China but also by the diverging views and preferences of individual ASEAN member states. While their external outlooks and emphasis on ASEAN unity and regional stability do converge to a large extent, each individual state prioritizes its own national sovereignty and interests.

In August 1995, the Philippines and China held a bilateral foreign ministry meeting at the undersecretary level in Manila. (This was an early effort to realize the COC as envisaged by the 1992 Declaration.) In the joint statement after the meeting, both sides emphasized the importance of abiding by the principles of a code of conduct and adopting a "gradual process of cooperation" which would lead to bilateral negotiations.[8] At the 29th ASEAN Ministerial Meeting (AMM) in July 1996, ASEAN foreign ministers endorsed the idea

---

[7]Cheng-Chwee Kuik, "Multilateralism in China's ASEAN policy: Its evolution, characteristics, and aspiration," *Contemporary Southeast Asia* 27(1) (2005): 102–122.

Cheng-Chwee Kuik, "China's evolving multilateralism in Asia: The aussenpolitik and innenpolitik explanations." In *East Asian Multilateralism: Prospects for Regional Stability*, edited by Kent E. Calder and Francis Fukuyama, pp. 109–142. The Johns Hopkins University Press, 2008.

[8]Leszek Buszynzki, "ASEAN, the declaration on conduct, and the South China Sea," *Contemporary Southeast Asia* 25(3) (2003): 343–362.

of a code of conduct to lay the foundation for long-term stability in the SCS.

These bilateral and multilateral efforts were hampered by differences, both within ASEAN and in relation to China, over several issues, including the geographical scope of the proposed code, as well as the provisions to govern activities within the disputed areas. For instance, Vietnam pressed for the inclusion of Xisha (the Paracels) in the Code, while the Philippines advocated the inclusion of provisions to ban the construction of new structures on the disputed islets. As the proposed inclusions were not supported by all ASEAN members, a deadlock ensued.

At the 35th AMM in Brunei (July 2002), Malaysia tried to break the stalemate by proposing that ASEAN and China issue a political declaration instead of a legally binding code of conduct. The ASEAN foreign ministers and the Chinese delegation eventually agreed. In November 2002, the DOC was announced at the Summit, with both sides reaffirming that the DOC would "promote peace and stability in the region" and agreeing to work "on the basis of consensus towards the eventual attainment of this objective."[9]

Reactions to the DOC varied. On one hand, some observers considered the DOC a breakthrough, in part because it was the first time China had agreed to a multilateral agreement over the SCS, despite its long-standing insistence on bilateral negotiations and approaches with the claimant countries. On the other, many analysts expressed disappointment and concern, not simply because the DOC is not legally binding, but also because of its other limitations. Scholar Ralf Emmers, for example, warned that "the document cannot be expected to prevent the occurrence of new incidents over territorial claims in the South China Sea."[10] He observed that the DOC "made no reference to its specific geographical scope, primarily because China opposed any mention of the Paracel Islands." He added:

---

[9]Ralf Emmers, *Cooperative Security and the Balance of Power in ASEAN and the ARF*, Routledge, 2003.
[10]Ralf Emmers, "ASEAN, China and the South China Sea: An opportunity missed," *IDSS Commentaries*, (2002): 1–3.

As a result of China's requests, the ASEAN members agreed to include 'on the basis of consensus' when referring to the eventual attainment of a code of conduct and to drop the phrase 'erection of structures' from the paragraph invoking the exercise of self-restraint. Vietnam had demanded that the declaration includes a commitment not to build new structures on the islands.

It took three years before the ASEAN states and China came up with the first draft of guidelines to implement the DOC and six more years before the guidelines were adopted. Another six years would pass before both sides agreed on a framework listing the issues to be addressed by the COC. In 2018, the ASEAN states and China finally settled on a single draft negotiating text for the COC.[11] Negotiations followed but were further delayed from 2020 to 2022 following the outbreak of the COVID-19 pandemic.

The same factors that resulted in the failure to attain a legal document in 2002 have continued, leading to a lengthy, lethargic process in concluding a COC in the subsequent 20 years and making it difficult to put forward a collective effort. A major reason was each claimant's unwavering stance on its own sovereignty. All the claimants have stood firm on the issues of sovereign jurisdiction and maritime rights. Moreover, the importance of domestic legitimation means that none of the ruling elites would concede on territorial issues. In addition, the protracted talks involving the COC over the past two decades have also been attributed to the differing threat perceptions and uneven sense of urgency among the Southeast Asian states. The result was a persistent lack of consensus over the SCS, even among the ASEAN claimant states. Consequently, the ASEAN states and China continue to struggle to bridge their divergent perspectives and interests in the disputed waters.

---

[11] Thi Ha Hoang, "Pitfalls for ASEAN in negotiating a code of conduct in the South China Sea," *ISEAS Perspective* 57 (2019b): 1–8; Rahul Mishra, "Code of Conduct in the South China Sea: More discord than accord," *Maritime Affairs: Journal of the National Maritime Foundation of India* 13(2) (2017): 62–75; Nian Peng and Ngeow Chow Bing, "Managing the South China Sea dispute: Multilateral and bilateral approaches," *Ocean Development & International Law* 53(1) (2022): 37–59.

III. Maintaining Dialogue (While Muddling through Tensions)

The 2002 DOC did not prevent tensions from arising in the SCS. Standoffs, accusations, and finger-pointing involving China and individual claimants (as well as among the big powers) occurred from time to time, especially since the 2010s. The DOC, however, through the "ASEAN Way" of conflict management, has played an important role in maintaining dialogue and mitigating risks at a time of increasing power rivalries and regional uncertainties in the SCS.[12]

As a political framework, the DOC has been ineffective. It is incapable of restraining the claimants and powers, especially the major ones, from asserting their sovereignty and acting unilaterally to maximize their interests. The big power rivalries (primarily between China and the United States, but also among other powers), particularly since 2010, have increased tensions in the disputed waters, limiting and undermining the implementation of the DOC.

Despite the DOC provisions, virtually all claimant states have advanced their sovereign and maritime rights by undertaking offshore oil and gas exploration and/or promoting tourism, while building up their maritime forces and presence.[13] Some have explored and pursued legal approaches.[14] In May 2009, Vietnam and Malaysia made a

---

[12] Yang Fang, "The South China Sea disputes: Whither a solution?" In *Territorial disputes in the South China Sea*, edited by Jing Huang and Andrew Billo, pp. 164–188. London: Palgrave Macmillan UK, 2015; Munmun Majumdar, "The ASEAN way of conflict management in the South China Sea," *Strategic Analysis* 39(1) (2015): 73–87; Kaewkamol Pitakdumrongkit, "Coordinating the South China Sea issue: Thailand's roles in the code of conduct development," *International Relations of the Asia-Pacific* 15(3) (2015): 403–431.

[13] Rahul Mishra, "Code of Conduct in the South China Sea: More discord than accord," *Maritime Affairs: Journal of the National Maritime Foundation of India* 13(2) (2017): 62–75; Carlyle A. Thayer, "ASEAN's long March to a code of conduct in the South China Sea," *Maritime Issues*, 2017, http://www.maritimeissues.com/politics/aseans-long-march-to-a-code-of-conduct-in-the-south-china-sea.html.

[14] Nguyen Hong Thao and Ramses Amer, "A new legal arrangement for the South China Sea?" *Ocean Development & International Law* 40(4) (2009): 333–349; Nizam Basiron Sumathy Permal, and Melda Malek. 2013. "Philippines arbitral

joint submission to the Commission of the Limits of the Continental Shelf (CLCS), claiming an extended continental shelf in the southern part of the SCS. In January 2013, the Philippines instituted arbitral proceedings against China, openly challenging China's maritime claims. Since the late 2000s, China has become more assertive in conducting maritime patrols, building artificial islands, and deploying assets to the contested areas.[15] China has also built artificial islands by reclaiming land around its outposts.[16] According to one account, China reclaimed "over 3,200 acres of land, nearly 19 times as much as all of the other claimants combined," while fortifying "those outposts with airfields, ports, radars, and other facilities."[17] These actions have continued even after the July 2016 Hague-based arbitral tribunal's ruling, which overwhelmingly favored the Philippines and rejected China's nine-dash line claim to historic rights in the South China Sea.

The actions–reactions between the claimant states have resulted in several standoffs at sea. In 2014, for instance, tensions erupted between Vietnam and China, when the Chinese deep-water oil rig *Haiyang Shiyou 981* was deployed by the China National Offshore Oil

---

proceedings against China," *Australian Journal of Maritime & Ocean Affairs* 5(1) (2013): 37–40; Viet Hoang, "The Code of Conduct for the South China Sea: A long and bumpy road," *The Diplomat*, September 29, 2020, https://thediplomat.com/2020/09/the-code-of-conduct-for-the-south-china-sea-a-long-and-bumpy-road/.

[15]International Crisis Group, *Stirring up the South China Sea (III): A Fleeting Opportunity for Calm*, Brussels: ICG, 2015; Cheng-Chwee Kuik, "Explaining the contradiction in China's South China Sea Policy: Structural drivers and domestic imperatives," *China: An International Journal* 15(1) (2017): 163–186; Christopher Roberts, "The South China Sea: Beijing's challenge to ASEAN and UNCLOS and the necessity of a new multi-tiered approach," (2017): 307. RSIS Working Paper.

[16]Andrew Chubb, "PRC assertiveness in the South China Sea: Measuring continuity and change, 1970–2015," *International Security* 45(3) (2021): 79–121; M. Taylor Fravel, "China's strategy in the South China Sea," *Contemporary Southeast Asia* 33(3) (2011): 292–319.

[17]Felix K. Chang, "Uncertain prospects: South China Sea code of conduct negotiations." Foreign Policy Research Institute, 2020, https://www.fpri.org/article/2020/10/uncertain-prospects-south-china-sea-code-of-conduct-negotiations/.

Company (CNOOC) to waters 120 miles off the Vietnamese coast, near islands claimed by both countries. Weeks-long standoffs ensued. Scholar Huong Le Thu observed that the incident was "the closest Hanoi and Beijing have come to escalating into open confrontation since the bloody incident over Johnson South Reef in 1988."[18] As a more powerful China asserts itself in the disputed waters, even friendly countries (like Malaysia) and friendly governments (like the Duterte administration in the Philippines) have not been spared. On May 31, 2021, 16 People's Liberation Army Air Force (PLAAF) aircraft flew into the airspace near Malaysia's Sarawakian coast off the South China Sea. When this episode occurred, nearly 300 Chinese militia vessels remained in the Philippines' waters. In recent years, Chinese vessels have also started sailing into Indonesia's exclusive economic zone off Natuna Island.

Although the DOC is ineffective in constraining assertive states, it still serves such important functions as: maintaining dialogue and consultations, managing expectations and pressure, as well as exploring cooperation and functional collaboration. While these functions do not resolve the SCS disputes, they help mitigate risks and uncertainties. Considering the deeply divergent interests and differences among the claimant countries and big powers, these roles of the DOC should not be taken for granted.

A counterfactual analysis of the situation would be instructive. Without the DOC, the ASEAN states and China would not have a mutually accepted political framework to engage each other and explore peaceful means to manage the SCS disputes, arguably the most difficult multi-nation problem in contemporary Asia.[19] Without

---

[18] Huong Le Thu, "Rough Waters Ahead for Vietnam–China Relations," Carnegie Endowment for International Peace, 2020, https://carnegieendowment.org/2020/09/30/rough-waters-ahead-for-vietnam-china-relations-pub-82826.

[19] Thi Ha Hoang, *From Declaration to Code: Continuity and Change in China's Engagement with ASEAN on the South China Sea*, Yusof Ishak Institute (2019a); Cheng-Chwee Kuik, "Multilateralism in China's ASEAN policy: Its evolution, characteristics, and aspiration." *Contemporary Southeast Asia* 27(1) (2005): 102–122; Lai To Lee, *China and the South China Sea Dialogues*, Praeger, 1999.

the DOC, the ASEAN-China SOM would be unable to actively engage in institutionalized dialogue and constructive negotiations. Without the DOC, the ASEAN states, which are smaller and weaker, would not have much collective space to bargain with their giant neighbor. All in all, without the DOC, the COC would remain a distant, even unattainable pipe dream.

The reality, while far from perfect, is that with the DOC, the ASEAN states and China have been able to make some progress out of their institutionalized (as opposed to *ad hoc*) and continuous (as opposed to stagnant or stopped altogether) consultation, engagement, and dialogue (as opposed to outright confrontation and estrangement). In addition, the Southeast Asian claimant and coastal states have paid more attention to managing intra-ASEAN differences, leading to rounds of attempts to talk among themselves before talking with China as a group on touchy sovereignty and maritime boundary issues. In the process, some concrete and potentially achievable areas of cooperation have been identified; some are gradually materializing, while other areas are being mapped out and will be implemented in stages when conditions are ripe.

Thus, the decades-long DOC process has kept the hope of sustainable peace and stability alive, mitigating multiple risks and dangers typical of territorial disputes among multiple claimants and multiple big powers. While the dangers of tension escalation, power entrapment, group marginalization, and regional polarization cannot be eliminated (by any mechanisms and means), they have been mitigated to some extent by the DOC *process* and related efforts at various levels.

IV. Maximizing Convergences and Mapping Cooperation: A Phased Process

The continuous communication and dialogue process among the 11 signatories of the DOC has managed expectations, maximized convergences, and mapped cooperation. Each of these functions complements the roles of other tools in the overall dispute management of the SCS, ranging from bilateral diplomacy and regional multilateralism to functional cooperation and multilayered strategic alignments with multiple partners.

(i) *Managing Expectations*

The DOC processes have bridged and managed expectations, not just between ASEAN states and China, but also among the ASEAN claimant and non-claimant countries. The major expectation across the 11 signatories is that, while the peaceful resolution of the multi-nation SCS disputes remains a long-term goal, the prudent and collective management of the disputes are increasingly pressing tasks. This shared expectation is further deepened with the establishment of the ASEAN–China Comprehensive Strategic Partnership in November 2021.

Other emerging and converging expectations between the two sides include the realization that dispute management is a cooperative *process*. All processes take time and all progressive processes require two-way accommodation and mutual adaptation, which typically involve gradual phases of negotiation and interaction. Decades ago, when the 2002 DOC was signed, Emmers (who, like most experts, preferred a COC), described the declaration as "an interim accord," "a step in the right direction," which can be used by the 11 parties "as the basis for developing a binding code of conduct."[20] In 2011, maritime expert Sam Bateman considered the DOC as "a necessary step in the process aiming at establishing and agreeing on a 'code of conduct' in the South China Sea," adding that it was "a pragmatic move to put the disputes in the background and bring ASEAN–China economic ties to the fore" while providing "an example of solidarity among the ASEAN members."[21]

---

[20] Ralf Emmers, "ASEAN, China and the South China Sea: An opportunity missed," *IDSS Commentaries*, (2002): 1–3.
[21] Sam Bateman, "Regime building in the South China Sea–current situation and outlook," *Australian Journal of Maritime and Ocean Affairs* 3(1) (2011): 25–33; Shicun Wu and Ren Huaifeng, "More than a declaration: A commentary on the

(ii) *Maximizing Convergences*

Despite their territorial claims, the ASEAN states and China converge on much of their external outlook: preserving regional peace, avoiding regional polarization, and enabling wider partnerships and cooperation. These convergences have been deepened, and arguably, institutionalized, by the DOC process.

Even though the DOC cannot prevent standoffs and tensions from erupting, the ongoing efforts by the 10 ASEAN states and China since September 2013 to reach a COC on the basis of the DOC provide momentum for the ASEAN–China SOM to engage in continuous negotiations. The dialogue has borne fruit, albeit gradually and partially, as the two sides reached a Single Draft Negotiation Text in June 2018.[22] Although the COC remains a work in progress, there are signs indicating that the convergence of outlooks between ASEAN states and China on the above-mentioned policy goals today remains considerably high.

(iii) *Mapping Cooperation*

As a mechanism of peaceful dispute management, the DOC process has helped identify, prioritize, and map cooperation across policy areas and over time. Among the areas of cooperation identified in the DOC are: marine environmental protection and scientific research, the safety of navigation and communication at sea, search and rescue operations, and combating transnational crime (e.g., trafficking in illegal drugs, piracy and armed robbery at sea, illegal traffic in arms).

V. Conclusion

Despite its shortcomings and inadequacies, the important role of the DOC as a mechanism for peaceful dispute management should not be

---

background and the significance of the Declaration on the Conduct of the Parties in the South China Sea," *Chinese Journal of International Law* 2(1) (2003): 311–319.
[22] Ramses Amer and Li Jianwei, "From DOC to COC," In *Routledge Handbook of the South China Sea*, edited by Keyuan Zou, pp. 357–375. Routledge, 2021.

underestimated. Indeed, as discussed above, the DOC is still a vital step in peaceful dispute management. It offers an indispensable, albeit inadequate, platform for the pertinent parties to explore, negotiate, and develop peaceful approaches in preventing the SCS dispute from escalating into direct confrontation, while allowing all states to promote their core interests and preserve regional peace stability. To sum up, even though the DOC has been ineffectual in restraining states and reducing tensions, it is still instrumental for performing several essential functions: a purposeful baseline for continuous negotiation, a progressive transitional vehicle for exploring the next achievable goal (in this case COC), and a potentially transformative platform for mitigating multiple risks and maximizing strategic convergences, thereby keeping the space for eventually adopting a code of conduct that will benefit all parties by promoting peace and stability in the region.

© 2025 World Scientific Publishing Company
https://doi.org/10.1142/9789811296031_0011

Chapter

11

A Stronger DOC toward the Successful Completion of a Reliable COC: The ADMM in the Context of the South China Sea Issue

U. Zeyar Oo

Bagan Vision Institute, Naypyitaw, Mayanmar
zeyarzeyaroo@gmail.com

Abstract

In coincidence with the 20th anniversary of the signing of the Declaration on the Conduct of Parties in the South China Sea (DOC), global politics has become increasingly complicated and complex more than ever in the post-Cold War era due to the COVID-19 pandemic, compounded by the Russia–Ukraine conflict which has drawn the strongest response from the United States and its Western allies. Fortunately, peace and stability in another global flashpoint, the South China Sea, has been maintained considerably under the wisdom of the Association of Southeast Asian Nations (ASEAN) and China, especially between China and four direct claimants: Brunei, Malaysia, the Philippines, and Vietnam, and as a result of the 20 years old DOC. However, some scholars assume that the DOC is a toothless document since the individual claimants cannot relinquish the respective entrenched positions on their controlled islands, islets, reefs, and rocks based on their national interest, though the DOC has, to some extent, contributed to safeguarding peace and stability in the South China Sea. Some other scholars argue that the lack of practical engagement in some serious areas of cooperation as prevailed in the DOC and the need for serious discussion on the sovereign right over the respective controlled islands by the individual claimants in the South China Sea has weakened the DOC and also affected the Code of Conduct in the South China Sea's (COC) negotiation process. However, there is a myriad of authors who do research on the issue of the disputed waters in the South China Sea from legal and political perspectives; therefore, this chapter will focus on the issue of the South China Sea from a different point of view and suggest the need for considerable acceleration of implementation on sensitive and serious areas of cooperation as prescribed in the DOC. Therefore, this chapter is to examine the progress that has been made by ASEAN and China as prevailed in the DOC that contributes to the successful completion of the COC and to identify ways and means, and areas of cooperation that should be implemented by ASEAN and China to strengthen the integrity and credibility of the DOC in order to support the realization of the effective and efficient binding COC as early as possible. The approach of this chapter may differ from other scholars' perspectives, and however, it is expected to contribute to promoting the level of trust and confidence among the claimants in making the COC become a politically, legally, and morally respectable, reliable, and qualified binding document. This chapter suggests that ASEAN Defence Ministers Meeting (ADMM) should be considered an appropriate and reliable platform to complement some tasks given by the DOC to enhance confidence-building measures and to avoid potential risks of conflict at sea and in the air. As a mature and qualified mechanism, the ADMM can fill the gap of adequate practical cooperation as given in the DOC that needs ASEAN and China to implement in the context of the South China Sea.

Keywords: ADMM, AUKUS, COC, DOC, Confidence-building measure, Joint Declaration, QUAD, South China Sea

I. Introduction

A new geopolitical shit has been drawn by an array of global strategic incidents compounded by the COVID-19 pandemic and the Russia–Ukraine conflict, which led to an unprecedented response from the United States and its allies. Following the Russia–Ukraine war, the tension between the United States-led North Atlantic Treaty Organization (NATO), European Union, and Russia has constituted an increase in geopolitical competition that results in the spillover effects on the other regions of the world, especially in the Asia-Pacific region where the United States and China have engaged in the strategic competition. The rest of the world is engulfed in massive panic, increased concern, and strong frustration to see if another strategic crisis that is likely to emerge from the potential unfortunate face-off between the two superpowers would surely affect the whole world. Some scholars fear that, among other potential conflicts, the South China Sea is a vulnerable venue where the two major powers may clash, and there is a potential risk of conflict if the former constantly keeps on unleashing pressure on the latter by asserting freedom of navigation operation in order to challenge the entrenched position over its controlled islands in the South China Sea. Fortunately, the Association of Southeast Asian Nations (ASEAN) and China are still able to maintain a *status quo* among the individual claimants by upholding the guidelines prescribed in the Declaration on the Conduct of Parties in the South China Sea (DOC) and promoting confidence-building measures while trying to expedite the Code of Conduct in the South China Sea (COC) negotiation process.

Among ASEAN members, four claimants: Brunei, Malaysia, the Philippines, and Vietnam, have disputes with China over sovereign rights over respective islands in the South China Sea. The first statement of ASEAN on the disputed waters of the South China Sea was issued in 1992. It was the very start of ASEAN getting involved formally in the issue of the South China Sea. The signing of the DOC in

2002 in Phnom Penh under the Cambodian chairmanship is a historic milestone for ASEAN and China and the golden key to unlocking the door of the COC negotiation process and safeguarding peace and stability in the region. However, there have always been ups and downs in engagements between ASEAN and China toward the realization of an effective and efficient COC in the South China Sea. Two major issues have been witnessed in the COC process in ASEAN's position on engaging with China: the united approach of ASEAN as a team and China's position to discuss with the claimants on a voluntary basis that has paused for some years until 2013 to resume the talks between the two parties for the realization of COC. Some analysts view that the DOC is just a political statement on the South China Sea and that the claimants have no desire to effectively implement the DOC since the individual claimants signaled a mere sign of moving away from their entrenched positions based on their respective national interests regarding the territorial rights of the controlled islands in the South China Sea.

Due to the nature of political and legal sensitivities and the tangibility of the issue of the South China Sea, individual claimants used to touch on less sensitive and serious areas of cooperation as stipulated in the DOC. Nevertheless, both ASEAN and China have been making their utmost efforts to make an early conclusion of an effective and efficient COC based on the very principle of peaceful settlement through negotiations and consultations.[1] Some scholars argue that the progress of discussions on the realization of the COC has been at a slower speed and is still far from an early conclusion, as suggested by China to finalize it by 2022.[2] Some scholars also view that the lack of effective implementation of the tasks given by the DOC has also weakened the spirit of the DOC, and ASEAN and China need to

---

[1] ASEAN Secretariat News, "Declaration on the Conduct of Parties in the South China Sea," May 2012, https://asean.org/declaration-on-the-conduct-of-parties-in-the-south-china-sea-2/.
[2] Bill Hayton, "After 25 Years, There Is still no South China Sea Code of Conduct," *Foreign Policy, FP News,* July 2021, https://foreignpolicy.com/2021/07/21/south-china-sea-code-of-conduct-asean/.

deepen confidence-building measures by pursuing serious discussions on sensitive issues such as maritime security cooperation in the South China Sea.

Therefore, this chapter will identify ways and means to seek practical cooperation in solving serious issues so as to make the DOC more mature, and to increase mutual trust and confidence between ASEAN and China, especially among the individual claimant members of ASEAN and China.[3] This chapter suggests that ASEAN Defence Ministers' Meeting (ADMM) platform, which is the highest consultative and cooperative mechanism on defense and security matters within ASEAN and also with dialogue partners, may be considered a confidence-building platform for ASEAN and China to solve non-traditional activities within the context of the South China Sea. Defence ministers of ASEAN and China have already started ministerial engagements annually under the framework of ADMM Plus One informal meeting since 2013 and are exchanging views on defense and security-related matters including the issue of the South China Sea.[4] Therefore, this chapter will suggest the role of ADMM and possible cooperation on some pending issues which are also relevant to defense and security establishments on how to implement based on the DOC and within the context of the South China Sea in order to support the COC negotiation process.[5]

---

[3] ADMM ASEAN, "Concept Paper on Establishing a Direct Communications Link in the ADMM Process," adopted at the *8th ADMM*, Nay Pyi Taw, July 2019, http://admm.asean.org/dmdocuments/Concept%20Paper%20on%20 Establishing%20a%20DCL%20in%20the%20ADMM%20Process%20(Final).pdf.
[4] ADMM ASEAN, *Joint Declaration on Defence Cooperation to Strengthen Solidarity for a Harmonised Security*, Phnom Penh, June 22, 2022.
[5] ADMM ASEAN, "Concept Paper on the Guidelines for Maritime Interaction," adopted at the *11th ADMM*, Clark, the Philippines, October 2017, http://admm. asean.org/dmdocuments/2017_October_11th%20ADMM_Clark_23%20 October%202017_Concept%20Paper%20on%20the%20Guidelines%20for%20 Maritime%20Interaction%20(as%20of%2019%20September%202017).pdf.

II. A Brief Overview of the 20-Year Journey of the DOC

ASEAN started its formal involvement in the issue of the South China Sea by issuing its first political statement on the South China Sea in 1992. A gathering of the ASEAN foreign ministers, which took place on July 21, 1996, in Jakarta, Indonesia, first endorsed the idea of concluding a regional code of conduct in the South China Sea to set up a political foundation for the long-term stability and to foster trust, confidence, and understanding among claimant nations. After many rounds of negotiations, ASEAN and China signed the "Declaration on the Conduct of Parties in the South China Sea" (DOC) in November 2002, in Phnom Penh, under the chairmanship of Cambodia. The DOC is a historic milestone document that attempts to resolve the territorial disputes claimed by some ASEAN members and China in the disputed waters of the South China Sea.[6] Analyst Mingjiang Li views that the DOC reveals three themes: promoting confidence-building measures, engaging in practical maritime cooperation, and setting the stage for the discussion and consultation to realize a legally binding document of the COC.[7] He further views that as the political goodwill of all parties, the DOC, by and large, maintains overall stability in the South China Sea and serves as a moral constraint on all claimant states in the South China Sea.[8]

The first joint working group meeting which was tasked to study and provide specific policy measures for the implementation of the DOC was held in Manila in August 2005.[9] During the meeting,

---

[6] Alice Ba, "Managing the South China Sea disputes: What can ASEAN do? Perspectives on the South China Sea," *Centre for Strategic & International Studies*, 202 (2014): 1–12.

[7] Embassy of the People's Republic of China in the Republic of Singapore, "Significant Progress Made in Implementing DOC and Pushing Forward Negotiation of COC," August 2015, https://www.mfa.gov.cn/ce/cesg/eng/jrzg/t1286517.htm.

[8] Mingjiang Li, "Managing Security in the South China Sea from DOC to COC," *Kyoto Review of Southeast Asia*, March 2014, https://kyotoreview.org/issue-15/managing-security-in-the-south-china-sea-from-doc-to-coc/.

[9] ADMM ASEAN, "Concept Paper for the Establishment of ADMM," adopted at the *Inaugural ADMM*, Kuala Lumpur, May 9, 2006, http://admm.asean.org/

ASEAN brought a draft document of seven-point guidelines for the implementation of the DOC. The second joint working group meeting was conducted in Sanya in 2006, which resulted in agreement among the parties to focus on six areas of cooperation. During the 44th ASEAN Ministerial Meeting held in 2011, China and ASEAN agreed on the Guidelines for the Implementation of the Declaration on Conduct of Parties in the South China Sea.[10] After a series of discussions and negotiations, ASEAN and China finally reached the conclusion of the DOC implementation guidelines in July at the China–ASEAN Foreign Ministers' Meeting. In 2012, ASEAN senior officials started working on the draft outlines of the COC and presented it during the July 2012 ASEAN Foreign Ministers' Meeting in Phnom Penh, and later reached an agreement with China to pursue the COC negotiation process.[11] Both parties identified four main areas of disagreement[12]: the geographic scope, restrictions on construction on occupied and unoccupied features, military activities in waters adjacent to Nansha (Spratly) Islands, and policies concerning the detainment of fishermen found in disputed waters.[13]

First, China–ASEAN Senior Officials' Meeting on the COC was convened on September 25, 2013 in Suzhou. During the Chairmanship of Cambodia, a draft COC was proposed by the Philippines and brought for discussion within ASEAN. Unfortunately, the 2012 version of the COC was responded to with a revised draft proposal from

---

dmdocuments/1.%20Concept%20Paper%20for%20the%20Establishment%20of%20an%20ASEAN%20Defence%20Ministers.pdf.

[10] ASEAN Secretariat News, "ASEAN and China Agreed on the Guidelines for the Implementation of the Declaration on Conduct of Parties in the South China Sea," May 2011.

[11] ASEAN Secretariat News, "ASEAN Foreign Ministers' Meeting in Phnom Penh," July 2012.

[12] Ministry of Foreign Affairs of the People's Republic of China, "China Adheres to the Position of Setting through Negotiation the Relevant Disputes between China and Philippines in the South China Sea," July 2016, https://www.fmprc.gov.cn/mfa_eng/wjdt_665385/2649_665393/201607/t20160713_679474.html.

[13] Carlyle A. Thayer, "ASEAN's code of conduct in the South China Sea: A litmus test for community-building?" *Asia-Pacific Journal-Japan Focus*, 10 (2012): 145.

Indonesia. On September 27, 2012, Indonesia presented the "Zero Draft a Regional Code of Conduct in the South China Sea" to ASEAN Foreign Ministers during a UN meeting in New York. In August 2017, ASEAN and China started to work on the COC framework, and both sides agreed on the Single Draft of COC in August 2018. The first reading of the COC Single Draft Negotiating Text was concluded by foreign ministers from China and ASEAN in 2019 in Bangkok, and they emphasized the need to maintain and promote an environment conducive to the COC negotiations and thus welcomed practical measures that could reduce tensions and the risk of accidents, misunderstandings, and miscalculations.[14] In 2019, Foreign Minister Wang Yi expressed optimism that the COC would be completed within three years.[15] According to Wang Yi, China supports a COC that has a "binding force" recognizing that the COC will have to be "an upgraded and strengthened version" of the DOC.[16] However, when the COVID-19 pandemic surged, the in-person scheduled meetings were prevented from being held until 2022. Chairman's statement at the 37th ASEAN Summit observed the continuously improving cooperation between ASEAN and China and further added that they were encouraged by the progress of the substantive negotiations toward the early conclusion of an effective and substantive COC consistent with international law including the 1982 United Nations Convention on the Law of the Sea (UNCLOS) within a mutually agreed timeline.[17] The second reading of the Single

---

[14] ASEAN Secretariat News, "Conclusion of the First Reading of the COC Single Draft Negotiating Text in Bangkok," 2019.

[15] Xinhua Staff, "ASEAN FMs Welcome Efforts, Progress on COC Negotiations," *Xinhua News*, August 2019, https://cambodianess.com/article/asean-fms-welcome-efforts-progress-on-coc-negotiations.

[16] Sebastian Strangion, "Chinese FM Pledges Progress on South China Sea Code of Conduct," *The Diplomat*, China Power, Diplomacy, East Asia, July 2022, https://thediplomat.com/2022/07/chinese-fm-pledges-progress-on-south-china-sea-code-of-conduct/.

[17] Lee Ying Hui, "Southeast Asia is Pushing Back on Beijing on the South China Sea," *Channel News Asia*, July 2020, https://www.channelnewsasia.com/commentary/asean-south-china-sea-vietnam-malaysia-indonesia-philippines-law-710856.

Draft COC Negotiating Text has been developed as a sign of progress.[18]

III. Shortcomings and the Need to Increase Practical Cooperation as per the DOC

Looking over the 20-years journey of the DOC, progress has been significantly made by both ASEAN and China in pursuing one of the tasks clearly suggested in the DOC which is to create a stronger binding document of a COC to settle disputes and conflicts among parties in the South China Sea. However, some analysts argue that the DOC has been disregarded and not fully abided by the parties concerned in the disputed waters of the South China Sea. Some further view that the DOC does not authorize legal power and rather bears moral constraints on the claimants of both ASEAN and China. Some analysts also see that claimant countries have been sticking to their entrenched positions and looking for their own national interests or security concerns which can only weaken the credibility of the DOC and affect the consultations on the early conclusion of the COC. Some scholars suggest that the DOC, to some extent, helps the claimant countries to refrain from activities that might lead to potential conflicts in the South China Sea; however, the parties directly concerned still need to seek serious discussion and promote practical maritime cooperation in areas such as environmental protection, search and rescue, navigation safety, law enforcement, military mutual trust, and humane treatment of fishermen.

Although the claimant nations of ASEAN and China have been engaging in various areas of cooperation as confidence-building

---

[18] Augus Haryanto and Arief Bakhtiar Darmawan, "Does the single draft of COC in the South China Sea matter?" *Intermestic: Journal of International Studies*, 4 (2020), http://download.garuda.kemdikbud.go.id/article.php?article=1717205&val=10271&title=Does%20the%20Single%20Draft%20of%20COC%20in%20the%20South%20China%20Sea%20Matters; Hoang Thi Ha, "ASEAN and the South China Sea Code of Conduct: Raising the Aegis of International Law," *Fulcrum*, September 21, 2020, https://www.iseas.edu.sg/media/commentaries/asean-and-the-south-china-sea-code-of-conduct-raising-the-aegis-of-international-law/.

measures according to the DOC, some incidents have ensured the shortcomings that affect the credibility and efficacy of the DOC, increase trust deficits between and among individual claimants, and also threaten ASEAN–China engagements and consultations for the COC in the South China Sea. The 2014 incident that occurred between a Vietnamese fishing vessel and a Chinese oil rig company was the most significant tension scraping the integrity of the DOC and became a shockwave against confidence-building measures that have been promoted by ASEAN and China to avoid any risk of potential conflicts in the South China Sea.[19] Analysts argue that the activities and infrastructure build-ups by individual claimant countries including China, in their respective occupied positions in the South China Sea, are major factors that raise concerns of other claimants and question the uncertainty of the DOC and its commitment to bringing peace and stability to the region. Therefore, the claimant countries have started seeking legal approaches to claim their sovereign rights over the disputed waters. That in turn impacts ASEAN's way of confidence-building measures and affects the credibility and efficacy of the DOC and also on the COC negotiation process. In 2013, the Philippines brought a case to The Permanent Court of Arbitration against China over the sovereign rights of the disputed waters that constituted ambiguity within ASEAN and resulted in the diversion of the ongoing COC negotiation process. Vietnam and Malaysia had also staged their cases to the International Commission of Continental Shelf against China over the overlapping claims when they faced the counterclaims of China. It is evident that the DOC that has been morally and politically committed by ASEAN and China does not offer a sufficient level of confidence between parties and that it can easily undermine a trust-building process.

Therefore, analysts remind that although ASEAN and China have made significant progress in implementing the DOC as a guiding

---

[19] SD Pradhan, "Bleak Chances of Progress on ASEAN–China on Code of Conduct in 2021: Implications for Vietnam," *The Times of India*, March 2021, https://timesofindia.indiatimes.com/blogs/ChanakyaCode/bleak-chances-of-progress-on-asean-china-on-code-of-conduct-in-2021-implications-for-vietnam/.

document to avoid risks of potential conflicts in the South China Sea, they still need serious discussions and effective practical cooperation in sensitive areas as prescribed in the DOC. According to Article 6 of the DOC, "pending a comprehensive and durable settlement of the disputes, the Parties concerned may explore or undertake cooperative activities that include marine environmental protection, marine scientific research, safety of navigation and communication at sea, search and rescue operation, and combating transnational crime, including but not limited to trafficking in illicit drugs, pricy and armed robbery at sea." In this sense, ASEAN and China should touch on the c, d, e of Article 6 of the DOC that are considered to be in connection with defense and security issues, which are quite sensitive for the parties directly concerned. Nevertheless, mutual understanding, trust, and confidence between ASEAN claimants and China must be built up to support the ongoing process of consultations of the COC in the South China Sea.

IV. Different Approaches Pursued by the Individual Claimants

ASEAN and China have started dialogues and talks on the COC since 1992 and finally reached a common ground with the DOC. However, there have been ups and downs in the implementation of the DOC and in upgrading the DOC to a realization of legally binding COC in the South China Sea. Looking at the approaches made by the individual claimants in pursuing a solution to their security concerns in the South China Sea, they can be classified into three categories: The first category is a unilateral approach in the search for its own solution; the second is a bilateral approach to avoid any risk of potential conflicts; and the third category is a multilateral approach through ASEAN and China dialogue framework, implementing the DOC and pursuing the COC negotiation process. Apart from that, some claimants try to internationalize the issue of the South China Sea and get international support. The claimant countries including China have their own positions to achieve legitimacy over the controlled islands, reefs, shoals, and rocks in the South China Sea and continue to build up activities and infrastructure, thereby increasing more trust deficits among the claimants.

Bilaterally, the claimants have established communication lines to reduce tensions in the disputed waters, avoid unexpected incidents in their respective territorial waters, and conduct cooperative activities in less sensitive areas like marine exploration and maritime seismic study. Among claimant countries, Vietnam and China have set up a line of communication and have started bilateral maritime activities such as maritime exploration. However, they have failed to go through serious discussions on the disputed waters and still need to cooperate in sensitive areas such as conducting joint activities in search and rescue, navigation safety, law enforcement, military mutual trust, and humane treatment of fishermen. Bilateral cooperation between China and other claimants is pursued considerably, but serious cooperation on the above activities is yet to be jointly conducted. Some analysts argue that the best way to solve the issue of the South China Sea is the multilateral approach through ASEAN, in particular, through the effective implementation of the tasks mentioned in the DOC and through consultations on the realization of the COC.[20] ASEAN sees the DOC as a common guiding document in managing the risk of potential conflicts in the disputed waters of the South China Sea and a significant step for the realization of the effective and efficient legally binding document COC that will contribute to safeguarding peace and stability in the South China Sea.[21] Therefore, ASEAN has been consistently and actively participating at the negotiation table with China on the consultation of the COC, even though the individual claimant member states uphold different positions over their own security concerns in the disputed waters. Individual claimants

---

[20] Bill Hayton, "How to Solve the South China Sea Disputes," *ISEAS Perspective*, 2022, https://www.iseas.edu.sg/articles-commentaries/iseas-perspective/2022-25-how-to-solve-the-south-china-sea-disputes-by-bill-hayton/.

[21] Edcel John A. Ibarra, *Revisiting the Need for a Legally Binding Code of Conduct in the South China Sea: Chasing a Moving Target*. CIRSS Commentaries, Vol. VII, March 2021, https://fsi.gov.ph/revisiting-the-need-for-a-legally-binding-code-of-conduct-in-the-south-china-sea-chasing-a-moving-target/.

have also staged their separate agendas in approaching the issue of the South China Sea in order to achieve sovereign rights over their respective islands, islets, reefs, and shoals, and therefore, the claimants are set to internationalize the South China Sea issue.

After the 2014 oil rig incident between Vietnam and China, the Philippines' case was brought to the International Arbitral Court, and the internationalization of the issue by the claimants has increasingly accelerated, thus constituting strategic concerns and ambiguity among the claimant countries and China. In December 2019, Malaysia made a partial submission to the International Commission of Continental Shelf (ICCS) regarding its continental shelf in the northern part of the South China Sea. In May 2020, Indonesia submitted a verbal note to the United Nations in response to the series of circular notes filed by China in relation to Malaysia's ICCS submission.

At the 36th ASEAN Summit held in June 2020, the Chairman's Statement contained an explicit mention of the 1982 UNCLOS as the basis for the settlement of disputes. Some argue that the DOC has actually contributed to several cases of cooperation in the South China Sea such as the tripartite joint seismic study among China, Vietnam, and the Philippines from 2005 to 2008.[22] Some analysts view that the relatively stable situation in the South China Sea before 2008 imposed little incentive on the claimant parties, individually or collectively, to take serious steps to implement the DOC. Initially, China preferred to discuss with the relevant parties while ASEAN continued its current practice of consulting among themselves before meeting with China.[23] However, ASEAN and China eventually agreed to conclude the DOC implementation guidelines in July 2011

---

[22] Robert Beckman, *South China Sea: How China Could Clarify Its Claims*, S. Rajaratnam School of International Studies, 2010, https://www.rsis.edu.sg/wp-content/uploads/2014/07/CO10116.pdf.

[23] Supalak Ganjanakhundee, "Wishful Thinking on Code of Conduct for South China Sea," *The Nation, Perspective*, February 2017, https://www.nationthailand.com/perspective/30306229.

at China–ASEAN Foreign Ministers' Meeting.[24] But the process of carrying out the cooperative projects enshrined in the DOC has greatly been slowed.[25]

V. External Powers as a Factor

Initially, external powers were not actively involved in the issue of the South China Sea since the overall situation in the South China Sea remained largely tranquil during those years, particularly from 2002 to 2009. However, external powers like the United States and its allies seemed to have stepped up their efforts in the management of security disputes in the South China Sea lately. Freedom of navigation in the region has become a principal idea of the external powers that have been largely exercised by the United States and its allies such as Australia, Britain, and France by sending their warships somewhere within 12 nautical miles of islands controlled by China in the South China Sea, and therefore lead to increased tensions between China and the United States.[26] The South China Sea is one of the possible battlegrounds where the United States has come to compete with China in the region as part of the former's Indo-Pacific strategy to contain the latter. According to the Joint Vision Statement issued at the recent Special Summit between ASEAN countries and the United States, it said that "We emphasize the importance of practical measures that could reduce tensions and the risk of accidents, misunderstandings and miscalculations." However, some analysts think that the involvement of the United States may not be beneficial to the COC negotiation process. Kimkong Heng, a senior research fellow at the Cambodia Development Centre, argues that the United States'

---

[24] Prashanth Parameswaran, "Will a China-ASEAN South China Sea Really Matter?" *The Diplomat*, August 2017, https://thediplomat.com/2017/08/will-a-china-asean-south-china-sea-code-of-conduct-really-matter/.

[25] ASEAN Archive, "Documents on ASEAN and South China Sea," June 2011, https://www.assidmer.net/doc/Documents-on-ASEAN-and-South-China-Sea-as-of-June-2011.pdf.

[26] Hoang Thi Ha, "Pitfalls for ASEAN in Negotiating a Code of Conduct in the South China Sea," *Think-Asia*, July 2019.

own agenda might exacerbate rather than facilitate the South China Sea negotiations.[27] Joint military exercises between claimants and external powers are increasingly intensified in the region as well.[28] In 2022, India and Vietnam jointly held a naval exercise in the South China Sea. The United States and the Philippines have resumed the annual Balikatan military exercise that had been postponed due to the pandemic. China also organized one of its largest-ever military exercises with Russia, involving 10,000 troops.[29]

Adding to the U.S.-led Freedom of Navigation program, the United Kingdom, Germany, and France have all sent naval vessels to the region that can surely affect the ongoing negotiations between ASEAN and China on the COC. The resumption of Quadrilateral Security Dialogue (QUAD) and the establishment of AUKUS (Australia, the United Kingdom, and the United States) which is a security and technological alliance has increased China's strategic concerns which would adversely affect peace and stability in the region. Both QUAD and AUKUS security pacts are designed to counter against rising China in the region. The Philippines argues that a stronger Western presence could deter moves from China in the South China Sea while Indonesia points out that AUKUS could provoke an arms race in the region, and Malaysia stressed the need to maintain dialogue with China.

At the QUAD Summit on March 12, 2022, the QUAD leaders committed to their shared vision of a free, open, and inclusive region anchored by universal values and unconstrained by coercive power which clearly targets China. However, China's position is quite clear, and it does not want to be influenced by countries outside the region in resolving the South China Sea issue, especially in the COC

---

[27] Kimkong Heng, "The Rise of China: Global Threat or International Peace?" *UC Occasional Paper Series* 1.1 (2017): 1–18.
[28] RFA Staff, "China, ASEAN to Hold South China Sea Code of Conduct Talks This Month," *Radio Free Asia*, May 2022, https://www.rfa.org/english/news/china/asean-southchinasea-05162022091755.html.
[29] Aristyo Rizka Darmawan, "AUKUS Adds Fuel to the South China Sea Dispute," *East Asia Forum*, November 2021. https://www.eastasiaforum.org/2021/11/01/aukus-adds-fuel-to-the-south-china-sea-dispute/.

negotiation process.³⁰ Chinese Foreign Minister Wang Yi stated in August 2019 that China would make unswerving efforts to safeguard the generally stable situation in the South China Sea that does not come easily and would not allow any country to cause chaos in the South China Sea. Wang Yi also reminded that the Chinese side would not accept any actions of sensationalizing, fomenting opposition, and making unfounded accusations, nor would the Chinese side accept any so-called initiative that promotes double standards under the disguise of justice.³¹

VI. The ADMM in the Context of the South China Sea Issue

As observed before, ASEAN and China have been making efforts to maintain peace and stability in the South China Sea through confidence-building measures based on the principles stipulated in the DOC and working on the realization of the COC in the South China Sea. However, analysts assume that the DOC is not being fully implemented by the parties directly concerned, and they lack practical cooperation in sensitive areas. Therefore, ASEAN and China need to consider other avenues for confidence-building measures beyond the DOC, particularly in areas such as non-traditional security, information sharing, and capacity building, as well as in defense diplomacy, to be able to gain more confidence and trust among the parties directly concerned. They also need to explore more opportunities for cooperation. As Baviera notes, the region's navies and enforcement agencies have already been receptive to information sharing and capacity building in the area of maritime safety. Two mechanisms already exist namely the Information Fusion Center in Singapore, which works

---

³⁰ Tin Sokhavuth , "Bid to Complete South China Sea Code of Conduct This Year," *Khmer Times,* January 2022, https://www.khmertimeskh.com/501001474/bid-to-complete-south-china-sea-code-of-conduct-this-year/.

³¹ Sebastian Strangion, "Chinese FM Pledges Progress on South China Sea Code of Conduct," *The Diplomat, China Power, Diplomacy, East Asia,*" July 2022, https://thediplomat.com/2022/07/chinese-fm-pledges-progress-on-south-china-sea-code-of-conduct/.

with more than 60 agencies and 30 countries to provide information toward the prevention of piracy and timely responses to maritime events, and the Regional Cooperation Agreement on Combating Piracy and Armed Robbery against Ships in Asia, which was created to promote and enhance cooperation against piracy and armed robberies in Asia.

ADMM is the highest ministerial defense and security consultative and cooperative mechanism in ASEAN and reports directly to the ASEAN Heads of Government on the development of cooperation in defense and security areas. According to the Concept Paper for the Establishment of an ASEAN Defence Ministers' Meeting, ADMM will be focusing on the exchange of views on regional and international security and defense issues; making voluntary briefings on defense and security policies; discussing related activities outside the ASEAN process; discussing interaction with external partners; and reviving of ASEAN defense cooperation. It will be guided by ASEAN fundamental principles enshrined in the Treaty of Amity and Cooperation in Southeast Asia. According to Article IV of Protocol to the Concept Paper for the Establishment of ADMM, the ADMM recognizes that the development of the ASEAN Security Community is open, flexible, and outward-looking. According to Article II of the protocol document, the ADMM elevates existing defense and military interactions to a higher plain from confidence-building initiatives to tangible defense and security cooperation within the ASEAN framework. The ADMM shall actively engage ASEAN friends and Dialogue Partners in dialogue and cooperation on defense and security matters through an ADMM-Plus mechanism at a pace comfortable to all ASEAN member countries while respecting the principles of consensus-based decision-making, independence, sovereignty, and non-interference in internal affairs.

Having such sensibility, ADMM agreed upon the proposal of the People's Liberation Army (PLA) of China to conduct an ASEAN–China Defence Ministerial Informal Meeting, and the first ASEAN–China of ADMM plus One meeting was held during the 7th ADMM in Brunei in 2013. Since then, ASEAN and China Defence Ministers' Informal Meeting has been held regularly. According to the meeting notes, ministers from ASEAN member states and China openly and frankly exchange views on a range of defense and security issues on the basis of confidence-building measures. It is said that the issue of the South China Sea has been the top agenda of the ministers from ASEAN and China to share their concerns on the risks of potential conflicts, to show their great support for the ongoing efforts of ASEAN and China on the realization of COC in the South China Sea, and to seek potential means of practical cooperation with China through ADMM in order to increase confidence-building measures in the South China Sea that would prevent the risks of conflicts that might occur at sea. ADMM-Plus Informal Meetings between ASEAN and China have become more and more mature and quite useful as confidence-building platforms in sensitive areas of cooperation such as security and defense. Looking at ADMM Joint Declarations issued annually by ADMM under the rotating chairmanship, the issue of the South China Sea and cooperation between China and ASEAN on the ongoing process of the COC negotiation process has always been mentioned in the preamble section of JD. It is a collective message of the ADMM ministers in an epilogue that highlights the will and attitude of the ADMM ministers to contribute to ASEAN's efforts on the issue of the South China Sea. According to the Joint Declaration of 16th ADMM on Defence Cooperation to Strengthen Solidarity for a Harmonised Security, the defense ministers of ASEAN member states declared that "The parties are committed in promoting maritime security, safety and freedom of navigation and overflight and creating a conducive environment for the peaceful settlement of disputes in the South China Sea."

The ADMM is a primary and principal platform for the defense and security engagements of the ASEAN, and its related platforms are ADMM-Plus, ADMM-Plus One informal and ASEAN Chief of Defence Formal Meeting (ACDFM). The ADMM mainly focuses on non-traditional security issues. However, as per the ADMM Three Year Programs, the ADMM highlights conflict prevention and conflict resolution through the development of cooperative mechanisms for peaceful settlements which is the area that can also be cooperated with China to reduce the risks of potential conflicts in the South

China Sea. According to ASEAN archival, so far, the ADMM has become mature within ASEAN and with the dialogue partners through its integral part of ADMM-Plus, and ADMM-Plus One informal. It has produced effective and efficient instruments that can be utilized in cooperating with China to intensify confidence-building measures and to avoid unwarranted and undesirable incidents at sea in the South China Sea. "The Concept Paper on Establishing A Direct Communications Link in the ADMM Process," "the Concept Paper on Guidelines for Air Military Encounters," "the Concept Paper on the Guidelines for Maritime Interaction," and "the Discussion Paper on Illegal, Unreported and Unregulated Fishing: Security Implications and the Role of Defence Establishments" are among other instruments adopted by the ADMM.[32] They are relevant and applicable in enhancing confidence and trust and are also useful in encountering any potential risks for conflicts at sea and in the air in the Asia-Pacific region. Such readiness of the ADMM should be considered a vital instrument which is supportive and contributive in establishing practical cooperation with any third country, particularly with China, through ADMM Plus One informal platform.

ASEAN and China already have cooperation experience in the maritime domain, and that was the first ASEAN–China maritime field training exercise conducted on October 22–28, 2018 in Zhanjiang in China's southern Guangdong province.[33] It featured several activities, including helicopter cross-desk landings and a joint search and rescue operation. It was jointly organized by ASEAN member states and China through coordination and communication at the ADMM-Plus

---

[32] ADMM ASEAN, "Concept Paper on Guidelines for Air Encounters," adopted at the *11th ADMM*, Clark, the Philippines, October 23, 2017, http://admm.asean.org/dmdocuments/2017_October_11th%20ADMM_Clark_23%20October%202017_(Singapore)%20Concept%20Paper%20on%20Guidelines%20for%20Air%20Encounters.pdf.

[33] ADMM ASEAN, "Discussion Paper on Illegal, Unreported and Unregulated Fishing: Security Implications and the Role of Defence Establishments," noted by the *13th ADMM*, Bangkok, 11 July 2019, http://admm.asean.org/dmdocuments/2019_July_13th%20ADMM_Bangkok,%2011%20July%202019_7.%20Final%20IUU.pdf.

One informal platform. According to Chinese Vice-Admiral Youan Yubai, the Commander of the People's Liberation Army Navy (PLAN) who is commander of the Southern Theater Command, it is not just a one-off engagement, but there will be more in the future also. Apart from that, China has jointly organized maritime field exercises with other ASEAN member states in promoting a community of common destiny between ASEAN and China. Therefore, the door is still for ASEAN and China to use the ADMM Plus One informal platform to start practical cooperation in maritime areas, as mentioned in the DOC. It is surely a vital platform to promote trust and confidence between the parties and thus support the ongoing efforts of consultations on the COC in the South China Sea.

VII. Conclusion and Suggestions

The DOC is a historic binding document for both ASEAN and China in managing risks of potential conflict and achieving peace and stability in the South China Sea and the entire region.[34] Although some analysts criticize the DOC as a toothless document which is merely abided by the claimant nations, it is an undeniable fact that the DOC has attained the credibility and confidence of the parties directly concerned and that it can be used to bring ASEAN and China to a negotiating table for a Code of Conduct acceptable to all parties in the South China Sea. On the other hand, the DOC has, to some extent, maintained a conducive atmosphere in the South China Sea despite individual claimants of ASEAN and China with their entrenched positions and the implicit pressures of external powers in the South China Sea. It is also an unquestionable fact that mutual trust and confidence between ASEAN and China is quite high at the conclusion of the first reading of the COC Single Draft Negotiating Text, and it gains further encouragement in realizing a COC through the second reading. However, ASEAN's position on having an effective and efficient

---

[34] Zong Haihe, "DOC: The Cornerstone for South China Sea Peace and Stability," *Global Times*, June, 2022, https://www.globaltimes.cn/page/202206/1268287.shtml.

COC is also relevant to other universal laws including the UNCLOS and China's position on its relevant documents. Different approaches of the individual claimants to achieve sovereign rights over the respective controlled islands in the disputed waters have also affected the COC process and undermined the credibility of the DOC.[35] Among other approaches, a multilateral approach through ASEAN in engaging with China is more relevant, effective, and efficient in solving the issue of the South China Sea. The most underlying factor that affects the credibility of the DOC and the slowdown of the COC negotiation process is that individual claimants are still interested in making serious discussions to politicize the issue and the failure to start practical cooperation in sensitive and vulnerable areas such as maritime security cooperation. In this situation, the credibility, maturity and relevancy of the ADMM can fill the gap of practical cooperation, and it can help promote confidence-building measures politically and give necessary political support for the successful holding of the COC negotiation process.[36] The ADMM Plus One informal platform should be considered a driving mechanism in undertaking practical cooperation between ASEAN and China. As shown in the past evidence, ASEAN and China should consider the potentiality of practical cooperation and the possible usefulness of the ADMM-Plus One informal platform to promote mutual cooperation in the serious part of cooperation areas such as maritime security cooperation as stipulated in the DOC. If the platform can be used smartly and intelligently, it can surely support and contribute to the early conclusion of a Code of Conduct in the South China Sea.

---

[35] Walter Lohman, "A critical Assessment of ASEAN's Diplomacy Regarding the South China Sea." In *Territorial Disputes in the South China Sea*, edited by Jing Huang and Andrew Billo, pp. 82–96. Springer, 2015.

[36] ADMM ASEAN, "Protocol to the Concept Paper for the Establishment of the ADMM," adopted at the *2nd ADMM*, Singapore, November 13–15, 2007. November 2007, http://admm.asean.org/dmdocuments/2.%20Protocol%20to%20 the%20Concept%20Paper%20for%20the%20Establishment%20of%20the%20ADMM. pdf.

© 2025 World Scientific Publishing Company
https://doi.org/10.1142/9789811296031_0012

Chapter 12

ASEAN, China, and the South China Sea

Ong Keng Yong* and Nazia Hussain[†]

S. Rajaratnam School of International Studies (RSIS),
Nanyang Technological University, Singapore
*amboky@ntu.edu.sg
†isnhussain@ntu.edu.sg

Abstract

ASEAN plays a pivotal role in promoting dialogue, cooperation, and confidence-building measures to manage maritime disputes in the South China Sea. However, despite protracted negotiations, the South China Sea issue continues to trouble relations between ASEAN and China as ASEAN strives toward an inclusive, open, and stable regional political and security community in Southeast Asia. The complexity of the issues involved means there are considerable difficulties in reaching an agreement between ASEAN and China on sharing the contiguous geography, managing ingrained perceptions of history, and apportioning responsibility in the maintenance of peace and prosperity in the South China Sea. At the same time, it is not possible to co-exist and work in partnership without rule-making and a rules-based framework for mutual benefit and progress. At the end of the day, both ASEAN, not just the claimant states in the grouping, and China stands to benefit from realizing the Code of Conduct in the South China Sea.

Keywords: ASEAN, Maritime Disputes, South China Sea, Code of Conduct

I. Introduction

The strategic significance of the South China Sea, or SCS in short, is indisputable. As the shortest route linking the Indian Ocean and the Pacific Ocean, the maritime corridor is crucial for free trade regimes — approximately 25% of world shipping transport moves through sea lanes that pass through the SCS — and for naval fleets traversing across the oceans. The SCS is endowed with rich fishery resources. Various reputable Western and non-Western sources have also estimated that there is so much untapped oil and natural gas beneath the seabed of the SCS, which is one of the largest seas on Earth. Increasingly, the ecosystems in the SCS and blue ocean/green plan development of the South China Sea natural environment are critical for managing climate change and rising sea levels of the littoral states.

The SCS is not only plagued by multiple overlapping claims of territorial sovereignty over islands, reefs, and other features but also by concerns pertaining to jurisdiction over territorial waters, exclusive economic zones, and continental shelves. Different islands, reefs, and features in Nansha (the Spratlys) are claimed by China, Vietnam, the Philippines, Malaysia, and Brunei, whereas most of Xisha (the Paracels) have been controlled by China since 1974, although Vietnam also claims ownership of the islands. Except for Brunei, all the claimant parties have some level of physical presence in the SCS.[1]

Maritime disputes in the SCS, influenced by economic, strategic, and geopolitical considerations, affect the regional security landscape and the role of the Association of Southeast Asian Nations (ASEAN) within it. Despite protracted negotiations, the South China Sea issue

---

[1] Quang Minh Pham, "The South China Sea security problem: Towards regional cooperation," *Asia Europe Journal*, 8 (2010): 427–434.

continues to trouble relations between ASEAN and China as ASEAN strives toward an inclusive, open, and stable regional political and security community in Southeast Asia.

II. Historical Context

Dating back to the time of the nationalist Kuomintang party, China had an 11-dash line on a map demarcating its territorial claims in the SCS, which included much of the whole sea — Dongsha (the Pratas) Island and nearby features, Zhongsha Islands (the Macclesfield Bank), Xisha, and Nansha. Subsequently, the government of the People's Republic of China (PRC) removed the portion encompassing parts of the Gulf of Tonkin, changing the map to the nine-dash line version, which Beijing cites to this day as the historical basis for its territorial claims in the SCS.

There was a gradual build-up of tensions, notably with the 1988 clash at Chigua (Johnson) Reef in Nansha, which saw Chinese and Vietnamese naval vessels exchange fire, culminating in many casualties. This incident marked China's first armed conflict with an ASEAN member state over Nansha.

China passed its Law on the Territorial Sea and the Contiguous Zone in February 1992. While Article 2 of the said Chinese law spells much of the SCS as China's internal waters, Articles 6, 7, and 12 require non-Chinese naval vessels to seek Beijing's permission before traversing the SCS, submarines to navigate on the surface of the sea and show their flags, and non-Chinese aircraft to obtain permission for overflight.[2] Article 8 permits Beijing to adopt all necessary measures to prevent and stop the passage of a ship deemed not innocent through its territorial sea.[3] Article 10 affords Beijing the right to

---

[2] "Law on the Territorial Sea and the Contiguous Zone," February 25, 1992, https://www.un.org/depts/los/LEGISLATIONANDTREATIES/PDFFILES/CHN_1992_Law.pdf.
[3] *Ibid*. Reference to Article 8 of the Law on the Territorial Sea and the Contiguous Zone.

order the immediate eviction of foreign naval vessels from the area.[4] Under Article 14, Beijing could authorize its navy to engage in hot pursuit of foreign naval vessels to the high seas.[5]

Turning China's claims in the SCS into law threatened to complicate any compromise or negotiation further, raising concerns within ASEAN circles of Chinese intentions. Malaysia's then Foreign Minister, Abdullah Badawi, was of the view that the Chinese law would obstruct efforts to negotiate a solution to the competing and overlapping claims in the SCS.[6] The general concern being that China would become more inflexible as a consequence. The then Malaysian Armed Forces Commander, General Tan Sri Yaacob Zain, issued a public warning that Malaysia would defend its claim to Nansha "even though we do not have the capability to go to war with China."[7] The then Chief of Staff of the Armed Forces of the Philippines, Lisandro Abadia, declared that the claimed islands were "vital to the nation," and that "the military would develop a credible defence force capable of safeguarding Palawan and the Philippine claim zone known as Kalayaan."[8]

Ali Alatas, the then Indonesian Foreign Minister, expressed concern that the "South China Sea would be the next flashpoint in Asia and pressed the Chinese to explain their new law."[9] He grew more pessimistic a year later in 1993, while presiding over the

---

[4] *Ibid*. Reference to Article 10 of the Law on the Territorial Sea and the Contiguous Zone.
[5] *Ibid*. Reference to Article 14 of the Law on the Territorial Sea and the Contiguous Zone.
[6] Leszek Buszynski, "ASEAN, the Declaration on Conduct, and the South China Sea," *Contemporary Southeast Asia* 25(3) (2003): 343–362.
[7] *Ibid*. Statement by then Malaysian Armed Forces Commander, General Tan Sri Yaacob Zain, on defending the country's claim to the Spratlys.
[8] *Ibid*. Similar sentiments put forth by then Philippine Armed Forces Chief of Staff, Lisandro Abadia, on defending their own claims in the disputed area.
[9] *Ibid*. The then Indonesian Foreign Minister, Ali Alatas, issued a warning of potential escalation of tensions in the South China Sea.

Indonesia-initiated annual Workshop on "Managing Potential Conflicts in the South China Sea," stating that the situation was "potentially explosive" and calling for action to avoid conflict.[10]

In response to China's Law on the Territorial Sea and the Contiguous Zone, ASEAN Foreign Ministers issued the Manila Declaration on the South China Sea at the 26th ASEAN Ministerial Meeting in July 1992. Point 4 of the Declaration highlighted ASEAN's wish to negotiate a Code of Conduct in the South China Sea. ASEAN Foreign Ministers attending the meeting "expressed the view that any adverse development in the South China Sea directly affects the peace and security in the region. They emphasized that any territorial or jurisdictional dispute should be resolved by peaceful means, without resorting to force. They urged all parties concerned to exercise self-restraint with a view to creating a positive climate for the resolution of these disputes."[11]

Subsequently, the idea of having a regional Code of Conduct in the South China Sea was deliberated and endorsed in "track one" mechanisms, such as the ASEAN Ministerial Meeting, the ASEAN Summit and the ASEAN Regional Forum (ARF), as well as "track two" fora, including the Council for Security Cooperation in the Asia Pacific (CSCAP) and the informal Workshop on "Managing Potential Conflicts in the South China Sea" initiated by Indonesia.[12,13,14]

---

[10] *Ibid.*

[11] 1992 Joint Communique of the 25th ASEAN Ministerial Meeting, Manila (July 22, 1992), https://cil.nus.edu.sg/wp-content/uploads/formidable/18/1992-25th-AMMJC.pdf.

[12] Wu Shicun and Ren Huaifeng, "More than a declaration: A commentary on the background and the significance of the Declaration on the Conduct of the Parties in the South China Sea," *Chinese Journal of International Law* 2(1) (2003): 311–319.

[13] Li Mingjiang, "Security in the South China Sea: China's balancing act and new regional dynamics," *RSIS Working Paper* No. 149 (2008).

[14] Leszek Buszynski, "ASEAN, the Declaration on Conduct, and the South China Sea," *Contemporary Southeast Asia* 25(3) (2003): 343–362.

III. Need for a Code of Conduct

Beijing's assertive presence on the Mischief Reef led to a change in stance by ASEAN. The Foreign Ministers of ASEAN issued a statement expressing their "serious concern" and urged the concerned parties "to refrain from taking actions that de-stabilize the situation."[15] The idea of a Code of Conduct as a means to manage relations with China *vis-à-vis* the SCS gained traction. The officials of the Philippines and China negotiated at the level of undersecretary of the foreign ministries. In the August 1995 joint statement from these talks, both sides agreed to abide by the principles of a Code of Conduct which included the peaceful settlement of disputes, the adoption of a "gradual process of cooperation" which would lead to bilateral negotiations and recognition of the principles of international law and the Law of the Sea.[16]

ASEAN Foreign Ministers at the 29th ASEAN Ministerial Meeting in July 1996 endorsed the idea of a Code of Conduct "to lay the foundation of long-term stability" in the South China Sea.[17] They accepted that the Philippine-China joint statement of August 1995 would serve as a basis for the draft.[18] Over the next three years, ASEAN member states finalized a draft Code of Conduct, which was then presented to China in 1999 for consideration at the first meeting of the Working Group of the ASEAN–China Senior Officials Consultations on the Code of Conduct.

ASEAN and China exchanged their respective drafts in March 2000 and agreed to consolidate them into one document.[19] The parties disagreed on four critical areas: the geographic scope, restrictions on construction on occupied and unoccupied features in the South

---

[15] Carlyle A. Thayer, "ASEAN's long march to a Code of Conduct in the South China Sea," *Maritime Issues*, July 18, 2017.
[16] Leszek Buszynski, "ASEAN, the Declaration on Conduct, and the South China Sea," *Contemporary Southeast Asia* 25(3) (2003): 343–362.
[17] *Ibid*. Principles to be included in drafting a Code of Conduct.
[18] *Ibid*.
[19] Carlyle A. Thayer, "ASEAN's Code of Conduct in the South China Sea: A litmus test for community-building?" *The Asia-Pacific Journal* 10(4) (2012).

China Sea, military activities in waters adjacent to Nansha Islands, and whether or not fishermen found in disputed waters could be detained and arrested.[20] There was also the preoccupation with the aftermath of the 1997–2000 Asian Financial Crisis, particularly on consolidating the competitiveness of the ASEAN economies to attract more foreign direct investment (FDI) and trade flows to and from Southeast Asia. As such, a formal ASEAN–China Code of Conduct remained elusive.

Nevertheless, ASEAN members and China signed the Declaration on the Conduct of Parties in the South China Sea (DOC) on the sidelines of the Eighth ASEAN Summit in Phnom Penh, Cambodia, on November 4, 2002. The parties to the DOC reaffirmed "that the adoption of a code of conduct in the South China Sea would further promote peace and stability in the region and agree to work, on the basis of consensus, towards the eventual attainment of this objective."[21]

China had previously insisted on bilateral negotiations with individual ASEAN claimant states. As such, the DOC was regarded by ASEAN as a positive step forward. It was Beijing's first multilateral declaration on the SCS. It seemed that China accepted the necessity to work with ASEAN to maintain the semblance of a peaceful neighborhood. According to then-Chinese Deputy Foreign Minister Wang Yi, "the deal actually symbolises new progress in China's relations with ASEAN. It also signals a new level of trust between the two parties."[22] Echoing similar sentiments, Chem Widhya, the then Permanent Secretary of the Ministry of Foreign Affairs and International Cooperation of Cambodia, noted that "the Declaration and related agreements mean we agree to come together in a kind of

---

[20] *Ibid.*

[21] Declaration on the Conduct of Parties in the South China Sea, https://asean.org/declaration-on-the-conduct-of-parties-in-the-south-china-sea-2/.

[22] Wu Shicun and Ren Huaifeng, "More than a declaration: A commentary on the background and the significance of the Declaration on the Conduct of the Parties in the South China Sea," *Chinese Journal of International Law* 2(1): (2003): 311–319. The then Chinese Deputy Foreign Minister, Wang Yi, emphasized that the DOC was a turning point toward progress in ASEAN–China relations.

political cooperation in the Asia-Pacific in terms of commitment to ensure security, to ensure stability, to ensure peace."[23]

The then Secretary-General of ASEAN, Rodolfo Severino, noted "this declaration that will be issued will embody the measures the countries are taking to avoid the disputes erupting into conflict … we have reached a kind of a set of behavioural norms that should govern the behaviour of parties pending the settlement of the jurisdictional and territorial questions."[24] The then President of the Philippines, Gloria Macapagal-Arroyo, highlighted "the signing would contribute significantly towards building trust and good neighbourliness among countries in the region … it manifests the parties' commitment to the maintenance of peace and stability, which are requisites to regional growth and development."[25]

Yet, the Guidelines to Implement the DOC, which ASEAN and China had agreed to draw up, took many years to settle and were only finally adopted by the two sides in July 2011. There were several distractions. The policy coordination to recover from the Asian Financial Crisis and toward an ASEAN Community based on the political/security, economic, and socio-cultural pillars was time-consuming. At the same time, two huge natural disasters hit ASEAN member states. There was the devastating Boxing Day tsunami of December 2004, with an epicenter off the west coast of northern Sumatra in Indonesia, killing more than 220,000 people across the region. The deadly Cyclone Nargis in Myanmar occurred in May 2008, and nearly 140,000 people died. In the SCS, tensions flared up from time to time over specific incidents involving China and individual ASEAN member states (the Philippines, Malaysia, and Vietnam). These problems were managed with diplomatic moves at the bilateral level.

---

[23] *Ibid.* The then Permanent Secretary of the Ministry of Foreign Affairs and International Cooperation of Cambodia, Dr. Chem Widhya, echoed similar sentiments about the DOC ushering in political cooperation in the Asia-Pacific.
[24] *Ibid.*
[25] *Ibid.*

IV. Significance of the DOC

While the DOC — described as a "non-binding political statement" — was not afforded the legal status that ASEAN had hoped to achieve, it nevertheless is an important document. The declaration shows that Beijing was cognizant of the strategic importance of Southeast Asia and the potential benefits of economic cooperation with the ASEAN grouping. The DOC signified that both ASEAN and China accepted the need to "promote a peaceful, friendly and harmonious environment in the South China Sea between ASEAN and China for the enhancement of peace, stability, economic growth and prosperity in the region."[26] The key principles listed in an ASEAN draft for the proposed Code of Conduct are incorporated into the DOC, that is, prohibition against the use of force and threats of force; exercise of self-restraint; peaceful settlement of disputes; search for and adoption of confidence-building measures; cooperation, consultation, and respect for the freedom of international air and maritime navigation.

The significance of the DOC cannot be over-emphasized. First, the DOC sought to address the fault lines between claimant and non-claimant states that were created by sovereignty and maritime jurisdictional disputes in the SCS. Secondly, despite the insistence on taking a bilateral approach to the South China Sea disputes, Beijing seems to see the DOC as a positive step forward. The official *People's Daily* in China proclaimed: "The Declaration, the first political document on the SCS between China and ASEAN, has positive implications for China to maintain its sovereign rights, maintain peace and stability in the SCS region, and enhance mutual confidence between China and ASEAN."[27]

The DOC was useful in checking the respective claimants from expanding their presence and resource exploitation in the SCS. For instance, when Vietnam reportedly planned to organize tourist

---

[26]Declaration on the Conduct of Parties in the South China Sea, https://asean.org/declaration-on-the-conduct-of-parties-in-the-south-china-sea-2/.
[27]Li Mingjiang, "Security in the South China Sea: China's balancing act and new regional dynamics," *RSIS Working Paper* 149 (2008).

activities in the SCS in 2004, the Chinese Foreign Ministry spokesman pointed to the DOC, saying that "we expect the party concerned to respect the bilateral consensus, respect the principles stipulated in the DOC, ... and avoid any action that might lead to further complication of the situation."[28] The same year, both China and the Philippines requested Vietnam to uphold the principles of the DOC when Hanoi started to construct an airplane runway on one island claimed by Vietnam.[29]

V. Toward a Code of Conduct

The DOC is the first step toward the establishment of a Code of Conduct in the South China Sea, which has been under discussion for many years. The eventual adoption of a Code of Conduct is spelled out in the DOC: "the Parties concerned reaffirm that the adoption of a code of conduct in the South China Sea would further promote peace and stability in the region and agree to work, on the basis of consensus, towards the eventual attainment of this objective."[30] Even as the DOC has managed to de-escalate tensions between claimant states and has engaged concerned parties through diplomacy as well as political and strategic cooperation, the potential for military confrontation remains. It is imperative to conclude a binding Code of Conduct in the South China Sea. The onus of implementing the principles outlined in the DOC is on ASEAN member states and China.

A Code of Conduct in the South China Sea is supported by all ASEAN partners and those seeking the preservation of free and open sea lines of communication for reasons outlined in the beginning of this essay. The DOC reaffirms the respect for and commitment of the parties to the freedom of navigation and overflight consistent with universally recognized principles of international law, including the

---

[28] *Ibid.*
[29] *Ibid.*
[30] Declaration on the Conduct of Parties in the South China Sea, https://asean.org/declaration-on-the-conduct-of-parties-in-the-south-china-sea-2/.

1982 UN Convention on the Law of the Sea (UNCLOS). The key is no derogation of UNCLOS provisions, as these provisions are the foundation of a durable and effective legal regime for an accessible and peaceful South China Sea.

It is germane to recall a few seminal statements. At the 17th ARF Meeting in July 2010 in Hanoi, then-U.S. Secretary of State Hillary Clinton opined: "The United States, like every nation, has a national interest in freedom of navigation, open access to Asia's maritime commons, and respect for international law in the South China Sea.... The U.S. supports the 2002 ASEAN–China declaration on the conduct of parties in the South China Sea. We encourage the parties to reach agreement on a full code of conduct. The U.S. is prepared to facilitate initiatives and confidence-building measures consistent with the declaration."[31]

The then Minister for Foreign Affairs of Australia, Alexander Downer, said, "I welcome the agreement.... This Declaration, which sets out the principles to guide conduct in the South China Sea, is good news for Australia. We have a strong interest in avoiding destabilizing conflict in our region and in ensuring freedom of navigation in an area through which much of our commercial shipping passes. Australia has been an advocate of a regional code of conduct for the South China Sea for several years... Australia will continue to encourage all parties to abide by their new undertakings in this Declaration."[32]

---

[31]Quang Minh Pham, "The South China Sea security problem: Towards regional cooperation," *Asia Europe Journal* 8 (2010): 427–434. Other external parties put forth statements too in support of the DOC and calling for a conclusion of the Code of Conduct. The European Union stated that it "supports the ASEAN-led process towards a Code of Conduct in the South China Sea, which should be effective, substantive and legally binding, and not prejudice the interests of third parties."

[32]Wu Shicun and Ren Huaifeng, "More than a declaration: A commentary on the background and the significance of the Declaration on the Conduct of the Parties in the South China Sea," *Chinese Journal of International Law* 2(1) (2003): 311–319. India raised the issue of the ongoing negotiations for the Code of Conduct in the South China Sea with Vietnam, "calling for the full and effective implementation of the Declaration on the Conduct of Parties in the South China Sea (DOC) in its

As regional countries and others around the world look forward to ASEAN and China finalizing a Code of Conduct, the COVID-19 pandemic brought person-to-person negotiations for the legally binding Code to a standstill. Nevertheless, Indonesia has offered to host the next round of negotiations between ASEAN and China. This is in line with the aspirations of the earlier generation of Indonesian advocates for a peaceful and resilient Southeast Asia. For ASEAN, Indonesia is the largest economy with the largest population in Southeast Asia. Indonesian strategic thinkers are focusing on the wider region and their country's role in realizing the ASEAN Community vision.

Indonesia took the initiative to invite counterparts from Brunei, Malaysia, the Philippines, Singapore, and Vietnam to a coast guards forum in February 2022 to foster harmony on maritime security issues and enhance cooperation among the coast guards of ASEAN member states.[33] This is a step toward increased coordination to manage challenges arising from developments in the SCS, including issues relating to IUU (Illegal, Unreported, and Unregulated) fishing in the area.[34] Indonesia's engagement with Vietnam in 2021 culminated in a memorandum of understanding (MoU) between the Vietnam Coast Guard and Indonesia's Maritime Security Agency, known as Bakamla. The MoU aims to improve collaboration and support temporary steps to demarcate the exclusive economic zones (EEZ) of the two countries.[35]

---

entirety and the substantive negotiations towards the early conclusion of a substantive and effective Code of Conduct (COC) in the South China Sea in accordance with international law, especially UNCLOS, that does not prejudice the legitimate rights and interests of all nations including those not party to these negotiations."

[33] Tom Abke, "Indonesia spearheading regional cooperation in South China Sea," *Indo-Pacific Defense Forum*, March 5, 2022, https://ipdefenseforum.com/2022/03/indonesia-spearheading-regional-cooperation-in-south-china-sea/.

[34] Sebastian Strangio, "Indonesia seeking Southeast Asian coordination on South China Sea disputes," *The Diplomat*, December 29, 2021.

[35] Tom Abke, "Indonesia spearheading regional cooperation in South China Sea," *Indo-Pacific Defense Forum*, March 5, 2022, https://ipdefenseforum.com/2022/03/indonesia-spearheading-regional-cooperation-in-south-china-sea/. Head of the Maritime Security Agency (Bakamla), Vice Admiral Aan Kurnia, said that it is important "to present a coordinated approach" in matters related to the South

"By settling territorial disputes, ASEAN member states could bolster their position in forthcoming talks involving Beijing on a South China Sea code of conduct,"[36] thus signaling to the international community that ASEAN governments are committed to protecting their sovereign rights while ensuring the region is secure and stable. "If some of the ASEAN member states wish to fulfill the original vision of having a unified position *vis-à-vis* the PRC in the code of conduct negotiations, then intramural unity is the key. At least the bilateral disputes between the Southeast Asian South China Sea parties ought to be ironed out first, and the Indonesia–Vietnam overlapping EEZ boundaries in the SCS being a good example."[37]

Going forward, there are considerable difficulties in reaching an agreement between ASEAN and China on sharing the contiguous geography, managing ingrained perceptions of history, and apportioning responsibility for the maintenance of peace and prosperity in the South China Sea.[38] At the same time, it is not possible to co-exist and work in partnership without rule-making and a rules-based framework for mutual benefit and progress. Freedom of navigation and overflight in the SCS is not just for the claimant states but also for the international community, given the strategic significance of the SCS and the volume of global trade and considerable movement of people relying on the essential routes through the SCS. Every ASEAN member state, not just the claimant states in the grouping, has a vital interest in realizing the Code of Conduct in the South China Sea. Ditto for China, as Beijing will also benefit from this joint venture with ASEAN.

China Sea, and "how to respond in the field when we face the same 'disturbance'…"

[36] *Ibid.*

[37] *Ibid.*

[38] The authors of this essay have benefitted from the detailed research in the book *Southeast Asia After the Cold War: A Contemporary History*, Singapore, NUS Press (2019) written by Professor Ang Cheng Guan. He discussed among other topics the arduous process through which the ASEAN member states, and China agreed on the Declaration on the Conduct of Parties in the South China Sea (DOC) in 2022, as a first step toward a Code of Conduct in the South China Sea.

Chapter 13

The DOC at 20: A Thai Perspective

Kavi Chongkittavorn

Bangkok Post and Institute of Security and International Studies, Bangkok, Thailand
kavihome2@gmail.com

Abstract

The 20th anniversary of the Declaration on the Conducts of Parties in the South China Sea (DOC) serves as a barometer of how all concerned players have been able to sustain their cooperative spirit in managing the conflict in a way that has stood up against the odds even at most critical times. Given the current shift in the geopolitical landscape throughout the world, the DOC reminds the regional and international community of the importance of nurturing goodwill and a conducive atmosphere for continued dialogue and negotiation. The ongoing implementation of the DOC, which outlines measures and steps to be taken to increase cooperation and coordination on issues of mutual concern, has been steady and is making progress, albeit rather slowly. All stakeholders are aware that further progress is needed if the disputed maritime areas have any chance of being transformed into a zone of peace, stability, and prosperity.

Based on interviews with senior Thai officials, both current and retired, this chapter examines Thailand's role and attitude toward the DOC since it was signed in Phnom Penh in 2002. The analysis also explores the strategies that the Thai government pursued at the time as the coordinator of ASEAN–China relations (2012–2015), especially focusing on the South China Sea, as well as its continuous efforts to promote functional cooperation and best practices among all stakeholders.

Keywords: DOC, South China Sea dispute, COC

I. Thailand's Motives Regarding South China Sea (2012–2015)

Although Thailand is not a conflict party in the South China Sea dispute, the country, a founding member of ASEAN, has been serving as a bridge to all concerned parties. Prior to 1996, when the idea of having the Code of Conduct (COC) was broached with China, Bangkok managed to do its bit to ensure that China and conflicting ASEAN members and the rest were on the same page. In 1995, with Vietnam's inclusion in the existing ASEAN claimants — Brunei, the Philippines, and Malaysia — the grouping felt more confident about engaging China. At the time, it was recognized by the ASEAN colleagues that then-Chinese Foreign Minister Qian Qichen had a close personal rapport with Thai Foreign ACM Siddhi Savetsila. Their relations had helped to reduce cleavages between China's attitude toward the grouping's new-found assertiveness following the admission of Vietnam a year earlier. That has been the pattern in later years during the Thai coordinating role.

Truth be told, China was comfortable with Thailand's role as it felt that Bangkok would remain neutral with those parties that had problems with China. For instance, during his visit to Manila for a joint ASEAN–China commission meeting in April 2013, Thai Foreign Minister Surapong Tovichakchaikul reiterated that the Philippines must not let its conflict with China over the overlapping claims in the South China Sea undermine comprehensive ASEAN–China relations.

According to senior Thai officials, like other ASEAN members, Thailand supported the collective ASEAN approach that would keep out external powers from meddling with maritime disputes. As a signatory to the 1982 UN Convention on the Law of the Sea and committed to the principles of the UN Charters, the country believed that it was the way to go. Quite often, Thailand was the conduit for the conflicting parties to smooth out positions that would allow for future agreements that could manage their dispute more effectively.

Bangkok sees itself as an honest broker as it has no interest vested in the resource-rich maritime areas. Similar to the international community's wishes, it hopes to see the disputed areas remain stable and peaceful. It was under the government of Prime Minister Yingluck Shinawatra (2011–2014) that Thailand assumed the role of coordinator of ASEAN–China ties. Bangkok realized that the success or failure of its role would depend on the progress made on the South China Sea disputes. Managing the growing economic dynamics of the ASEAN–China ties would also be one of its top priorities. Another important role was preventing possible spillover effects emanating from the disputes in the South China Sea. The government instructed the Ministry of Foreign Affairs to make full use of the ASEAN–China coordinating role to display the country's diplomatic finesse in bridging the gap and differences over the disputes in the South China Sea.

II. Thailand's Role as the Coordinator of ASEAN–China Ties

Interviews with senior officials who were involved at the time revealed three important insights related to Thailand's role as the coordinator of ASEAN–China ties. First, as a non-conflict member of the South China Sea dispute, Thailand seriously perceived itself as a "non-provoking" and "neutral" player. With this approach, Thailand was quickly taken up by ASEAN and Chinese colleagues. During his visit to Bangkok in November 2012, Chinese premier Li Keqiang praised Thailand's "leading and exemplary role" within the ASEAN framework during his meeting with Prime Minister Yingluck Shinawatra.

In addition, Thailand believes that it can serve as a genuine "interlocutor" in ASEAN–China relations as originally intended when the coordinating country's role was created to facilitate bilateral ties with the other dialogue partners. As such, Thailand will treat the ASEAN–China relations as a multidimensional entity without isolating any conflict or inconvenience. In other words, these important bilateral relations should not be held hostage by the ongoing dispute over the South China Sea. Bangkok is fully aware that the global media and attention have been focusing on the maritime dispute.

Finally, unlike other coordinating countries, Thailand is proud to highlight its excellent ties with China and was confident it could create sufficient "comfort level" and "mutual trust" to permit ASEAN and China to sit at the negotiating table and stay engaged during its coordinating timeframe. Bangkok was very hopeful that the improved bilateral ties would further promote progress in the negotiation of the code of conduct in the South China Sea.

In retrospect, after Thailand took over the role in July 2012, Bangkok successfully convened a series of meetings — one at the senior official level and the other two at the ministerial level. Bangkok was taken by surprise when Beijing announced in September 2012 that official negotiations with ASEAN on the COC had already started. After nearly a decade of implementation of the DOC, the beginning of COC negotiation represented a big leap forward. Furthermore, Thailand was instrumental in persuading China to take part in the dialogue, moving beyond the current brawl with the Philippines.

Lest we forget, under the Thai coordinating role, it was the first time that both sides had met after the ASEAN chair, Cambodia, failed to issue a joint communique in July 2012 due to the disagreement over the wording related to the South China Sea dispute. There were lots of blame games as to the real reasons behind the maleficence. Thailand was unable to do much as the ASEAN chair had the prerogative over the outcome. It was interesting to note that at the Phnom Penh meeting, Indonesia and Singapore tried to push for the issuance of the joint communique, with Thailand involved as a coordinator.

The second meeting broadened to include the discussion with experts — a one-and-a-half track approach. The first High-Level Forum to commemorate the 10th anniversary of ASEAN–China Strategic Partnership (August 2012), was a timely occasion to bring new stakeholders into the discussion. The closed-door meeting was useful for taking stock of what was accomplished and looking toward the future.

Then came the third meeting, which was considered the ASEAN foreign ministerial retreat that Brunei failed to host earlier in 2013. The ministers convened a preparatory meeting for their trip to Beijing for a conference with the newly appointed Foreign Minister Wang Yi to commemorate the 10th anniversary of the ASEAN–China Strategic partnership. The meeting was considered a family gathering as the ASEAN leaders were preoccupied with their international developments to the point that they could have done more in reviewing their common positions on various regional and international issues. Thailand was given credit for organizing the retreat and for ensuring that ASEAN would be able to speak with one voice and preserve solidarity when they met their Chinese counterparts.

III. Beyond the DOC: Searching for a Middle Ground

The DOC served as a foundation for ASEAN and China to continue their commitment to engage with one another. These two decades of engagements had helped to suppress provocation and lack of self-restraint in maintaining peace and stability in the South China Sea. Thailand has been treating the DOC as a milestone document because it also helped all conflicting parties identify areas of cooperation and collaboration.

In addition, the DOC has been able to create a conducive atmosphere for all concerned parties to take up practical cooperation, especially in maritime areas. Thailand has been one of the earlier recipients of projects related to maritime environment protection. Others have chosen law enforcement, coastal environment protection, and maritime research. In the near future, Thailand plans to have an in-person seminar on maritime environment protection to take advantage of the post COVID-19 pandemic.

Commemorating the 20th anniversary of the DOC, both ASEAN and China should seriously consider whether the DOC could serve as a building block for a broader cooperative framework. At the moment, the DOC is one of the components of ASEAN–China cooperation in the South China Sea. After a decade of implementation, the DOC could further expand the code of conduct and incorporate more areas of cooperation. Certain salient measures in the DOC are considered win–win and should be retained and developed further. Other measures could be redefined or updated to respond to the fast-changing environment surrounding maritime logistics and communications. At this juncture, the negotiators from ASEAN and China are working on the second reading of the single draft text. Progress has been slow due to the impacts of COVID-19 preventing all concerned parties from meeting face-to-face.

The DOC is considered a non-binding regional rules-based order in the South China Sea. It is a political document derived from mutual trust and mutual respect between ASEAN and China, which share a strong desire to ensure the South China Sea becomes a sea of peace, stability, and prosperity. The ongoing negotiation on the code of conduct in the South China Sea is reaching a critical point, as both sides are considering issues related to self-restraint measures and rights of the third parties and disputed settlements among others. Since the COC negotiations kicked off in 2012, it has been clear that the COC would be a regional effort formulated by regional countries to settle their disputes in peaceful ways. However, these efforts have evolved over the past years and have picked up pace with conflicting parties putting forward their positions and reservations.

As the conflicting parties continue to negotiate on the single draft text, Thailand sees the need to strengthen functional cooperation in the South China Sea as a means to promote trust and confidence among conflicting parties as well as a part of ongoing efforts to reduce the confrontational tension. In addition, Thailand wants to nurture the current positive momentum so that it can transform the South China Sea into that desired sea of peace, stability, and prosperity in the long run. Before ending the coordinating role, the Thai authorities held a brainstorming session with selected ASEAN members to push for the so-called best practices and non-binding guidelines for cooperation in the South China Sea. Bangkok has already proposed five areas of cooperation: policy support and governance; capacity-building; research and innovation; public awareness and outreach; other matters. These measures aimed to promote enhanced cooperation in all areas related to marine environmental protection in the South China Sea. For instance, one of the proposals is exploring the formulation of a joint plan of action to combat and mitigate marine debris as well as respond to oil spill incidents. The other calls for improvement of capacity for early warning and predicting natural hazards to make communities more resilient to the impact of climate change.

IV. Conclusion

As the negotiation of the code of conduct has almost reached its final act, Thailand wants to ensure the COC will serve as a standard document governing ties between small and large states. It will be the first document on which conflicting parties in the troubled sea agreed. Indeed, the COC will also remind the global community that regional countries can work on and agree on common solutions to their challenges no matter how difficult this might be. In coming years, the COC could be transformed into a key regional-based order that aims to promote peace and progress. For the time being, ASEAN and China are on the same page concerning the full implementation of the DOC. However, the ongoing COC negotiations still have to overcome many hurdles before ASEAN and China can reach an all-round consensus. Therefore, for the time being, expanding and strengthening functional cooperation in the South China Sea is desirable.

Chapter 14

ASEAN's 20 Years of Continued Efforts to Engage China on the South China Sea: Lessons from the DOC and the Way Forward*

Nguyen Hung Son

Diplomatic Academy of Vietnam
nguyenhungson2005@yahoo.com

Abstract

In 2002, an important milestone was laid on one of the central-most security issues of Southeast Asia when ASEAN and China signed the Declaration of Conduct of the Parties on the South China Sea (DOC). The document soon became a frequently talked about topic relating to the regional security architecture, one that raised much hope but also questions about the management of one of the most enduring security challenges of the region.

---

*Views expressed in this chapter reflect the author's personal perspective.

This chapter seeks to review ASEAN's approach to building a set of codes to regulate the conduct of the stakeholders in the South China Sea, and how the Declaration of Conduct of the Parties on the South China Sea (DOC) influenced ASEAN engagement with China after its signing. The chapter would also assess the DOC's implementation over the past 20 years, reviews current efforts to upgrade the DOC into the supposedly superior Code of Conduct, and suggest a way forward.

Keywords: South China Sea dispute, DOC, Norms, ASEAN-China relations

I. ASEAN's Efforts to Forge a Code on the South China Sea

The South China Sea was not an issue ASEAN had to deal with immediately after its inception nor through its formative years. During the Cold War, ASEAN had far more important strategic and security challenges to deal with than territorial or maritime disputes. Those were navigating through major powers rivalry and confrontations, preserving Southeast Asia as a Zone of Peace and Neutrality, keeping the region free from nuclear proliferation, and so on. Only after the Cold War ended and geostrategic rivalry subsided did maritime competition become a security issue that concerns ASEAN.

The first time ASEAN hinted at the need for a document to regulate claimants' behavior on the South China Sea was in Manila, in July 1992, when ASEAN Foreign Ministers issued a joint declaration calling for parties to resolve the dispute by peaceful means, without resorting to force, and call on all "parties concerned to apply the principles contained in the Treaty of Amity and Cooperation in Southeast Asia as the basis for establishing a code of international conduct over the South China Sea."[1] The declaration was issued in response to what was perceived as China's increasing expansion of presence and influence over the South China Sea. Earlier in 1992, China had passed the Law on the Territorial Sea and Contiguous

---

[1] "1992 ASEAN Declaration On The South China Sea," https://cil.nus.edu.sg/wp-content/uploads/2017/07/1992-ASEAN-Declaration-on-the-South-China-Sea.pdf (Accessed December 15, 2018).

Zone, reiterating its claims on the whole of Nansha (the Spratlys). The same year, it contracted Crestone, a U.S. oil company, to explore the Southwestern part of the South China Sea. The Philippines had reasons to worry because it was a claimant in Nansha and was afraid it would soon have to confront China. All this occurred while Russia and the U.S. — a key ally of the Philippines — the two Cold War powers were withdrawing from the region after the end of the Cold War, leaving a power vacuum that China wanted to fill.

ASEAN at the time had just 6 members, the original 5 members plus Brunei Darussalam, which joined the grouping in 1984. Vietnam, another important claimant, was not part of ASEAN at the time. Faced with the new geopolitical challenge of a post-Cold War order, ASEAN made the declaration on the South China Sea to show solidarity with the Philippines, to assert its role in the changing regional environment, but most importantly, to assert its interests and principles as laid out in the Treaty of Amity and Cooperation and be the guiding principles for inter-state relations in the post-Cold war arena. These principles would later become key elements of the DOC as well as other agreements ASEAN conducted with external partners.

ASEAN tried to invite the then Chinese Foreign Minister Qien Qichen, who was present at the time of the ASEAN declaration, to sign the declaration but Minister Qien declined on the basis that China was not part of the drafting process of the declaration.[2]

ASEAN was united again on the South China Sea in March 1995 when the ASEAN Foreign Ministers issued a strong statement after China erected a structure on one of the features in Nansha, the Meiji (Mischief) Reef. The reef was claimed by the Philippines and had been used as shelter by Filipino fishermen.[3] The Philippines was shocked to find a concrete structure with a Chinese flag on it. The Philippines instigated ASEAN's first "statement on recent developments on the South China Sea."[4]

---

[2] Rodolfo C. Severino, "ASEAN and the South China Sea in Security Challenges," *Institute for Regional Security* 6(2) (2010): 42.
[3] *Ibid.*, pp. 37–47.
[4] Marites Danguilan Vitug, "Rock solid: How the Philippines won its maritime case against China," *Bughaw* (2018): 32.

In July of the same year, ASEAN Foreign Ministers' annual joint communiqué reiterated the statement.[5] The difference in the later statement on the South China Sea was that Vietnam had just been admitted to ASEAN, hence added weight to the statement because it also voiced Vietnam's concern on the South China Sea. ASEAN was as territorial as they were strategic in issuing the statement. Although no specific country was named in the criticism, it was obvious to whom the statement was directed.

It was the Meiji incident that motivated ASEAN member states, most notably the Philippines, to start the process of drafting a code of conduct for the South China Sea. In 1996, the ASEAN Foreign Ministers "endorsed the idea of concluding a regional code of conduct in the South China Sea which will lay the foundation for long term stability in the area and foster understanding among claimant countries."[6]

The admission of Vietnam into ASEAN resulted in ASEAN's expansion to include all 10 Southeast Asian countries in 1999 eventually. The expansion was ASEAN's response to the post-Cold War order in the region, when regional integration and trade liberalization were a high priority, while the small and medium countries of Southeast Asia, now freed from the Cold War division, also looked to join a regional grouping to elevate their national standing and development.

While ASEAN's expansion to include Vietnam emboldened its position and views on the South China Sea territorial and maritime disputes, it also diversified its approaches on the South China Sea and made a unified stance sometimes harder to achieve. ASEAN's common perception at the time (2000) was that the South China Sea issue was a territorial problem involving a few of its members. Within ASEAN, a subset group of claimant states was created, consisting of

---

[5] The 28th ASEAN Foreign Ministers' Joint communiqué, ASEAN Secretariat, https://asean.org/?static_post=joint-communique-of-the-twenty-eighth-asean-ministerial-meeting-bandar-seri-begawan-29-30-july-1995.

[6] 29th ASEAN Foreign Ministers Joint communique, 1996, https://cil.nus.edu.sg/wp-content/uploads/2019/03/29th-ASEAN-Ministerial-Meeting.pdf.

the four claimants (Brunei Darussalam, Malaysia, the Philippines, and Vietnam). South China Sea-related business was usually first given to the claimants' group, and ASEAN as a group would then proceed to endorse what the claimants could agree on.

ASEAN saw that if the territorial dispute was not properly managed, it could threaten regional stability and affect all members. ASEAN therefore wanted the claimants to handle the dispute with China in a way that would not affect the security environment of the whole region. ASEAN supported international law and UNCLOS as the basis for the claims and the management of their disputes, but the claimants were left to interpret and apply that law themselves.

ASEAN supported the idea of building the Code of Conduct with China (COC) to create a cooperative framework to manage the issue for regional stability rather than to help the claimants find a resolution to the dispute. Therefore, despite being endorsed by the ASEAN Foreign Minister in 1996, the code of conduct drafting process was championed mostly by the claimant states within ASEAN: Brunei Darussalam, the Philippines, Malaysia, and Vietnam.

ASEAN's earlier proposed draft code of conduct only received lukewarm responses from China. According to a memo sent to the Philippines secretary of foreign affairs in 1999, after seeing the ASEAN draft, the Chinese embassy in Manila stated that it would never agree to such a draft because of the inclusion of Xisha (the Paracels) in the scope of application, and because the draft encouraged other countries and international organizations to subscribe to the principles that the draft code proposed.[7] China instead produced its own draft but declared it was not in a hurry to conclude the negotiation,[8] because of China's long-standing preference to handle the South China Sea bilaterally, arguing that the "code at any

---

[7] Marites Danguilan Vitug, "Rock solid: How the Philippines won its maritime case against China," *Bughaw* (2018): 121.
[8] Leszel Buszinsky, "ASEAN, The Declaration of Conduct and the South China Sea," *Contemporary Southeast Asia* 3 (2003): 352.

multilateral forum can only lead to further complications of the matter."[9]

The 9/11 terrorist attack on the U.S. in 2001 strategically realigned the U.S. and China's foreign policies. China turned its charm offensive toward ASEAN to take advantage of U.S. inattention to the Asia-Pacific while redirecting its focus on the war on terror. China subsequently took a more open stance and agreed to negotiate the code of conduct with ASEAN collectively. ASEAN saw the opportunity and moved quickly to finalize the draft code. It was due to unresolved differences over the explicit inclusion of Xisha in the scope of application, and on a clause demanding no new occupation of any features in the South China Sea, that prevented the code to be concluded.

The Declaration of Conduct of Parties in the South China Sea (DOC) was a compromised text, but it was watered down into a political declaration which did not meet the expectations of the key ASEAN claimants who had originally planned for a legally binding international treaty.[10]

The difficult birth of the DOC showed that it took giant steps by both ASEAN and China to come to such an agreement. Both ASEAN member states and China went beyond narrow national interests in pursuance of broader regional and common strategic interests in forging the Declaration.

II. The DOC's Influence on ASEAN's Approach to the South China Sea

After the DOC was signed, ASEAN tried to stay low on the South China Sea issue. The name "South China Sea" would not appear officially on ASEAN's agenda, and the issue is customarily placed under

---

[9]"China rejects ASEAN 'Code of conduct' for Spratlys," *Asian Political News*, August 2, 1999, http://business.highbeam.com/435555/article-1G1-55364474/china-rejects-asean-code-conduct-spratlys.
[10]Rodolfo C. Severino, "ASEAN and the South China Sea in Security Challenges," *Institute for Regional Security* 6(2) (2010): 37–47.

the discussions on "Regional and International Issues" in a discrete way. The South China Sea issue also appeared indirectly under discussions on the "Progress on the implementation of the DOC." The security aspect of the South China Sea would not be discussed; only confidence-building and technical cooperation projects were on the agenda. ASEAN Foreign Ministers' joint communiqués usually carried a paragraph or two on the South China Sea issue but focused mainly on the implementation of the DOC and other cooperative activities. The text stayed more or less the same over the years without any direct correlation to what was happening on the ground. For the period between 2003 and 2009, ASEAN wanted to believe that the South China Sea was properly managed and that the remaining issues should be handled bilaterally between a few claimants and China. Most ASEAN member states were not concerned about the overlapping maritime claims, the interpretation and application of UNCLOS, or geostrategic competition between the major powers.[11]

While tensions in the South China Sea were gradually building up, especially after China formally announced the 9-dash-line in its note verbale to the United Nations,[12] many ASEAN members still hoped that effective implementation of the DOC could help. By this time, several ASEAN members saw the South China Sea issue as a result of a strategic trust deficit; they were convinced that confidence building measures would reduce mistrust, promote cooperation, and reduce tension. In 2011, most ASEAN members continued to prioritize working with China to develop a set of Guidelines to implement the DOC, now with a greater sense of urgency. However, the draft Guidelines for the DOC could not be endorsed by ASEAN while China demanded the removal of a clause which allowed members to meet before meeting with China. China reasoned that this was an ASEAN custom that need not appear in an ASEAN– China agreement. ASEAN insisted that having its own meeting before meeting

---

[11]Interview with various ASEAN officials between 2000 and 2008.
[12]China Note verbal CML/1/2009 sent to the UN on May 7, 2009, https://www.un.org/depts/los/clcs_new/submissions_files/mysvnm33_09/chn_2009re_mys_vnm_e.pdf.

any dialogue partner was part of the "ASEAN way." To overcome the deadlock, ASEAN finally agreed to drop that clause in exchange for a commitment from China to regularly review and report on the implementation of the DOC to the ASEAN–China Foreign Ministers meeting. This was a way of bringing about transparency in the implementation of the DOC. ASEAN and China adopted the Guidelines in 2011, nine years after the DOC was signed.

The Philippines, however, was not convinced that the Guidelines or the DOC would resolve the South China Sea problem. The Philippines had been having problems with the Chinese at Reed Bank in 2011, where its oil exploratory vessels were harassed, forcing them to desist. The Philippines proposed the idea of a ZoPFF/C, "a Zone of Peace, Freedom, Friendship and Cooperation," of which the core idea is to segregate disputed maritime areas from undisputed areas based on UNCLOS.[13] ASEAN, however, was not interested in overlapping maritime claims, as members did not want to risk bilateral ties and economic benefits with Beijing.[14] ASEAN reacted with hesitation and eventually did not endorse the Philippines initiative, probably because certain members anticipated a collision course with China. At a key working-level meeting in which Manila initiated to advance the ZOPFF/C, Cambodia, and Laos did not send their representatives.[15]

On the other hand, ASEAN member states have been working together since 2011 to push ahead with a binding Code of Conduct to replace what was perceived as an inadequate DOC. Rounds of talks among the ASEAN officials and experts have been taking place to

---

[13] Statement of the Philippines Secretary of Foreign Affairs Albert F. del Rosario to the ASEAN Foreign Ministers meeting on the FoPFF/C, November 15, 2011, https://www.officialgazette.gov.ph/2011/11/15/the-secretary-of-foreign-affairs-on-the-west-philippine-sea-november-15-2011/.

[14] SCMP Reporter, "Hanoi eyes ASEAN Card on the South China Sea," September 4, 2010, https://www.scmp.com/article/710496/hanoi-eyes-asean-card-south-china-sea (July 30, 2021).

[15] Barry Wain, "Towards Peace and Prosperity in the South China Sea: Pathways for Regional Cooperation," paper presented at Forum on the South China Sea, Manila, October 17, 2011.

discuss possible elements of the COC. ASEAN Senior Officials agreed to adopt a blueprint of the Code of Conduct, titled the "ASEAN Proposed Elements of a Code of Conduct between ASEAN Member States and China" in June 2012. A noticeable difference in ASEAN's second attempt to draft the COC, compared to its effort a decade earlier, was the emphasis on handling maritime disputes and incidents rather than disputes over territories, reflecting a shift in ASEAN's perception of the South China Sea issue. Problems that were encountered in the discussions on the COC in 2002 such as the geographical scope and whether the COC covered Xisha, did not come up during these discussions. Instead, ASEAN was looking for a common interest shared by all members such as compliance with the rule of law, especially UNCLOS, and the prevention of incidents that might destabilize the whole region. The blueprint asked the parties to clarify the disputes in accordance with international law and UNCLOS, and called for their proper management to prevent escalation. ASEAN's priority in the South China Sea thus shifted toward incident prevention and management. ASEAN Foreign Ministers' joint communiqué in 2013 noted the suggestions for establishing communication hotlines and search and rescue missions for people and vessels in distress at sea.[16]

Despite a parallel process of COC drafting and negotiation, ASEAN and China continue to agree, even to these days, that the DOC remains to be "the" only agreement between China and ASEAN and, therefore, its full and effective implementation is necessary.

III. Achievements of the DOC and Criticisms

The DOC's past 20 years' performance should best be assessed based on the motivations and objectives of the DOC's signatories.

---

[16]The 46th ASEAN Foreign Ministers Joint Communiqué, ASEAN Secretariat website, https://www.asean.org/storage/images/2013/news/jointcommunique ofthe46thASEANforeignministersmeeting46thamm–final-30june2013.pdf (Accessed December 15, 2018).

For ASEAN, although the DOC was not a legally binding Code of Conduct as originally wanted, it still served many purposes.

Firstly, the DOC was the first document ever signed by all 10 ASEAN member state on the South China Sea. The DOC was an important milestone for ASEAN itself in accepting that the South China Sea needed to be dealt with by ASEAN as a group and not just by the claimant states alone. It was to serve as a document to formulate ASEAN's common position on the South China Sea issue and was especially helpful to newer members of ASEAN who are not a party to the maritime or territorial disputes in the South China Sea, such as Laos, Myanmar, and Cambodia. Although occasionally, there were still denials to the official inclusion of the South China Sea issue on ASEAN's agenda, no member states refused to discuss the issue under the chapeaux of the DOC's implementation. The principles laid out in the DOC were always the fallback position all ASEAN member states resort to in order to find common grounds in a tense situation or heated debate on the topic.

Secondly, the DOC was the only instrument, and therefore a very important one, for ASEAN to engage China on the South China Sea in a multilateral setting. The DOC process was also seen as an effort in the claimant states' broader strategy to multilateralize the dispute, first by regionalizing and then internationalizing the issue. These views saw that ASEAN not only tried to bring the issue formally to ASEAN–China meetings but also to the newly established ASEAN Regional Forum (ARF) and other international gatherings, e.g., the Non-aligned Movement (NAM).[17] The DOC indeed helped draw international attention, expectation, and cooperation to support its implementation, at the least through capacity building for the stakeholders involved, thus in the process of "internationalizing" the dialogue and cooperation but not the dispute itself. The DOC also generated several multilateral and minilateral cooperation, such as the tripartite joint seismic study among China, Vietnam, and the Philippines from 2005 to 2008. Under the context of the DOC,

---

[17]Rodolfo C. Severino, "ASEAN and the South China Sea in Security Challenges," *Institute for Regional Security* 6(2) (2010): 42.

a declaration on coastal and marine environmental protection in the South China Sea was issued on the occasion of the 20th ASEAN–China Summit; ASEAN and China established a hotline communication platform among senior officials of the Ministries of Foreign Affairs in response to maritime emergencies, and agreed to apply the Code for Unplanned Encounters at Sea in the South China Sea.[18]

Thirdly, ASEAN wanted an instrument to promote and solidify norms based on the 1982 UNCLOS in the region. At the time of the start of the negotiation of the COC between ASEAN and China, China had just ratified the Convention in 1996. The rules and norms stipulated in the Convention, such as the regimes of exclusive economic zone and archipelagic state, were young and needed enforcement. Engagement and cooperation from China were fundamental. Although a binding code was not achieved, the DOC as a signed political document that recognized the centrality of the 1982 UNCLOS was useful for that purpose. After the signing of the DOC, all parties frequently cited UNCLOS as the basis for maritime cooperation and engagement, as well as when there are differences. The DOC also served as a platform for many maritime cooperative ideas — scientific research, safety of navigation, humanitarian assistance, etc. — where UNCLOS were further discussed, interpreted, and applied in the specific context and areas in the South China Sea, which helped promote its norms.

Fourthly, the most important expectation out of the DOC was that it would serve as a confidence-building measure to promote peaceful resolution of disputes in the South China Sea, prevent incidents among the claimants, and preserve the *status quo*. There was a sense of emergency to prevent such incidents after what happened in the Meiji Reef. Many observed that the DOC did contribute to this objective by maintaining the goodwill of all the parties,[19] serving as a

---

[18]Zong Haihe, DOC: the cornerstone for South China Sea peace and stability, https://www.globaltimes.cn/page/202206/1268287.shtml
[19]Li Mingjiang, "Managing Security in the South China Sea: From DOC to COC," https://kyotoreview.org/issue-15/managing-security-in-the-south-china-sea-from-doc-to-coc/.

mechanism for dialogue and preventive diplomacy to preserve regional stability. Despite its vagueness and occasional gaps in interpretation, all parties continue to commit to the fundamental "rules of the road," that is respecting the UN Charter, the 1982 UNCLOS, TAC, the 5 principles of co-existence; peaceful resolution of dispute, without resorting to the threat or use of force; respect for freedom of navigation and freedom of overflight, and obligation to exercise restraint. Critics would deny these as just rhetorical, but under the context of the current global geopolitical upheavals, these political commitments remain important.

And lastly, ASEAN also needed to compartmentalize the South China Sea issue in order to remove what was perceived as the remaining stumbling block that stood in the way of further ASEAN–China cooperation. Some ASEAN member states had perceived the South China Sea as an unwanted problem for ASEAN–China relations and therefore wanted to set it aside. Despite its shortcomings, the DOC gave ASEAN the hope that the South China Sea problem had been framed and contained. ASEAN–China relations indeed took off thereafter. China acceded to the Treaty of Amity and Cooperation in 2003 and became ASEAN's first strategic partner the same year. The DOC, however, was not able to fully contain and compartmentalize the South China Sea issue between ASEAN and China. Developments in the South China Sea over the past 20 years on several occasions went much above the capacity of the DOC, spilled over to other areas and at times overshadowed the trust and confidence between ASEAN and China. At such times, the DOC still served as a reference point and mechanism to maintain communication and dialogue between ASEAN and China.

China's motivation was to manage the South China Sea debate within the ASEAN–China framework, thereby preventing "interference" from external powers on the issue (ha, p. 3). Talking with ASEAN, and only ASEAN, was also a way for China to prevent the South China Sea from being further "multilateralized" or "internationalized." Former Secretary-General of ASEAN Rodolfo C. Severino observed that "even as China yielded to the ASEAN states and consented to deal with them as a group, Beijing managed, by that very concession, to get the U.S., Japan and everyone else out of the multilateral discussions on the South China Sea and the whole issue out of the ASEAN Regional Forum."[20]

If managing the U.S. and its allies' interference was China's primary concern, the DOC might have been useful in the time period immediately after its signing in 2002, up until around 2006–2007. In this period, the South China Sea was seen as relatively quiet and low profile, without much incident and little attention being paid to at major international for a.

China also had much broader strategic objectives and needed to ensure the South China Sea issues did not implode those. As the Cold War ended, global order shifted, and China was admitted to the WTO, China saw an opportunity to expand China's strategic influence through trade and development, and the ASEAN–China Free Trade Area would be an important stepping stone. China understood that in order to gain ASEAN's strategic trust to embark on this deal, it must respond to ASEAN's security concern regarding the South China Sea.

Overall, although the DOC was not useful at all times and for all purposes, it was certainly useful at certain times for certain purposes. However, the DOC also faced much criticism for its shortcoming, especially from external observers.

First, the DOC was not able to prevent massive operations that upset the *status quo* in the South China Sea. This raised the question of how much political will is actually placed on the political declaration. Many questions arose about the legal power of the document, or if there is any way to sanction non-compliance.[21] This was also the reason why there were calls for a more legally binding instrument to replace the DOC.

---

[20]Rodolfo C. Severino, *Southeast Asia in Search of an ASEAN Community*, Singapore: Institute of Southeast Asian Studies, 2006, p. 189.
[21]Li Mingjiang, "Managing Security in the South China Sea: From DOC to COC," https://kyotoreview.org/issue-15/managing-security-in-the-south-china-sea-from-doc-to-coc/.

Secondly, despite 20 years of dialogues on UNCLOS as the foundation for maritime rules and norms, ASEAN and China's understanding of key elements of the UN Convention has not narrowed. In fact, positions on certain regimes within UNCLOS were further divided, such as on archipelagic base lines, the regime of exclusive economic zones, legal status of low tide elevations, submerged features and artificial islands, etc.

Thirdly, despite both ASEAN and China's willingness to promote cooperation on less sensitive areas to build confidence and address common challenges, there were very few practical activities implemented, such as to protect the environment or to address IUU fishing. One of the reasons why cooperation under the DOC has been less effective than desired is the lack of legal clarity on the applicable maritime zones. On the one hand, it was understood that the DOC would cover the whole of the South China Sea. On the other hand, there are no clearly defined areas in the South China Sea where all parties accept as disputed areas based on maritime entitlement derived from the 1982 UNCLOS. As a result, all activities proposed hit the fundamental question of jurisdiction, that is if the zone of cooperation is indeed disputed.

IV. Conclusions and the Way Toward a Legally Binding Code of Conduct

The DOC provided valuable lessons for both ASEAN and China. It illuminated the pathway forward toward the goals of the early conclusion of an effective and substantive code of conduct that is in accordance with international law, including the 1982 UNCLOS.

First, "if there is a will there is a way." Political will and sincerity are the precondition for both the DOC's full and effective implementation and a successful negotiation of the COC. There must be genuine belief that ASEAN and China are to successfully find common ground in their interpretation and application of UNCLOS to the South China Sea. If either ASEAN or China is only half-hearted in the process, half-committed to the "ground rules" and allow its narrow interests to take over, the confidence could quickly evaporate.

Secondly, a whole-of-government approach would be needed from both sides. The spirit of dialogue and cooperation enshrined in the DOC must be carried on to the COC negotiations and be understood by all stakeholders and at all levels of government. After all, it is the diplomats that talk the talk, but activities "on the ground" are undertaken by a multitude of government, non-government, and para-government agencies. Without these actors' cooperation, no matter how much consensus and agreement was reached "up there," there could still be much dis-order "down there" in the South China Sea.

Thirdly, ASEAN and China should never lose sight of the strategic environment and their broader goals in handling the South China Sea. They also need to have an open mindset in setting their visions, not least because of the gigantic changes that are taking place, such as how disruptive technologies might affect the maritime domain. The competition for hydrocarbon resources might ease, and China might soon emerge as a leading force for green energy. Fish stock degradation might force fishing industries into more sustainable fish farms. Unmanned vehicles might change the way countries need to be or show "presence" at sea. A code of conducts that is "future proof" and relevant must not ignore these very critical developments.

The global pivot toward the Indo-Pacific means that the South China Sea would continue to be the central geopolitical and geostrategic focus for years to come. It is in ASEAN and China's interest to reap the opportunity by keeping the sea a medium for connectivity and cooperation and not a theatre for competition or confrontation. It is in China and ASEAN's interests also to objectively assess the success and shortcomings of the past 20 years of implementation of the DOC so as to repeat the successes and avoid the shortcomings being repeated, for a small misstep might easily cost ASEAN and China decades of missed opportunities and fortunes.

www.ingramcontent.com/pod-product-compliance
Lightning Source LLC
LaVergne TN
LVHW022314291224
800089LV00002B/49